The Waite Group's®

C++
Programming
Second Edition

The Waite Group's®

C++ Programming

Second Edition

John Thomas Berry

SAMS

A Division of Prentice Hall Computer Publishing
11711 North College, Carmel, Indiana 46032 USA

To my wife Nancy and my daughter Rebecca
for their patience, help, and, above all, love.
To my students at Foothill College who understood
if their projects were sometimes a little bit late.

Trademarks

All terms mentioned in this book that are known to be trademarks or service marks are listed below. In addition, terms suspected of being trademarks or service marks have been appropriately capitalized. SAMS cannot attest to the accuracy of this information. Use of a term in this book should not be regarded as affecting the validity of any trademark or service mark.

ANSI is a registered trademark of American National Standards.

IBM is a registered trademark of International Business Machines Corporation.

MS-DOS is a registered trademark of Microsoft Corporation.

Smalltalk is a trademark of Digitalk Inc.

UNIX is a registered trademark of UNIX Systems Laboratories.

From The Waite Group:

Development Editors
Mitchell Waite
James Stockford

Content Editor
Harry Henderson

Editorial Director
Scott Calamar

From SAMS:

Publisher
Richard K. Swadley

Publishing Manager
Joseph B. Wikert

Managing Editor
Neweleen A. Trebnik

Acquisitions Editor
Gregory Croy

Development Editor
Stacy Hiquet

Production Editor
Andy Saff

Editors
Lori Cates
Anne Clarke
Katherine Stuart Ewing
Jodi Jensen

Technical Reviewer
Brad Jones

Editorial Assistants
Rosemarie Graham
San Dee Phillips

Production Analyst
Mary Beth Wakefield

Book Design
Michele Laseau

Cover Art
Ron Troxell

Production
Jeff Baker
Michelle Cleary
Mark Enochs
Bob LaRoche
Laurie Lee
Anne Owen
Juli Pavey
Linda Seifert
Dennis Sheehan
Lisa Wilson
Phil Worthington

Indexer
Jeanne Clark

Composed in Palatino and MCP Digital
by Prentice Hall Computer Publishing

Printed in the United States of America

Overview

Contents

Preface

Since the first edition of C++ *Programming,* much has changed in the software development world. C++ now holds an even stronger position than before and is used by ever increasing numbers of programmers and software designers. At the college where I teach, C++ has evolved from an experimental course in advanced programming techniques to a bread and butter computer science class offered and filled every quarter. The people taking this course are primarily software professionals in the Silicon Valley of Northern California.

C++ itself has evolved from a young, vigorous, and experimental programming language into a refined and well-developed programming tool. The days of slow and sometimes unreliable translators have given way to a series of slick, powerful, and convenient compilers, many of which have integrated editors and debugging facilities. In addition, C++ has spread to a wider range of machines and operating system environments. Originally found only on UNIX, C++ compilers can now be found on the MS-DOS, Macintosh, and Amiga platforms.

What hasn't changed is the need for a good, practically oriented introduction to this powerful programming language. This is precisely what we offer in this current edition. We have eliminated discussion of C++ syntax that is no longer used, added chapters to cover new topics such as multiple inheritance, and reorganized the presentation to allow a smoother path to the mastery of this software design tool. In addition, there is a new emphasis on object-oriented programming techniques. What we haven't altered is the emphasis on every day examples that put the syntax of C++ in a problem solving context.

John Thomas Berry
San Francisco

Acknowledgments

The task of trying to make the C++ programming language understandable in something as short as a book is an overwhelming one; it could not have been accomplished without a great deal of help. I can't even begin to acknowledge the time and effort that went into helping me make this book possible, but I would like to personally thank the following individuals:

- Scott Calamar for getting the second edition off the ground and running.

- Harry Henderson for still being the best editor around.

- Louise Orlando for her ability to make the frantic last minute details fall into line with a minimum of stress.

I would also like to thank the following companies for their cooperation and help:

- Borland International

- Comeau Computing

Also, I don't want to forget my students at Foothill College. Their intellectual curiosity has kept me going when I sometimes stumbled in a forest of details. And finally my wife Nancy and my daughter Rebecca whose cooperation and willingness to share really made it all possible.

1

Using C++ as a Software Design Tool

1

Using C++ as a
Software Design Tool

This book explores the C++ programming language. Although the focus is on the syntax and techniques used with C++, the book also explores this programming platform as a software development environment. As such, there are two important elements of C++ that you must keep in mind:

C++ is a superset of the earlier C programming language.

C++ is a vehicle for a new programming paradigm based on the notions of object-oriented design.

Although these distinct characteristics are not mutually exclusive, they influence the way you write C++ programs. Note that the discussion in this chapter and the rest of the book presupposes a reasonable knowledge of C.

The Object-Oriented
Design Paradigm

Object-oriented analysis and design have become trendy new "catchwords" in software technology. These techniques, however, are also an effective way of creating large, complicated systems. In fact, these techniques are effective enough to have captured the attention of a significant number of designers who choose to work with this new and developing software technology, but this paradigm is still new enough that it takes some effort to determine what is hype, what is dream, and what is reality.

One problem with *OOP* (*Object-Oriented Programming*) is that it has been implemented on top of a variety of software and hardware systems. Besides C++, these systems include Smalltalk, LISP, Pascal, and even nonprocedural languages such as PROLOG. In each of these implementations, a certain flavor of the underlying language persists, embodied especially in the notation and syntax. These disparate platforms make it difficult to come to general conclusions when comparing OOP software. What works well on one system might be impossible on another. This is why I focus on C++ as an OOP vehicle and what you can do with it.

The Elements: Encapsulation, Polymorphism, and Inheritance

OOP is changing the way people look at program design. In traditional programs, functions accept, transform, and return data in the form of variables and their values. In OOP design, however, data and the functions needed to work with the data are bound together in a structure called an *object*.

An object is a tangible part of the program, much like a structure variable in C. As a representation of data, an object contains elements that store values: variable members. An object also has methods, however, that act on these stored variables. In C++, these methods are the member functions. Instead of sending a variable down to a function to have an action performed on it, in OOP languages—including C++—you ask the object to perform the action. The relationship among objects is akin to a message-passing system; although in C++, you need to be careful not to carry this analogy too far.

An object represents an autonomous part of a program. It is complete in itself and includes the capability to act on its internal members. An object, however, still can communicate with the outside world. To make this concept complete, it's necessary for the object also to bar outside access to its internal parts except through a carefully controlled interface. This represents the first element in OOP: *design encapsulation*.

Encapsulation extends a capacity that has been used often in programming design: *modularity*. In C, functions and files have been used to create autonomous areas within a program that can be accessed only by a carefully controlled interface. In the case of a properly constructed function, for example, only the function name and the parameter list offer a way to export or import values. A global variable modified with the static declaration cannot be accessed outside the file. These are both cases of encapsulation. C++ supports functions and file scope, but it also adds the class as another area with a controlled interface.

The second element, *polymorphism,* is something that's found in nearly every programming language. In its simplest terms, polymorphism is the use of a name or symbol—for example an operator—to stand for more than one action. In C, certainly—but also in Pascal and FORTRAN—the arithmetic operators represent a perfect example of this characteristic. The + symbol, when used with integers, stands for a different set of machine instructions than it does when the operands are double values. The operations are similar enough in broad outline to justify using the same symbol. I might suggest that it would be misleading for these operations not to share a symbol. In OOP-based design, this polymorphism is extended throughout the language. In C++, as you will see, it becomes a particularly important element in the internal design of objects.

The final element that defines the base level of OOP theory is *inheritance.* This is a simple concept that allows the designer to take existing objects and create new ones that inherit the properties of the earlier object. This principle has the practical benefit of simplifying design. For example, after you have a linked list object defined and debugged, you can use it seamlessly in a variety of contexts by creating new objects that inherit its linked list properties but add the specialized items it needs to complete its current task. On a theoretical level, inheritance makes it easier to construct models of real-world relationships that often exhibit the property of inheritance.

Objects as Solutions

One thing that the creation of objects does is to help organize the complexity that you face in writing even moderate-sized software systems. Because objects are complete and communicate only through a well-behaved interface, you can use them to divide a problem into smaller tasks, with each one implemented as some kind of object. Then the construction of the system becomes one of connecting objects. It's a divide-and-conquer strategy: Deal with one task at a time.

Polymorphism is an important tool for the designer. It allows a design to remain open to receive new kinds of data and values even after it has been created, coded, and debugged. You will see concrete examples of this in subsequent chapters. Polymorphism also allows the designer another important tool. User-defined data types are treated exactly the same as built-in types: They use the same syntax. These data types are not treated in a special way. An OOP-based programming language is extensible in the fullest sense of the word.

From the designer's point of view, *inheritance* represents an increased efficiency of design. Existing parts can be reused in a safe way — one that does not lead to obscure bugs later in the design phase or even after the program is finished.

Even if you are uninterested in the theoretical notions about object-oriented design, the techniques associated with it are practical enough to be of interest to you. OOP is an effective technique for creating solid software in a minimal amount of time.

C++ Is an OOP Design Tool

C++ is an object-oriented programming language. It contains the OOP elements that I talked about previously: encapsulation, polymorphism, and inheritance. Everything that I've mentioned before can be done in C++. Moreover, C++ does these things with a C flavor, which makes it an attractive step into OOP technology for the practical designer who already is familiar with C.

Creating Objects in C++

Objects are created in C++ through the mechanism of the *class*, which is a data type similar to the C structure. However, it differs from the C structure in many important ways. The most obvious—and perhaps, most important—is that it contains not only variable members (integers, real numbers, and character strings), but also function members, which are the methods that act on the variable members.

Besides carrying their own functions, C++ class objects also contain *private* areas—parts of the class that are available to the member functions but that cannot be accessed from outside the function. A class is divided into two basic sections: a private section and a *public* section. This public section defines an interface between the class object and the rest of the program. The C++ class fulfills the first object-oriented criterion: encapsulation.

Polymorphism also is well-supported in C++. Any function name can be overloaded, which means the function name can be shared among different functions. The compiler takes responsibility for matching the name with the proper code. This overloading is particularly important within the class. Member functions, which are the internally defined methods that operate on class values, frequently are overloaded. Moreover, the overloading syntax extends to the set of operators common to both C and C++. Any symbol in this set can be associated with a function in the context of a particular class. For example, you can create a class of complex numbers and redefine the + operator to work with these objects. C++ thus meets the second object-oriented criterion: polymorphism.

Finally, a C++ class can serve as a base class to a subsequently defined derived class. The derived class shares the characteristics of the base class, but adds its own private section and member functions. Because the derived class can access only the restricted parts of the base class, there is no restriction on which or how many classes can serve in this capacity. Furthermore, a class can be derived from more than one class, hence, *multiple inheritance*. Multiple inheritance increases the flexibility and the options of the software designer. All three criteria — encapsulation, polymorphism, and inheritance — are thus met by C++.

Designing with
Object Definitions

The *class* data type becomes the focus of C++. Everything in the language revolves around this user-defined data type. Instead of being collections of independent functions connected by often complex sequences of program statements, programs tend to be clusters of classes. Each class, in turn, handles the complexity necessary for its part of the program. As a result, the statements that are not part of any class are minimized and the connecting code often seems simple in comparison to the complicated system that is being implemented.

Examples of the class data type range from ordinary objects, such as a name or address class, to graphical objects such as windows and menus. Figure 1.1 illustrates some of these possibilities.

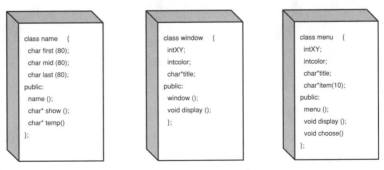

Figure 1-1. Typical class examples.

7

It takes a shift in perspective to use class types when you are designing code. The old habits of creating variables and passing them to functions for action and results are often hard to break. This is particularly true because C++ doesn't entirely abandon the notion of functions and function definitions. In the new context, however, functions perform their services inside classes instead of taking the dominant role they have in more traditional languages such as C.

Of course, it's possible to write C++ code that looks like C code. The temptation is there because the new syntax contains numerous improvements to traditional C: for example, the function overloading that I mentioned earlier. You can ignore the object-oriented features and just write programs that are conglomerates of functions, albeit with better syntax. If you do this, however, you'll miss the power and the beauty of the C++ programming language. In the pages that follow, I discuss the syntax of C++, but I also frequently revisit the perspective of object-oriented design. I encourage you to try from the beginning to think in terms of class objects and their connection.

C++ Is a Superset of C

Chapter 2 contains an overview of the C++ language. This overview focuses on the innovations and object-oriented features of the language. Before you can embark on this journey of discovery, however, you must understand that C++ is not a completely new language. It is instead an evolutionary step up from C. In fact, much of its syntax is identical to that of C.

Basic features and syntax that C and C++ share include

- The `main()` function
- The use of function arguments
- Arithmetic and logical operators
- Control and looping statements
- Bitwise manipulation
- Basic data types

These basic statements and operators work identically in C and C++, but other more complex parts of the syntax also are shared. Some of these bear review before you move deeply into the syntax of C++.

Storage Classes in C++

Scope, or the area within which a variable is defined, is only one of the factors of which designers must be aware when they create applications. The storage class of a variable affects also the way a program uses the variable. Basically, the storage class of a variable or other data object determines the length of time that the object exists. The four C++ storage classes are the same as those in C: auto, static, extern, and register. In the next chapter, you'll see that C++ adds a fifth storage class in the form of dynamically allocated objects.

A variable of an *automatic* storage class exists only when the program executes the block in which the variable is defined. For example, in

```
example()
{
   int  i = 0;
     .
     .
     .
}
```

i is an automatic variable. Space is allocated for it while the function example() is executing. That space is deallocated, however, as soon as control returns to the function that called example(). You can declare an automatic variable by using the modifier auto in the declaration. Because this is the default for a local variable, however, the explicit declaration rarely is used.

You can declare a variable also as static. A static variable comes into existence when the program begins execution and lasts until the program ends. This permits the variable to retain its value even though program execution has passed beyond its scope. Consider the following code fragment:

```
example()
{
  static int  x = 0;

  x++;
     .
     .
     .
}
```

In this case, static modifies the declaration of a variable local to a function. Note that the scope of the variable x hasn't changed; it is still accessible only while the program is executing `example()`. Because x is `static`, however, its memory locations are maintained from function call to function call, and the value stored in x is retained indefinitely. This feature is useful for functions that need to maintain counters or information about their previous execution.

You can declare also a variable of file or global scope as `static`.

```
static int  i;

example()
{
   .

   .

}
```

This declaration restricts the scope of the variable i to the file in which it is declared. In C++, as in C, large applications often encompass several files. A `static` declaration restricts the scope of a global variable to its file of origin. No other file in the program can reference this particular variable, even if the variable subsequently is declared as `extern`. This is a useful feature that supports modularization.

Note that the `int` type declaration in the two previous examples is redundant. A declaration of `static x` assumes the data type to be `int`. A `static` declaration of any other data type, however, must be declared explicitly. For example, you must declare a real number value as `static double x`.

You declare a variable or function name in a program as `extern` to reference a definition or declaration that is found in another file. This was designed originally to facilitate the separate compilation of files. In C++, however, any variable or function name that has a scope outside of a function that you do not explicitly declare `static` is implicitly of type `extern`.

A `register` declaration works the same way as it does in C. It is, after all, only a suggestion to the compiler—one that is ignored if no registers are available. A `register` value must be an integer type—`char`, `int`, `long`, and so on—with a size that fits into the register. (The maximum size is, of course, hardware-dependent.)

The Declaration of a Constant Value in C++

In traditional C, the preprocessor macro facility creates a kind of constant value. The statement

```
#define RATE 1.5
```

on a line replaces the character string RATE with the value 1.5 throughout the program. This is done at the preprocessor stage before the compiler is called. The replacement is a purely textual substitution.

Both ANSI C and C++ offer a true constant object. By prefixing a declaration with the const specifier, you can create a data object that has variable-like scope and visibility, but also has a value that the program cannot change. Thus, in the code fragment

```
const x = 1.2;

example()
{
    .
    .

    int y = x * 23;
    .
    .
}
```

x is a constant integer value that you can use anywhere you can use a variable, except on the left side of an assignment statement.

The primary advantage that the const modifier has over the more traditional #define construction is that the constant is a memory location like a variable. It is not merely a substitute identifier. This distinction is an important consideration when you are using pointers, because you can combine this modifier with a pointer variable declaration.

Pointers in C++

Pointer variables—variables that contain the address of another variable—operate in analogous ways in C and C++. You must declare a pointer variable as a pointer to a built-in or user-created type. The most commonly used pointer variable in C++ is the character pointer, which is the base type for the character string. Almost as common are pointer variables to the complex data types that dominate a C or C++ program. These include *structures, arrays,* and (in C++ only) classes. The syntax of a pointer is the same in both languages. The * operator in a declaration designates a pointer variable. For example, the declaration char* x creates a character string variable. The * operator causes the declaration of the variable x to allocate space, not for the character value, but for the address of the memory location that holds such a value. Remember, the declaration of a pointer variable doesn't create the space needed to store a value. It creates only the place to store an address. To store the value, you must use the new operator or assign the value of some preexisting variable to the pointer variable.

The same two operators that manipulate pointer variables in C—& and *—are available also in C++. Figure 1-2 illustrates the use of these operators in C++. The address-of operator (&) puts the address of an existing variable into a pointer, as follows:

```
int x = 123;

int* y = &x;
```

After this code executes, the variable y contains the address of the variable x. The dereferencing operator (*) performs the complementary operation of obtaining the value at the location that has its address stored in the pointer. The following code:

```
int x, y = 123;

int *z = &y;

x = *z;
```

copies the value in y into x by way of the pointer z. The * operator performs an indirect memory access: It reads the value at location z and uses this value as an address to find a location that contains another value. This last value is the one the assignment operator uses.

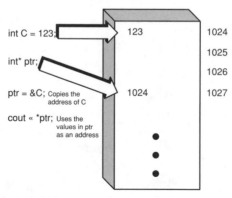

*Figure 1-2. The use of * and & in C++.*

Pointer access to functions is the same in C++ as it is in C. An extra set of parentheses performs the necessary indirect access. For example, the declaration of a pointer to a function might look as follows:

```
int (*f)();
```

You must use parentheses around the variable name to ensure that the correct indirection is performed. Note that the declaration

```
int *f()
```

specifies a function that returns a pointer to an integer, which is not the same operation shown in the preceding example. The address-of operator (&) assigns a value to the pointer as follows:

```
int (*f)();

f = &example();

(*f)();
```

This code fragment assigns the address of the function example() to the variable f, which has been declared as a pointer to a function. The third statement calls the function through the pointer variable by using the indirection operator enclosed in parentheses. As with the declaration, you must use the parentheses to generate the correct dereferencing operation. Of course, if example() has any parameters, you must include them also in the function call.

void **Pointers in C++**

One new development shared by ANSI C and C++ is the void pointer. The void data type, which specifies functions that don't return a value to the calling function, has long been common in C. Now, however, you can declare pointer variables to be of this type. Although you can't dereference these pointers, you can assign other pointer variables to them. In fact, they are useful because they are compatible with all types of pointer variables and therefore can serve as generic pointer variables in situations in which code must handle several different data types. Then you can use a type cast or merely assign the void* variable back to variables of the original types to return accessibility.

You declare a void pointer as you would any other pointer variable.

```
void *x
```

You use the void pointer in an assignment statement as you would a normal pointer. Although you can't use the & and * pointer operators on it, you can assign it another void pointer variable or a pointer of any other type. For example, in the following code fragment:

```
int y = 123;

int* p = &y;
int* q;

void *vp;

vp = p;

q = vp;
```

the pointer p contains the address of an integer value, in this case y. The pointer vp accepts the value of this address and passes it to the third pointer variable q.

The void pointer type gives you an important advantage: the ability to write more general programs. Now you can create code that handles a variety of different data types without having to "wire in" this information early in the development process.

What's Unique About C++

So far, this book has focused on the many similarities between C and C++. Many elements, however, are unique to C++. Such elements are not found in the traditional C syntax, even in a modified form. These include an enhanced input/output system, function overloading, and, above all, the class, which is the central concept of C++. It's time to turn our attention to the C++ syntax.

Chapter 2 contains an overview of the C++ programming language. In subsequent chapters, attention is focused on each important characteristic of this object-oriented programming tool.

- Chapter 3 discusses the class data type.

- Chapter 4 covers function definition and overloading.

- Chapter 5 contains more advanced class definitions.

- Chapter 6 introduces the friend function.

- Chapter 7 discusses the question of operator overloading.

- Chapter 8 introduces inheritance and the derived class.

- Chapter 9 adds the technique of multiple base classes.

- Chapter 10 talks about the `iostream` library.

Finally, in Chapter 11 an exploration of class design and use rounds out the discussion of C++, including the important topics of object-oriented programming and software recycling.

2

C++: An Overview

C++: An Overview

C++ is a superset of C. It contains the syntax and features of its predecessor language but adds some rules and constructions of its own. In this chapter, I survey in outline form the ways in which C++ diverges from C. In subsequent chapters, you explore each new area in detail. Note that the discussion in this chapter presupposes a reasonable knowledge of C. Even if you have limited experience with C, you still can benefit from reading about the new C++ features.

C++ Is Derived from C

One of the strengths of C++ is that it is derived directly from the C programming language, and thus it is based on familiar ground. C is a subset of C++. Because of this, C++ is not a completely new programming language that requires a long learning curve. If you already know how to program in C, you know most of the basic syntax of C++. You have little to unlearn, so you can concentrate on the wealth of features that C++ adds to the previous language. Figure 2-1 illustrates the relationship between C and C++.

It is impossible to include in this book a discussion of the complete syntax of C, so I assume you have a basic familiarity with that language. The following brief summary, however, highlights some important programming elements and points out some of the differences introduced by C++.

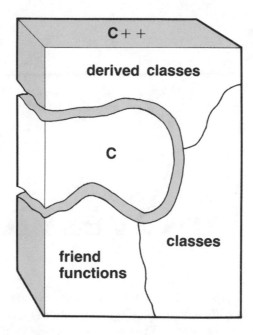

Figure 2-1. The relationship between C and C++.

The Form of a C++ Program

A C++ program consists of a series of one or more functions. These functions can be combined in a single file or can be spread throughout several disk files. There must be one, and only one, function called main(). Although main() is where execution of the program officially begins, this is not an absolute. Later discussions show that it's possible to execute code both before main() is called and after it finishes executing. C++ also permits greater modularity in programming through several interesting additions to the usual C syntax. One feature—the class—integrates functions into data structures. Another permits the "overloading" of function names, enabling two or more functions to share a common calling sequence.

The Overall Similarity of C and C++

C++ is closely linked to C: It contains the same programming statements and constructions. It has essentially the same scope and storage class rules, and even the operators are identical. Of course, C++ offers more, but it's important for you to recognize the similarities. These similarities are best demonstrated by an example program that clearly shows the superset-subset relationship. To drive the point home, day.cpp (Listing 2-1) is a legal program in C and in C++.

Listing 2-1. A legal C and C++ program: day.cpp.

```
#include <stdio.h>
#include <stdlib.h>

char* days[] = { "Monday", "Tuesday",
                 "Wednesday", "Thursday",
                 "Friday", "Saturday",   "Sunday"};

main(int argc, char* argv[])
{

  int jdate;

  char* day;

  if(argc == 1)   {
    printf("format: list1 <julian date>\n");
    exit(1);

  }

jdate = atoi(argv[1]);

day = days[ (jdate % 7) ];

printf("day = %s\n",day);

}
```

This simple program accepts a Julian calendar date (defined here as the number of days since January 1) and returns the appropriate day of the week. The key to this program is the external character string array, days[], which contains the days of the week. The Julian date is divided modulo 7. This division returns a number between 0 and 6, which is the remainder after dividing by 7. This remainder is used as an index into the array. The arrangement of the days of the week in the array is not random: The first day of the week in the list is the last day (December

31) of the previous year. The second cell in the array—index 1—is set for the day of the week on which January 1 falls. Counting continues from there. Another interesting feature of the program is the command line interface. If you run the program without the required argument, it displays the correct command line format and exits.

Although day.cpp is a legitimate C and C++ program that compiles with either language translator, you would do some things differently if you were to write this program purely in C++. Consequently, when you compile this program using a commercial C++ translator, the program generates some warning messages. Nonetheless, it is a good illustration of the close relationship between these two programming languages.

Basic features and syntax that are shared by C and C++ include

- The main() function

- The use of function arguments

- Arithmetic and logical operators

- Control and looping statements

- Bitwise manipulation

- Basic data types

Keep in mind, however, that even these similar areas have distinctive C++ characteristics. The power that's packed into C++ makes it more than just another version of C. This power dictates a new approach to programming. Thus, the example in Listing 2-1 is *legal* C++, but not *good* C++.

C++ Is Not Only C

Do not overestimate the similarities between C and C++. The two languages have significant differences, some of which are easy to overlook. Any comparison of these languages is complicated by the fact that C is in a transition period. The industry-wide standard for C differs in some respects from traditional C syntax. This standard often mirrors some of the changes introduced by C++. Therefore, this book concentrates on C++ and does not compare it to any great extent with the C standard. This way, you gain a feeling for the spirit of C++ without having to spend time reconciling different programming constructions and styles. At the same time, let's look briefly at similarities between C++ and the ANSI C standard.

Variables in C++

Because C++ and ANSI C share a common base syntax, the rules that apply to variable declaration and creation are the same. There are, however, some unique variations that are used in C++ but not in ANSI C. It's important to discuss these differences early in your study of this object-oriented programming language.

Declarations in C++

One of the most obvious differences between the two languages is in the declaration of variables. Although variables still are declared in C++ with a type name and a variable name (for example, `int x`), the positioning of the declaration within the program is more flexible. Recall that in C all declarations must occur at the top of a function block or a block created by a pair of braces ({ and }). You must declare all variables, not only before they are used, but before any executable statement. For example, a function that calculates the mean of a set of numbers might look like this:

```
double mean(double num[], int size)
{
  int loop;
  double total = 0;

  for(loop = 0 ; loop < size ; loop++ )
     total += num[loop];

return total/size;
}
```

Inside the braces, the function is divided into two parts—a declaration section and an action section.

In C++, however, declarations can be placed anywhere in the program. In fact, as a matter of C++ style, you should keep declarations as close to their point of use as possible. This placement underscores their relationship to the statements that use them and reminds the programmer of their scope. In C++, the `mean()` function would look like this:

```
double mean(double num[], int size)
{
   double total = 0;
```

```
   for( int loop = 0 ; loop < size ; loop++ )
      total += num[loop];

  return total/size;
}
```

The integer variable loop occurs only inside the `for` statement. Therefore, you can delay declaring it until you initialize the `for` statement.

The Scope of a Variable

The scope rules of C++ are similar to those of C. There are three possible scopes for a variable or other data object: `local`, `file`, and `class`. I discuss the C++ class later in this chapter. For now, let's examine the other two scopes.

A local variable is used exclusively within a block. Blocks are defined by a pair of braces. For example, in

```
example()
{
   int x,y;
      .
      .
      .
}
```

the variables x and y are local to the function `example()`.

A block can be defined also within another block, as follows:

```
example2()
{
    int x,y;
   {
     int p;
        .
        .
   }
      .
      .
}
```

In this example, x and y are local to `example2()`; however, the variable p is local to the inner block defined by the second set of braces. This is the same in C++ as it is in C. This form is used rarely in either language, however, because it is hard to read.

The primary issue with scope is the visibility or accessibility of the variable. A local variable is known only within its block. In the last example, p can be accessed only inside the inner block; it is invisible to other blocks. The variable y, however, illustrates another aspect of the visibility rules: its relativity. Whether a variable is local or global depends on the context. The y object is available inside both the outer and the inner block. In other words, something declared in an enclosing block always is accessible in the enclosed block, but not the other way around.

In contrast to a local variable, a variable of file scope is declared outside any function or class. The availability of this kind of data object extends from the point of declaration to the end of the source file in which it is declared, regardless of the number of blocks involved. For example, the following code:

```
int count;

example()
{
    .
    .
}

example2()
{
    .
    .
}
```

defines an integer variable, count, which can be accessed in both example() and example2(). This corresponds to the global variable of other programming languages.

One important aspect of the scope of variables concerns the notion of data- or variable-hiding. Consider the following code fragment:

```
int count = 5

example()
{
    int count = 10
    .
    .
}
```

There appears to be a conflict between two objects with the same scope. Which version of count does the function use? The answer is simple, and it's the same in both C and C++. The most local name takes precedence. Here, the `count` that is declared within `example()` is used inside the function. What's new in C++ is the ability to bypass this restriction and to refer to a variable or other name outside the current scope, even if a local name hides that object. You can do this by using the scope resolution operator (`::`).

The scope resolution operator changes the reference of a name from a local variable to one of file scope. The following `scope()` function illustrates the use of this operator:

```
#include <iostream.h>
int count = 5;
main()
{
 int count = 10;
 cout << "inner count = " << count << "\n";
 cout << "outer count = " << :: count << "\n";
}
```

By placing the `::` in front of the variable, you force it to refer outside the defined scope to the file. Of course, if no variable by that name exists in the global scope, an error occurs. (The `cout` statement is a simple output statement that displays text and variable values; more on this later.)

Free Store Objects—The *new* and *delete* Operators

In addition to `automatic`, `static`, `extern`, and `register`, C++ actually has a fifth storage class: objects created using the C++ new operator. This operator dynamically allocates a specified number of memory locations. When these objects are allocated, they remain in existence until you use the `delete` operator to deallocate them specifically. For example, to create an array for a character string (a common use of the new operator), you need to execute the following code:

```
char* ch;
ch = new char[100];
```

new allocates 100 contiguous locations, each one large enough to hold a single character. The beginning address of that space is assigned to the string pointer variable `ch`.

Objects manipulated by the `new` and `delete` operators are not `automatic` because they are not destroyed when the program leaves their scope; however, they also are not `static`. A `static` data object exists for the full term of the program's execution. A variable created by new can be destroyed and its memory allocation returned to the pool of available locations at any point in the program. This capability gives the programmer complete control over dynamic memory use.

Simple I/O in C++

Like C, C++ doesn't have any built-in I/O statements. It maintains maximum flexibility by using functions in the standard library to support all such activities. C++ was designed to be upwardly compatible to C. Therefore, C++ implementations in practice make available all the familiar I/O functions, including getchar(), putchar(), scanf(), and printf(). In fact, a C program that depends heavily on these capabilities compiles as well under C++ as it does with an ordinary C compiler.

C++ greatly enhances the input and output of values, however. This enhancement includes a great improvement in convenience and a more streamlined interface to the outside world. This new interface eliminates the need for using large functions, such as scanf() and printf(), which carry extra baggage. The object-oriented nature of C++ led to the creation of routines for getting values from the keyboard and putting them on the display screen that are as general as their C counterparts yet are much more efficient and simpler to use. The details of the implementation of this subsystem are covered in Chapter 10. Basically, C++ gives you access to a series of small general-purpose input and output routines that can be tailored to the specific values you need to use. In addition, the convenience of these routines rivals that of the printf() and scanf() routines because the system automatically chooses the proper routine for the desired operation.

An Introduction to the *iostream* Library

The basic I/O declarations are in the standard header file iostream.h, which you must include in any program that uses the routines. This header file defines an interface to the I/O subsystem that consists of the three standard files and special C++ objects—cin, cout, and cerr—that are attached to these files. When a program begins execution, it automatically opens these files, associates them with the iostream objects, and initially attaches cin to the keyboard and cout and cerr to the display screen. Coupled with these files is a set of I/O operators that is truly unique to C++. Two operators connect the specified output values with the appropriate file: << sends values to cout or cerr, and >> retrieves values from cin.

In both cases, the operator acts as a mediator between a variable or expression and the outside world. The code fragment

```
#include <iostream.h>

main()
{
    char x;

    cin >> x;
       .
       .
}
```

reads a character value from the keyboard and puts it in the variable x. The following code:

```
#include <iostream.h>

main()
{
  char x = 'a';

  cout << x;
     .
     .
}
```

performs the complementary operation: It takes the value of x and displays it on the screen.

I/O Objects: *cout* and <<, and *cin* and >>

There is a twofold advantage in using the operators for I/O rather than the function call syntax found in C. First, this notation is more natural to write and thus is easier to read. The double greater than signs compel you to see the direction of the flow of characters. This visual cue is not available with the C-style function call. More importantly, the operators give I/O statements a more fluid style, enabling them to be combined into complex I/O expressions. Thus, C++ offers two new operators with the same economy of style and power as the increment operator (++) and makes them part of I/O notation.

These specialized operators are an integral part of the C++ programming philosophy. Later chapters show how C++ gives the program designer an almost unlimited capability for redefining the operator symbols available in the language. You can use this capability to create code that is both exact and concise. As a result, your code is easier to maintain.

Another important aspect of these I/O operators is that they do data conversion. This results from their flexibility in using only two operations to get and put data. The two previous examples used declarations of the most basic character data type. As a matter of fact, you can retrieve or display any type of value. Consider the lines in io.cpp (Listing 2-2).

Listing 2-2. Using the I/O operators: io.cpp.

```
#include <iostream.h>

main()
{
  double x = 1.23, y;

  cin >> y;

  cout << "the answer is " << x * y << "\n";
}
```

This actually is a complete C++ program. It defines two real number variables—one with an initial value and one that receives a value from the keyboard. The latter operation is accomplished by using the input operator >> with the object cin. The operator implementation performs the necessary conversion to a double. Note that in an earlier example this same operator handled a character value. The output also illustrates more of the capabilities of this input/output subsystem. You use the output operator << to group together several values and send them to the screen as part of a single operation. These pieces need not be the same data type, because each use of the operator represents a separate call to the operator code. For example, io.cpp displays a character string, a double value, and a special character. The special character is merely a new-line character that you should recognize from its common use with the C printf() function.

This brief introduction should help you get started writing C++ programs that communicate with the outside world. However, you can do much more with cin, cout, cerr, <<, and >>. Chapter 10 contains a complete discussion of these important C++ elements.

The Class Data Type

The focus of the C++ programming language is the class, a data type that supports both modular design and the exciting new notions of object-oriented programming. It is the class data type that defines the functionality of the C++ programming language and marks it as a significant improvement over C.

The advantage offered by the class is manifest even in its most basic form. Consider the following declaration:

```
struct square  {
    int side;
    int area();
};
```

This is a declaration of a simple class. Obviously, the basic form of this data type is derived from the familiar notion of a structure or a heterogeneous collection of contiguous variables. Like a C structure, the C++ class has a variable part that stores a value. Unlike the C struct type, however, the square class also has an associated function. In the example, the declared function returns an integer value. A class is complete: It contains both a storage location to contain values and the functions that manipulate those values. This format is a necessary condition for the creation of object-oriented programs.

Much of this book is devoted to exploring the ramifications of the class definition. It shows how to create and then use these classes to solve common, yet complex, programming problems. The C++ class is not limited to this first basic definition. You can use it to create arbitrarily complex objects. By exploring this exciting new territory, you will discover the practical side of this abstract concept.

Simple and Not-So-Simple Classes

So far, you have seen only the simplest kind of class definition—a declaration. However, even this simple form can be enhanced and expanded. Now, let's talk about implementation, for example, how to create an object that reflects a defined class.

Let's expand the previous class declaration into a complete definition of a new data type. With such a simple construction, this is a straightforward matter. Consider the struct square definition (Listing 2-3).

Listing 2-3. An expanded `struct` definition: square.cpp.

```
struct square  {
     int side;
     void set(int);
     int area();
};

void square::set(int x)
{
     side = x;
}

int square::area()
{
     return side * side;
}
```

A complete definition must include not only the declaration but a definition of the functions that are members of the class. In this case the only member functions are the easily implemented `set()` and `area()`. The set() function initializes the variable part of the class, whereas the `area()` function returns the area of a figure. Note that in this context, the scope resolution operator (`::`) associates a function definition with the function name declared in the structure. One important advantage of the class becomes apparent when you use the definition in some code.

```
main()
{
     .

     .

  square x,y;

  x.set(2);

  cout << "area of figure x = " << x.area() << "\n";

  y.set(3);

cout << "area of figure y = " << y.area()  << "\n";
     .

     .
}
```

Each object that you create by declaring a class variable (often called an *instance* of the class) is an independent region of the program. For example, when the function set() is invoked, it alters only the values in the object that calls it. This frees the program designer from worrying about passing variables back and forth to a function. The function belongs to the variable; it's a member function.

Classes as Objects

The class defined by the keyword struct is only the most basic of such objects. It lacks one of the most important advantages of the class: privacy. A more complete object uses the keyword class in its declaration, as in class.cpp (Listing 2-4).

Listing 2-4. A complete class declaration: class.cpp.

```
class  precord  {
     char* name;
     char* id;
     long salary;

public:
     precord(char*,char*);
     void set_sal(long);
     char* display();
};

precord::precord(char* nm, char* i)
{
     name = new char[strlen(nm) + 1];
     strcpy(name,nm);
     id = new char[strlen(id) + 1];
     strcpy(id,i);
}

void precord::set_sal(long s)
{
     salary = s;
}

char* precord::display()
{
     temp = new char[strlen(name) + strlen(id) + 31];
```

```
    sprintf(temp,
        "name = %s\nid number = %s\nsalary = %ld\n",
        name,id,salary);

    return temp;
}
```

This example is still a simple class. Unlike the previous examples, however, it has all the elements of this data type. The most important thing to notice is that it is divided into two sections—a public part that contains the member functions and a private section. In the example, the private section contains only variable members. Note that only the members that are declared in the public part of the class definition are known to other parts of the program. The members in the private part are hidden. The only way to access the variable members in this example is through the member functions, which form a well-controlled interface to the class.

Member functions of a class can serve as an interface because they have special access to the private part of the class. The simple member function set_sal() can take its parameter and store that value directly into the member variable salary. The members in the public part of a class serve as a bridge between the rest of the program and the hidden part of the class object. The simple class created by a struct declaration lacks this private part; all of it is public. The members of such an object are freely available to be set and unset by any part of the program. Such lack of control invites problems and makes any particular error more difficult to trace.

The private part of a class adds a new dimension of modularity to a C++ program. Now you can hide the details of the class implementation from the rest of the program. In the precord class (Listing 2-4), this includes data items. In other definitions, however, some member functions also might be included. Thus, you can create programs that more fully approach the ideal of a series of independent objects, which is the goal of object-oriented design.

Although the code in this example is straightforward and easy to understand, it contains another concept that you should be aware of before moving on to other topics. The function precord() might seem a little strange to the traditional C programmer. That's because precord() is a special member function called a *constructor*. A constructor is called each time you create an object of this class, either by a declaration or through dynamic allocation. It represents a kind of initialization routine in which the designer supplies the code to put the values into the multifaceted class. A complementary destructor function automatically is called as soon as a class object is destroyed. Neither constructors nor destructors are required for a class definition. All but the simplest classes usually have them, however. Constructors and destructors are covered more fully in Chapter 3.

Derived Classes

Another important feature of C++ is that it gives you the ability to create hierarchies of class objects. In other words, you can define a class *A* and a class *B* in such a way that everything that is in *A* also is in *B*, yet *B* contains some additional elements. The advantage of this is obvious to anyone who has had to solve programming problems in database design or in similar fields, such as expert systems. This capability offers advantages for even the most mundane programming tasks. For one thing, in C++, you can create a class and compile it. Even if you distribute only the object form of your program, another programmer can create a derived class based on your original definition without having access to your source code; this enormously increases the flexibility of the programming language.

The mechanism for creating a derived class is easy to use. First, you create an ordinary C++ class, as in base.cpp (Listing 2-5).

Listing 2-5. A base class: base.cpp.

```
class new_rec  {
    char *name;
    char *id;

public:
    new_rec(char*, char*);
    char* display();
};
```

This class becomes your base. A derived class must specify this as its base. You then can add anything to the derived class to supplement this base, as in derived.cpp (Listing 2-6).

Listing 2-6. A derived class: derived.cpp.

```
class rec : private new_rec  {
    char *address;
    char *city;
    char *state;

public:
    new_rec(char*,char*,char*,char*,char*);
    char* show();
};
```

In the class definition header in Listing 2-6, the phrase

```
: private new_rec
```

marks this class as one derived from the earlier defined new_rec. Although the declared rec object also is a new_rec object, the rec object's access to its parent class is limited. Specifically, it can't access the private part of new_rec. Its members can access the member functions of the base class, however, without any further dereferencing.

Derivation is not limited to a single base class. In Listing 2-7, I define a second base class (name), rewrite the derived class, and incorporate it into the previously defined base (Listing 2-5).

Listing 2-7. A derived class with multiple base classes.

```
class name   {
    char* first;
    char* mid;
    char* last;

public:
    name(char*, char*, char*);
    char* show_name();
}

class rec : private new_rec , private name {
    char *address,
        *city,
        *state;

public:
    new_rec(char*,char*,char*,char*,char*, char*, char*, char*);
    char* show();
};
```

The use of more than one base class (multiple inheritance) adds flexibility to an already powerful capability. I discuss this aspect of class definition more fully in Chapter 9.

Function Definition in C++

Although the main design module in C++ is the class, the function is still an important tool for organizing program code. Functions permit the program designer to create local regions within a program and then to carefully control the entrance to and exit from the code in these regions. More importantly, the programmer can create libraries of compiled general-purpose routines and then use them in many different programs. Of course, a major component of a class is the member function.

The declaration of parameters in the header line differs from pre-ANSI C, which requires that you use a separate line. As with ANSI C, a function must be declared before it's called. In this declaration, the type and number of the parameters also are included. The following example demonstrates this declaration syntax:

```
main()
{
   int example(int,int);
   .
   .
   .
}
```

In contrast to the function definition header, in the declaration you do not need to explicitly mention the parameter name, only the data type. You can include the parameter for clarity, however. In the remainder of this book, I will include only parameter data types in the declaration. C++ requires that you declare each function before you call it.

The syntax of a C++ function definition follows the same prototyping format as the ANSI C standard. A function definition starts with a header line that contains a declaration of the return value of the function and a list of declarations for any of the parameters, as follows:

```
int example(int x, int y)
```

In this declaration, the function returns an integer value and takes two integer values—x and y—as arguments. Note that the parameter declarations are done in a single step within one set of parentheses.

Call by Reference in C++

Another C++ feature that expands the versatility of functions and function calls is the provision for *call by reference* parameters. Although this term might be foreign to many practical C or C++ programmers, the action that it implies is used every day. When a function with an associated list of parameters is called from another function, the variables represented by the parameters must be supplied with values. Ordinarily, you do this by calling the function with a set of variables, expressions, or other values—one per formal parameter—although C++ also lets you specify a default value that doesn't need to be supplied explicitly. Often, these formal arguments are in the form of variables. When you invoke the following function:

```
x = example(x,y);
```

the variable x is associated with the first parameter of example(), and y is associated with the second parameter.

Parameters that are declared in the function definition have a scope that restricts them to the function. In the following example:

```
int example(int x, int y)
{
    int z;
       .
       .
    return z;
}
```

x, y, and z are local variables. Using a variable in the calling sequence is identical to initializing a variable in the declaration statement within the function being called. The values that are passed to the parameter are copies of the formal arguments. For example, if you call the example() function with the following setup:

```
int p = 2, q = 4, w;
w = example(p,q);
```

the value in p is copied into x. Similarly, q is copied into y. These two sets of variables are connected only in that they share the same values. Values move in only one direction—from the calling function to the called function. Any changes that occur in the variables in the function are not passed back to the caller. This syntax is known as a *call by value*.

In C, the call by value is the default operation. You can achieve a call by reference, however, by using a pointer as a parameter. In a call by reference, you pass the actual variable (in other words, the memory storage address) to the function. When you use a pointer, the address of the actual argument—not its value—is sent to the function. In the following example:

```
void example(int *x)
{
    int z;
       .
       .
    *x = 2*z;
}
```

a change in the parameter *x has a permanent effect in the calling function because it changes the value of the variable x. This is one way to retrieve values from a function without using the return statement. It also is a common alternative to using global variables when two functions must share data.

Declaring Reference Variables

C++ provides an alternate form of call by reference that is easier to use than pointers. First, let's examine the use of reference variables in C++. As with C, C++ enables you to declare regular variables or pointer variables. In the former case, memory is actually allocated for the data object. In the latter case, a memory location is set aside to hold an address for an object that will be allocated at another time. C++ has a third kind of declaration—the reference type. Like a pointer variable, it refers to another variable location, but like a regular variable, it requires no special dereferencing operators.

The syntax of the reference variable is straightforward.

```
int x;
int& y = x;
```

This example sets up the reference variable y and assigns it to the existing variable x. At this point, the referenced location has two names associated with it—x and y. Because both variables point to the same location in memory, they are in fact, the same variable. Any assignment made to y is reflected through x. The inverse also is true: Changes to x occur through any access to y. Therefore, with the reference data type, you can create an alias for a variable.

The reference data type finds its greatest use in parameter declarations. For example, in the function header

```
int funct(int& x)
```

the parameter x receives not a copy of the actual argument, but rather, a reference back to the actual variable within the scope of the calling function. The reason for this is simple: When a parameter is created at the time a function is called, the syntax is identical to a variable declaration with initialization. In Listing 2-8, ref.cpp illustrates this syntax.

Listing 2-8. A program that illustrates the function call syntax using the reference data type: ref.cpp.

```
main()
{
    void func1(int&);
     int x = 123;

     cout << "x = " << x << "\n";
     func1(x);
     cout << "x = " << x << "\n";
}

void func1(int& p)
{
    p += 24;
}
```

In ref.cpp, after declaring the function func1() and declaring and initializing an integer variable x, you print the value of the x before it's used as a parameter in the function call. The parameter in the function is declared as a reference type. This means that when the actual call is made, the variable p, although it is local to func1(), contains a reference to the variable x back in the main() function. Any assignments or changes made to p are reflected in x (in this case, the value of x is increased by 24). Reference data types give C++ an enhanced capability for parameter passing.

Overloading

With function overloading, which is a unique part of C++'s function syntax, you can create a family of similar functions that operate on different types of data. All functions in the created family share the same name, but each has an independent code definition. Each overloaded function must have at least one parameter that differs in type from the other functions. In other words, the data type of at least one parameter must be unique to each version of the function. Parameter lists that contain different numbers of arguments, even if they are the same type, also differentiate overloaded functions. When the function is called, the parameter list that is passed to it causes the system to choose the proper body of code. Thus, you don't need to add program statements that choose the correct function. Function overloading eliminates also the need for devising strange names to indicate the differences and the similarities of several related functions.

Function overloading is accomplished by creating different functions with the same name. Their declaration alerts the compiler to their status as overloaded functions. For example

```
int cube(int);
double cube(double);
```

declares a group of two overloaded functions called cube(). These functions differ in the value they return and the data type of their single parameter. It is this parameter that determines which cube() is used by any particular function call. Remember, overloaded functions must differ in either the type of parameters in the parameter list or the number. The return value has no part in distinguishing overloaded function names.

An important caution must be added before leaving the subject of function overloading. As useful and powerful as it seems, this feature can be abused easily and can lead quickly to incorrect and misleading code. In any case, function overloading should be used sparingly and with caution, especially by programmers who are new to the C++ language.

Function Overloading in Classes

Function overloading is used most successfully within the context of a class. Far from becoming a dangerous and ambiguous technique, it can be used to increase the modularity and readability of a program. Class constructors often are overloaded to accommodate different formats of class object initialization.

In Listing 2-9, a simple class is created with three versions of the constructor, including two different ways of putting initial values into the variable members. The first constructor is defined as the default constructor. This constructor is called if no values are offered to the class. The default constructor sets each member to a harmless value. The special character '\0' (the null mark that indicates the end of a character string) is put into the first position of each of the character string arrays. The second constructor accepts three individual character strings representing the three elements of a name: the first name (first), the middle name (mid), and the last name (last). Finally, a third constructor is called that accepts a line of the form

```
"Sally Sara Smith"
```

and extracts the three components in order to initialize first, mid, and last. This constructor uses the standard library function strtok() to break the string into its three constituent substrings. It works by dividing a character string based on a specified delimiter character (in this case the delimiter is a space).

Listing 2-9. Illustrating overloaded member functions: oname.cpp.

```cpp
class name   {
   char first[80];
   char mid[80];
   char last[80];

public:
   name()   { first[0] = mid[0] = last[0] = '\0'; }
   name(char*, char*, char*);
   name (char*);
   char* show();
};

name::name(char* f, char* m, char* l)
{
   strcpy(first, f);
   strcpy(mid, m);
   strcpy(last,l);
}

name::name(char* nm)
{
  strtok(first, strtok(nm, " ");
  strtok(mid, strtok(0, " "));
  strtok(last, strtok(0, " "));
}

char* show()
{
  char* temp = new char[strlen(first) + strlen(mid) +
                                    strlen(last) +26];
  sprintf(temp, " First: %s\nMiddle: %s\nLast: %s\n",
                        first, mid, last);
   return temp;
}
```

An alternative to using overloaded constructors would be to create a single constructor that contains code for all three possibilities. The single constructor would be more complicated, harder to read, and more prone to errors. Using three different constructors produces a much cleaner, easier-to-follow design.

Function Overloading Outside Classes

The overloading of function names is not restricted to class member functions. Any function can be subject to this treatment. For example, in Listing 2-10, a simple function that adds two real numbers is overloaded to handle two different kinds of parameters. In the first case, the parameter list contains two double values, which are added together to produce the result. In the second case, the input is a character string that contains an expression of the form: "3.4 4.1" (two real numbers separated by a space).

Listing 2-10. An example of non-member function overloading: over.cpp.

```cpp
#include <iostream.h>
#include <string.h>
#include <math.h>

main()
{
  double add(double, double);
  double add(char*);
  double x = 1.2;
  double y = 3.4;
  char* ch = "3.4 4.1";

  cout << "Result is " << add(x,y) << "\n";

  cout << "Result is " << add(ch) << "\n";
}

double add(double p, double q)
{
 return p + q;
}

double add(char* expr)
{
 double p = atof(strtok(expr, " "));
```

```
double q = atof(strtok(0, " "));

return p + q;
}
```

In the second add() function, the character string is broken into its constituent parts again using the standard library function strtok(). After two substrings of digits are released from the expression, the library routine atof() converts them to double values initializing the automatic variables p and q. The return statement sends back the result of adding these two values.

Operator Overloading

Another important capability made manifest by the class definition is overloading operators. This simple concept is used frequently in the internal design of programming languages; C++ merely extends its scope. The basic idea behind operator overloading is to redefine a commonly used symbol so that it applies to a new set of values. For example, the + operator represents the addition operation. Furthermore, you can use this simple operator with any type of numeric data. You can add two integer values, or you can add doubles or longs. (In C++, you can add even two character values together if the operation makes sense in the context of the program.) The C code that adds two double values is quite different from that which adds integer values. Thus, C uses an overloaded + sign with its built-in data types. If you define a class data type, you can overload any of the common operators so that they apply to the new class. Therefore, C++ gives you the same capability with user-defined types that C offers with the built-in data types.

The key to redefining an operator is to associate the appropriate operator function with a class object. (One important restriction on operator overloading is that it must involve an object of type class.) You could accomplish this association by defining an operator function and passing it a class as a parameter. The simplest method, however, is to make the operator function a member of the class itself. After it is declared, the operator function can be defined like any other function. For example, suppose you have defined a class with three components: x, y, and z. Furthermore, you want to define the addition of two objects of this type as the sum of their corresponding parts. The x values are added, then the y values, and so on. Although this can be accomplished by definition and the addition function, it is more convenient to use a traditional symbol for addition and expand it to embrace this new definition, which is accomplished easily in overload.cpp (Listing 2-11).

Listing 2-11. A class with an overloaded operator: overload.cpp.

```cpp
#include <iostream.h>

class triad {
  long x, y, z;

public:
  triad(long, long, long);
  void show();
  void operator + (triad p);
};

triad::triad(long p, long q, long r)
{
  x = p;
  y = q;
  z = z;
}

void triad::show()
{
  cout << "x = " << x << "\n";
  cout << "y = " << y << "\n";
  cout << "z = " << z << "\n";
}

void triad::operator + (triad p)
{
  x += p.x;
  y += p.y;
  z += p.z;
}
```

For clarity, this example defines only a single operator function. The function `operator+()` redefines the + operator, but only in the context of this class. Note the format of the function redefinition. Each of the symbols available in C++ has a corresponding operator function. The redefinition is no more exotic than writing a function to handle its details. The following example brings in one object of type `triad` as a parameter and changes the object that calls the +. This calling sequence is the same as if you were adding two integers

```
main()
{
 triad a(2, 3, 4);
 triad b(3, 4, 5);

a + b;
a.show();
}
```

This similarity to traditional uses of the symbol is what makes operator overloading a convenient tool for program design.

As with function overloading, operator overloading is fraught with potential dangers. It is an easy facility to abuse, particularly through overuse. Its inherent dangers are compounded by the fact that it is too easy for you to overload an operator in one context and then try to use its older meaning in another context. Always use operator overloading with caution.

Compiling and Linking with C++

The process of producing a C++ program is an important consideration to the software designer. Editing the text, compiling, and linking are all subjects sure to rouse interest in anyone who produces code. There are few universals, however, when discussing this part of the subject. Many of the details depend not only on personal taste but also on the particular implementation of C++ and any attendant tools that you use.

Many factors can cause a particular individual to choose one style of programming over another or even one particular implementation of a compiler over another. It's difficult to do justice to each possible combination of compiler and development environment. There is no way to make a value judgment concerning one particular choice over the other.

Integrated Environment Versus Command-Line Invocation

As noted previously, most platforms provide a choice in implementations of C++ compilers and translators. There are still a few in which you have to use the one version that's available, but these development-poor environments are disappearing rapidly. It makes sense, therefore, to look around at what's available and try to find a platform that suits your personal taste. One important choice to make is between a stand-alone compiler and one that comes embedded in a software development environment.

Stand-alone C++ compilers usually are invoked in the traditional way from a command line. The source files, object files, libraries, and options are all arguments to the command line. This type of compiler is reminiscent of the original C compilers, particularly as found on UNIX. The advantages of such a compiler are not always as obvious.

- It's easy to use in concert with the operating system.

- You have maximum freedom to choose and configure your own software environment.

- It's easier to customize the operation of the compiler, particularly in an operating system that permits background processing.

If C++ is an addition to an old and familiar software development environment, a stand-alone compiler might be the best choice.

C++ compilers also come as part of an integrated software development environment, which typically includes an editor, a debugger, the compiler, the linker, and its support libraries. An integrated compiler can be a bargain if it includes everything needed to develop sophisticated software. As another advantage, the parts of the environment, because they are being supplied by the same vendor, are optimized to work together and usually require minimal installation and setup. In addition, such integrated environments usually are implemented with a graphical user interface that speeds the process of program creation.

Many times a compiler that comes with its own development environment also has a command-line mode or option. This can be used if the compiler specifications are impressive, but you don't want the environment. It's useful also in the more likely situation in which you occasionally may need to interface the compiler to some other command or program or provide for automated (batch) compilation.

Whichever type of implementation you choose, the compiler specifications should compel the choice. The format and the peripheral files and programs should be secondary. It is more difficult to make up the deficiencies of a mediocre compiler than to add missing libraries or utility programs.

Separate Compilation and Linking

One important technique that is used often in C is the practice of compiling functions and collections of functions independently of any program. When these functions are needed, they are linked into the source that contains the `main()` function. One important advantage here is that the functions become general-purpose resources that serve a number of different programs. Under some operating systems, these independently compiled files can be compressed into libraries, where they perform the same function but in a format that saves disk space.

In C++, the technique of separate compilation is used even more frequently. The nature of a class is ideal for this treatment, because the philosophy behind object-oriented programming favors the kind of modularity that such implementation produces. The techniques are modified only slightly when used with a class.

Consider the way you use a class in a program. Each program module must have a copy of the class definition—in this respect it is similar to using C structures. However, it is not necessary to include the code that implements the member functions in each file. Instead, this code can be compiled once and the resulting object code can be linked when the program is completed. Each class then consists of two parts, the class definition and the member function code.

Listing 2-12 contains the contents of a file, name.h, which has the definition of a simple name class. Wherever you need to access or use this class, name.h is included using the preprocessor `#include` command. Note that only the declaration of the class is found in this file.

Listing 2-12. The definition of a simple name class: name.cpp.

```
class name  {
    char first[80];
    char mid[80];
    char last[80];

public:
    name(char*, char*, char*);
    char* full_name();
};
```

Listing 2-13 shows a file that contains the source code definitions for the member functions of name. You first include the declaration using the preprocessor command #include. Each function is defined in the file name.cpp. When this file is compiled, it produces an object module that can be linked into any subsequent source file that needs to use the name class. Of course, it is necessary to have this object file to use the class. After it has been compiled, the source code no longer is necessary.

Listing 2-13. The source code file that implements the name class: name.cpp.

```
#include <string.h>
#include "name.h"

name::name(char* f, char* m, char* l)
{
  strcpy(first, f);
  strcpy(mid, m);
  strcpy(last, l);
}

char* name::full_name()
{
  char* temp = new char[strlen(first) + strlen(mid) + strlen(last) + 3];
  strcpy(temp, first);
  strcat(temp, " ");
  strcat(temp, mid);
  strcat(temp, " ");
  strcat(temp, last);
  return temp;
}
```

Listing 2-14 shows how this class would be used in a program. Again, you need to include the class declaration through the file name.h. When you compile the program, it is necessary to link in the object code. As long as you take these two steps, you can use the class in the program without further ado.

Listing 2-14. A simple program that uses the `name` class: sname.cpp.

```
#include <iostream.h>
#include "name.h"

main()
{
  name x("John", "Jacob", "Smith");

  cout << x.full_name() << "\n";
}
```

Listing 2-15 is another example that uses the name class. This time it's being used in a file that defines a new class, address, derived from name. Again, I've split the implementation into two files: a definition, address.h, and a source file, address.cpp (Listing 2-16).

Listing 2-15. Another example using the `name` class, this time as a base for a derived class: address.h.

```
#include "name.h"

class address : public name  {
   char street[80];
   char city[80];
   char state[80];
   char zip[80];

public:
   address(char*, char*, char*, char*, char*,char*,char*);
   char* full_address();
 };
```

Listing 2-16. The source code file for the `address` class: address.cpp.

```
#include <string.h>
#include "address.h"
```

continues

Listing 2-16. continued

```
address::address(char* f, char* m, char* l, char* s,
                char* c, char* st, char* z) : name( f, m, l )
{
  strcpy(street, s);
  strcpy(city, c);
  strcpy(state, st);
  strcpy(zip, z);
 }

char* address::full_address()
{
  char* temp = new
           char[strlen(street)+strlen(city)+strlen(state)+strlen(zip)+5];

  strcpy(temp, street);
  strcat(temp, "\n");
  strcat(temp, city);
  strcat(temp, ", ");
  strcat(temp, state);
  strcat(temp, "  ");
  strcat(temp, zip);
   return temp;
}
```

Listing 2-17 is an example of a program that uses the address class. It includes the file that defines address. It has to be linked to the object module that contains the address class function code and the object module for name.

Listing 2-17. A program that uses the address class: xdress.cpp.

```
#include <iostream.h>
#include "address.h"

main()
{
  address y("Sally", "Sara", "Smith",
           "123 El Monte Road",
           "Los Altos Hills", "CA", "94022");

  cout << y.full_name() <<"\n";
  cout << y.full_address() << "\n";
}
```

The use of separate compilation adds a component of modularity that complements the already high degree of data abstraction inherent in C++. In its most complete development, this separate compilation leads to the creation of a class library on the model of the already existing standard library functions. Most C++ compilers are supplied with some class libraries already implemented. These are good models to emulate.

Summary

This chapter explored some of the differences and advances of C++ over C. In the process, you've had an overview of the syntax of this object-oriented language. Specifically, you've looked at

- Enhanced modes of declaration

- The definition of a new data type, the class

- Enhanced parameter processing, including reference data types

- Function definitions including function name overloading

- Operator overloading

- Separate compilation of classes.

The rest of the book looks at each of these basic topics in depth. In the process, you explore the details of C++.

3

Focusing on the Class

3

Focusing on the Class

Chapter 2 gave a broad overview of the C++ programming language. You have seen how the new features of C++ and those features inherited from C fit together to form an organic whole. Now you need to focus more narrowly on each of these important C++ features to discover the power and elegance of the language. Central to C++ and these discussions is a new kind of data type, the *class*. The class offers a programmer the tools to create internal data objects that more closely match the behavior of the real-world objects and systems that the program must manipulate. Whether the application involves nuclear physics or sales records, the software designer's main task is to create more accurate ways of representing the real world within the limited domain of the computer. The class data type makes this mapping easier and more powerful.

C provides basic mechanisms, such as header files and separately compiled functions, to help programmers divide a program into modules that are functionally related, yet separately maintainable. Truly modular program design requires more than this, however. The programmer also needs to control how the modules are accessed and to determine which parts of each module are private (internal) and which are public (external). Through the mechanism of the class, C++ provides a new degree of control for specifying the relationship among the various objects in a program, as well as a way to specify how each class of objects is used.

The C++ class represents an improvement over C; it combines flexible data representation with fully controllable modularity. Thus, a new concept is established—the object—that honors both issues. After a discussion of the existing facilities in C, this chapter introduces the structure and design of the class in C++, focusing first on issues of data representation, then on the subject of modularity.

When most programmers think of data types, they tend to think of the built-in ways that C and C++ represent such things as integers, floating-point numbers, or characters. However, one often must take into account objects that consist of many different, yet related, kinds of data. A simple example of this is a client record, which might include character data (name and address), integers (inventory), and financial data (dollar amounts). Although the computer must use different methods to manage these different basic types of data, the programmer needs to have a way to handle the data record as a single entity, as well as by individual data items.

Structures in C represent a first step toward this higher level of data organization. Using C's structure definition facility you can combine many different variables into a kind of "super" data object that has two aspects. On one hand, the entire object can be manipulated: You can send it as a parameter to a function, for example. On the other hand, you can access also the individual components of such a structure data type. Thus, the capability of structures to mirror the complex "real-world" entities that they represent makes them an indispensable part of a C programmer's repertoire.

A structure definition in C, however, refers only to the storage of values, because a structure data type is merely a collection of variables. For each set of data, the programmer must provide a set of tools to manipulate the data. For example, you need tools to allocate memory for a new data record, to move data into and out of the record, to perform operations on the various fields, and to free memory when the record is no longer needed. Traditional C has no internal way to relate the data to the tools that work with the data. The best it can do is permit you to put both structures and related functions into one header file or a separately compiled module.

C++ expands this notion of a structure data type to include not only the members that store values but also the member functions that operate on those variables. The result—a complete object called a class—is the basis for calling C++ an *object-oriented* programming language. Thus, C++ can be seen as a quantum advance from the more commonly used "functional" or "procedural" languages such as C, in which data and algorithms are strictly separated.

The Simplest Class

The C++ class is an evolutionary step forward from the C structure data type. In C, you're used to using struct to create customized data types, particularly those of a compound nature. A data processing record, for example, combines whatever personal information in which you are interested in such a way that you can either treat it as a whole (such as by storing it on a disk file) or look at its individual parts.

The following code is a common example of a structure. This one stores a person's name and might serve as part of a more complicated structure definition. Because an important goal of C++ is to maintain upward compatibility with C, it should come as no surprise that this particular example is correct also in C++.

```
struct name  {
    char first[80];
    char middle[80];
    char last[80];
 };
```

So, you can have structures in C++ that behave the same way as those used in C. The issue, however, doesn't really end at this point. Although a structure definition in C is usable if you promote the C code to C++, the true C++ structure is a different kind of thing; it has greater functionality and flexibility.

The *struct* Keyword

The keyword struct in C++ actually defines a class. Just like a structure in C, a class can contain members that stand for storage locations. In the following example, first[] indicates an array of characters that is 80 members long. The same is true of middle[] and last[]. One important difference between a class and a structure is that a class also can contain a different kind of member, a *function member*. In the following example, I've taken the earlier structure definition, but this time, I've added a function to the list of members. The function show_last_name() returns a character string that contains the contents of the member last[].

```
struct name  {
    char first[80];
    char middle[80];
    char last[80];
    char* show_last_name();
};
```

Defining a class creates a template that will be used later when actual objects of that type are allocated. The easiest way to create a class object is a simple declaration:

```
name x;
```

in which name is a previously defined class. This declaration uses the previously defined class template to allocate contiguous storage for its variable members, just as a C structure definition would. One important difference to note is apparent from the declaration. It's no longer necessary to use the keyword struct when declaring the variable. Class names occupy the same addressing space as variables in C++. Access to the variable members follows the C mechanism. Listing 3-1 shows a program that uses the class defined in the previous example. Individual members of the class are accessed through the variable name, using the dot notation. Note that the function member `show_last_name()` also is accessed using the dot notation. In this example, the access appears as an expression within a chain of values that is being passed to `cout`.

**Listing 3-1. A `main()` function
that uses the `name` class.**

```
#include <iostream.h>
main()
{
   name x;

   cout << "Enter Names Below:\n";
   cout <<  "   First..........";
   cin >> x.first;
   cout << "   Middle.....";
   cin >> x.middle;
   cout << "      Last.........";
   cin >> x.last;

     cout << " Last Name  " <<  x.show_last_name() << "\n";
}
```

The Difference Between a Structure and a Class

The previous section focused on the similarities between the C structure and the C++ class. The only differences noted were the existence of the function member and the fact that structures no longer have a unique name space, but instead they coexist with the other variable names. This section focuses more on these differences and what they mean when you begin to use classes to design programs.

One important issue that I've glossed over is the question of defining function members. So far, all that I've done is declare them and then offer an example that uses the member function. A function must be defined before it can be used, of course. In fact, highlighting the definition syntax serves to underscore the different nature of a C++ class. In the following example, you can see a more complete rendering of the previous example.

```
struct name  {
    char first[80];
    char middle[80];
    char last[80];
    char*  show_last_name();
 };

char* name::show_last_name()
{
    return last;
}
```

As undramatic as the preceding example is, it still shows the basic elements of defining a member function. The important point to note is the use of the *scope reference* operator (::) along with the class name in the header of the function definition. It is this combination that identifies the function as a member of this particular class. Without this qualifier, the definition would create an ordinary function, subject to the usual function rules of access and scope. You could define an additional show_last_name() function that has no connection to the class. Beyond this, the function definition is the same as the function that you're used to defining in C.

Let's look at a more ambitious class definition. The following example defines a circle class.

```
const double pi=3.1415;

struct circle  {
  double rad;
  void set_radius(double);
  double get_area();
  double get_circum();
 };

void circle::set_radius(double r)
{
 rad=r;
}
```

```
double circle::get_area()
{
 return pi * rad * rad;
}

double circle::get_circum()
{
 return pi*2*rad;
}
```

Because the `circle` class refers to a geometric figure, `pi` is defined as a `double` constant with the appropriate value. The `struct` keyword indicates that the definition that follows is the class named by the tag field on the same line; in this case, the tag name is `circle`. The `double` variable `rad` is an ordinary variable that contains the value of the circle's radius. The C++ class definition is different than the C structure because it also contains function members. In `circle`, these members are

```
void set_radius();

double get_area();

double get_circum();
```

The first function sets the radius variable `rad`. The second member function returns the value of the area of the circle, which is calculated from the current value of `rad`. Finally, the last member function returns the current circumference. The definitions of these members are straightforward. In each case, they are single-line functions that perform a calculation and then return the results.

As before, to create a circle object, a declaration is necessary.

```
circle x;
```

Also as before, the members of the class are accessed using the dot notation.

```
cout << x.rad << "\n";
```

The preceding line displays the contents of the `rad` member. The same is true of function members

```
cout <<  "Circumference = " << x.get_circum();
```

This expression prints the value of the circumference of the circle.

Function Members
and Data Members

One area you have not yet explored is the relationship between a function member and other members of the class. This is a key element of the concept of a class and a subtle difference separating C++ and C. The members of a class have a special interlocking relationship—each one of them knows about and can access each data member implicitly. Furthermore, the scope of the class defines an autonomous region in the program that includes all of its members. Remember, although this example uses the `struct` keyword, it still creates a class. What's true for this example is true for all classes.

Take another look at the previous example. The member function `set_radius()` takes as a parameter a `double` value and assigns the value of its argument to the `rad` member of the class. Note further that no dereferencing is required. Because `set_radius()` is a member, it can access directly the other member, `rad`. No other part of the program has this privilege. To access any member of the class, the variable and the member name need to be mentioned. Looking ahead to fully articulated classes that can hide members, this capability of member functions becomes an even more striking feature.

As with structures, you also can declare a pointer variable to a class, as in the following:

```
circle* p;
```

The arrow notation manipulates any of the members as it would in a C structure. Thus, `p->rad`, `p->set_rad()`, `p>get_area()`, and `p->get_circum()` are all legal expressions.

The Mechanics
of the C++ Class

Classes defined with the `struct` keyword are only the beginning. They offer only a limited benefit from the new class types that are possible in C++. In this section, you begin to explore more fully the flexibility offered in C++. This flexibility is available through two new and important keywords: `class` and `public`.

As you'll see shortly, among the other things that it does, the class in C++ offers a new tool for modularization. It does this by defining an autonomous region within a program that maintains two important characteristics:

A local scope that is larger than a function but smaller than a file

A controlled interface to the rest of the program.

Through the class, the designer has an enhanced ability to control the complexity of a project by dividing it into subtasks and assigning each of these subtasks to a module in the program.

The *class* Keyword

The full benefits of the class type in C++ are activated by using the keyword `class`. Listing 3-2 shows the declaration of a simple class that keeps track of time.

Listing 3-2. A true class: `s_time`.

```
class s_time {
   long secs;

 public:
  void set_time(char *);
  void get_time(char *);
 };


void s_time::set_time(char *time_day_24)
{
 long hours;
 long minutes;

 minutes=atol(&time_day_24[2]);
 time_day_24[2] = '\0';
 hours = atol(time_day_24);

 secs=(hours*3600)+(minutes*60);
}}


void s_time::get_time(char *tod)
{

 static char *tday[]={"MIDNIGHT","P.M.","NOON","A.M."};

 int hours;
 int minutes;
 int amflag=0;
```

```
hours = secs/3600;

minutes= (secs % 3600)/60;

if(hours == 24)  {
  hours = 0;
  amflag = (minutes == 0) ? 0 : 3;
 }
else if(hours > 12)  {
  hours = hours - 12;
  amflag = 1;
 }
else if(hours == 12 )
  amflag = 2;
else
  amflag =  3;

sprintf(tod,"%2d:%02d %s",hours,minutes,tday[amflag]);
}
```

This package consists of three parts: a long variable that stores the number of secs since midnight and the two member functions set_time() and get_time(). The set_time() function initializes the secs variable; it converts into seconds the character string that contains the proposed time in a 24-hour format. The function get_time() returns the time as a character string and displays it in the familiar a.m./p.m. format.

In addition to the use of the keyword class rather than struct, the primary difference between this version and the classes previously defined using struct is the word public:, which appears in the middle of the definition. This keyword divides the class into two parts: the public part, which is fully available to the rest of the program, and the rest of the definition, which is restricted to member functions of the class. This forms a barrier that divides the class into two sections: an internal section available only to the other members of the class and a section that contains member functions that can be accessed from outside the class.

Access to the private part of a class is barred to any but the class's own member functions—and special functions called *friends*, which I discuss in Chapter 6. The class's own member functions have the same special relationship as those in the structure type. Functions that are not members of the class can access the members of the private part only through the functions in the public part. Thus, a program cannot rely in any way on the details of the implementation of the class, which are hidden. S_time represents a typical situation. The data part of the object is defined within the private part of a class. The functions that operate on it are defined in the public section. These public functions form an interface to the rest of the program, thus allowing controlled access to its value sections (see Figure 3-1).

Figure 3-1. The difference between public and private sections of a class.

By hiding the implementation details of a class, a designer can program maximum flexibility into programs and systems of programs. Because no other part of the program can access the private part of a class, the interface always remains the same. You can change the details of implementation in a class—even radically change them—without affecting all the code that depends on that class. As long as you maintain the same access format, everything continues to work. For example, in the s_time class, you might decide to store the current date as the number of minutes since midnight, or even as the minutes and seconds since January 1. In each case, as long as get_time() and set_time() use the same calling format and return values, you don't need to change anything else. Without the privacy offered by the class, an element from somewhere else in the program might directly access the secs variable, in which case, any change to the storage structure would be disastrous.

A secondary benefit of this controlled interface design results from the way C++ classes often are used. It is easy to write general-purpose classes that can be used in many different programs and systems. Indeed, programmers often make a class the focus of a library of routines. This capability strongly supports structured design techniques. As another example of a C++ class, consider s_date (in the next example). This example defines a simple date class; it holds the value for a complete date as a series of integer values that represent the day, the month, and the year. This constitutes the private part of the class. With the new_date() function defined in s_date, the programmer can set the date and give_date() displays the current value of the date. Note that the character string array mname[], which contains the names of the months indexed by their number (January is 1, June is 6, and so on) is a constant because it never changes during program execution.

The member function give_date() allocates memory whenever it is called, which may worry some designers. One advantage to using dynamic memory allocation is that the value then can be passed to some other part of the program, even a part out of the scope in which the value initially was created. Along with this convenience comes the responsibility to deallocate this memory, which also is passed on. Including the buffer in the class would undermine its design and make the current value members redundant.

Listing 3-3. A simple date class: s_date.

```
const char* mname[]={ "illegal month","January","February","March","April",
                      "May","June","July","August","September","October",
                      "November","December"};

class s_date  {
    int day;
    int  month;
    int year;
```

continues

Listing 3-3. continued

```
public:
  void new_date(int,int,int);
  char* give_date();
};

void s_date::new_date(int d,int m,int y)
{
 day=d;
 month=m;
 year=y;
}

char* s_date::give_date()
{
 char *buf=new char[80];
 sprintf(buf,"%s %d,%d",mname[month],day,year);
 return buf;
}
```

The Parts of a Class:
Public and Private

The preceding examples demonstrate that the C++ class is a powerful tool for modularizing programs. A class represents a part of a C++ program that is intentionally isolated from all other parts. This is often a point of confusion. The items in the private part of the class have a scope that extends to the entire class— private and public parts—but no further. You cannot access a variable in this private part, for example, from outside the class. This is similar to the relationship of a function to its local variables. A class, however, can appear anywhere within a program—even in the middle of a function. Remember, the primary function of a class is to modularize a program; this is the key to using it effectively.

What should you put into the private part of a class? This is sometimes one of the hardest design questions to answer. The general pattern for simple classes is to make the value part of the data type private, and make the access functions public. The previous class examples all have followed this plan. In the class defined in s_time (Listing 3-2), the variable member that holds the current time in seconds (secs) is hidden from view, as are the three integer members in the s_date class (Listing 3-3). The functions that manipulate these variables, however, are public.

Although this pattern is common, you should not view it as a rule. There are situations in which a private function member is best. Some classes even require a public value part. However, this typical arrangement often makes sense for practical reasons. Usually, the data section of any data type is likely to change. For example, porting a program to a different machine can make a difference in the size of a value. On the other hand, you might implement a high-level data structure as an array in one instance and as a linked list in another. Functions are usually public for the simple reason that a program must have access to the data type if it's going to be useful at all.

The class defined in the following example is a definition of a stack data type implemented as a C++ class. This class is more complicated than the previous examples, but it still represents a typical class definition. It implements the stack, which is a LIFO (last-in, first-out) data structure, as a small array (stak[]) and uses an integer variable (top) to indicate the current start of the array. When you push a value onto the stack, top is incremented. A call to the pop() function decrements top, which moves between 0 and a maximum value set by the constant MAX_ELEMENT. The function error_rep() provides a simple error-reporting facility. The error_rep() function and the two limit variables are hidden in the private section of the class. The public section consists of three stack access functions: stack(), the constructor, which initializes the class by setting top to an appropriate value; push(), which puts a value onto the stack; and pop(), which removes a value.

Listing 3-4. A stack class: stack2.

```
#include <iostream.h>
#include <stdlib.h>

#define MAX_ELEMENT 10

class stack  {
  double stak[MAX_ELEMENT + 1];
  int top;
  void error_rep(int);

public:
  stack() { top = -1; }
  void push(double);
  double pop();
};

void stack::error_rep(int mes_num)
```

continues

Listing 3-4. continued

```
{
 static char* messages[] = { "NOP",
                             "ERROR: STACK overflow condition",
                             "ERROR: STACK underflow condition"};

 cout << messages[mes_num] << "\n";
}

void stack::push(double x)
{
 if(top < MAX_ELEMENT)
     stak[++top] = x;
 else
     error_rep(1);
}

double stack::pop()
{
 if(top >= 0)
  return stak[top-];
 else
  error_rep(2);
 return 0;
}

main()
{
 stack y;

 cout << y.pop() << "\n";

 y.push(23);
 y.push(4.3);
 y.push(2.1);


 cout << y.pop() << "\n";
 cout << y.pop() << "\n";
 cout << y.pop() << "\n";

}
```

First, push() checks for an overflow condition. Then this value increments the top variable. Finally, it uses this value as an index into stack, in which it assigns the value passed from the member. The pop() function checks for underflow and passes the current value of the array back to the caller. Then, top is decremented.

The algorithms that are defined in this class could be used to create a stack type using just the C-compatible part of C++. The array stak[] could be defined as a static global array in a separate file with the push() and pop() functions. error_rep() also could be declared as static to hide it from the rest of the program. The big distinction between the stack as defined in this C-like way and as defined in C++ is that with the former, you can have only one stack in the program. To create multiple stacks, you would have to make multiple copies of the file that contained the code and then rename each function. As a result, you might have a dpush(), a dpop(), an fpush(), and an fpop(). Using the stack class defined in C++, you can declare as many stacks as you need.

```
stack x;

stack y;

stack z;
```

Each stack variable is unique and each has access to all of the powers and capabilities of the stack. No extra selection code is necessary. You push values onto them by specifying the stack object you want to work with, as follows:

```
x.push(2);

y.push(3);

z.push(4);
```

You pop values from them in a similar manner.

```
cout << x.pop() << "\n";

cout << y.pop() << "\n";

cout << z.pop() << "\n";
```

In both cases, the same functions and the same syntax apply to each object.

Note that the data section and one function reside in the private part of the class. All the other functions are located in the public part. The design criteria for the public part is obvious: The programmer needs to have access to the stack. There must be some kind of push and pop operation at least, or it's not a stack at all. These two functions represent the "interface" to the rest of the program. Almost as clearly, the rest of the program must be kept at a distance from the implementation of the stack. This avoids code that directly manipulates the array stak[] for the sake of efficiency. Because you might want to reimplement the stack as a linked list later, for example, you must keep the rest of the program in the private part so that neither another programmer nor forgetfulness can destroy your work.

But what about error_rep()? Why is it private and hidden from the rest of the program, even though it has no particularly important role in the basic operation of the stack? Only the member functions use the error-reporting function in this stack data type. error_rep() is not directly called by any other part of the program. Therefore, as a purely internal member, it belongs in the private part of the class. As a rule of thumb, you should restrict the public section to those members that control access to the class. Unnecessary access to the inner functioning of the class increases the risk that a program will use the class object in a nonportable and unwise way.

Class Initialization: Constructors and Destructors

The examples thus far have not required explicit memory allocation. Often, things are not so simple. To help you thoroughly understand the concept of class, let's examine how C++ actually allocates memory and manages it for a class. First, recall how C allocates memory for variables in general. When you declare an integer or double variable, C allocates storage space for it somewhere in memory—sometimes on a stack or in a particular memory segment. Where and when this space is allocated depends on the interaction of the storage class and the scope of the variable. For example, C might put extern and static variables in one location, and auto (automatic) variables in another. This allocation is a straightforward operation because variables and other data objects in both C and C++ are not dynamic. The compiler creates them before any action is performed on them, whether they are at the beginning of the program (static and extern variables) or at the entry to a function (automatic values). C always knows the parameters of the allocation—sizes and so on—before it actually allocates memory. The same is true for arrays and structure classes that do not have any member functions.

C also performs the same kind of allocation for user-defined structure types. A struct definition specifies a set of variable locations in a particular order. These variables are contiguous in memory. C allocates the structure as a whole, with the important exception of member variables that are pointers. The only memory allocated for a pointer is for the storage of an address, and it does not include the location that the member variable points to. The following example

```
struct info  {
   char *name;
   char *address;
   char *phone;
} x;
```

allocates three pointer variables, but it does not allocate the space for the character strings to which they point. If you want to assign a name to the name member, you first must call the allocation operator new or find some other way to fill name with the address of a character string. Creating complete class objects is more involved, however, because they have an internal structure that includes both data storage members and functional members, as well as the further complication of having private and public sections. An even greater level of complication arises when a class contains pointer variables that need to be initialized.

To handle the greater complexity of class allocation and to enhance its power, the class declaration mechanism includes the capability of executing a special, class-specific function known as a *constructor*. The syntax of the constructor function is simple: It always has the same name as the class. For example, if the class is named link_node, the constructor is link_node(). This function always is executed when you create an object of the class type. For a variable of storage class extern, the constructor is called once at the beginning of the program. In contrast, if the variable is automatic, the constructor is called each time the scope is entered. Note that C++ automatically calls the constructor function without any explicit action by the program code. Thus, you do not need to worry about where or when you should use it. C++ does not allow an explicit call of the constructor.

The programmer, however, determines the contents of the constructor function. No special restrictions apply, and it can perform a wide range of initial actions on both the class and its constituent members. Some typical initialization actions include

- Allocating internal pointer variables (for example, creating character string variables)

- Assigning specific values to member variables

- Executing machine- or device-specific start-up code

This list by no means exhausts the possibilities. To better understand the use of constructors, consider the name class defined in the following example.

```
#define SPA   " "

class name  {
   char* first;
   char* mid;
   char* last;

public:
   name(char*, char*, char*);
   char* show_name();
};

name::name(char* f, char* m, char* l)
{
    first = new char[ strlen(f) + 1 ];
    strcpy(first, f);

    mid = new char[ strlen(m) + 1 ];
    strcpy(mid, m);
    last = new char[ strlen(l) + 1 ];
    strcpy(last, l);
 }

char* show_name()
{
    char* temp = new char[ strlen(first) + strlen(mid) + strlen(last) + 3
];
    strcpy(temp, first);
   strcat(temp, SPA);
   strcat(temp, mid);
    strcat(temp, SPA);
   strcat(temp, last);

   return temp;
}
```

The constructor for this example takes three string values as arguments. These values are used to set the three variable members first, mid, and last. But before any assignments can be made, memory must be allocated to hold the strings. This memory is allocated through the C++ allocation operator new. Note the use of strlen() from the standard library, which allows the class constructor to allocate precisely the correct amount of memory—with one additional space for the end-of-string character.

The only other member function for this class is show_name(), which returns a character string consisting of the three variable members concatenated together into a single string. As with the constructor, strlen() and new are put to use to create a memory location. Then strcpy() and strcat() fill the location with the appropriate values.

The code in the previous example also highlights an important characteristic of constructor functions: If a constructor requires an argument, you must supply that argument at the time the constructor is called. These values are supplied in a number of ways. The most common circumstance, however, is to give these arguments at the time the variable is declared.

```
name x("John", "Jacob", "Smith");
```

The three values between the parentheses are passed as parameters to the constructor.

Each class also can have another special member function: the *destructor*. Unlike the constructor function, the destructor is called at the time the class object is destroyed, for example, when a class variable of the automatic storage class goes out of scope. The destructor takes no parameters and is formed by putting a tilde (~) in front of the name of the class. The main use for the destructor is to tidy up after a class variable is no longer needed. In the following example, the previous class has been rewritten to include a destructor.

```
class name  {
   char* first;
   char* mid;
   char* last;

public:
   name(char*, char*, char*);
 ~name();
   char* show_name();
};

name::~name()
{
  delete first;
  delete mid;
  delete last;
}
```

Here the design of the destructor is obvious. Whenever a name object is destroyed, the destructor returns the memory allocated for its variable members back to the system. This is a typical—and necessary—use of the destructor function.

Recall that memory allocated with the new operator exists until a subsequent call to delete. This memory could be lost easily if a class variable passes out of its scope without releasing it. The memory would still be allocated, but you couldn't access it because the class variable would be gone.

Often, destructor functions are the complements of constructors. If you had to allocate a member variable with the new operator, you would deallocate it with a corresponding destructor. You also can use the sequencing created by the execution of this function to close any open files or to shut down any devices or subsystems of the computer that were opened on behalf of the class. This important use can be effected by sending a deinitialization string to a printer or a port, for example. Even something as basic as logging off could effectively be executed by a class destructor.

Classes Within Classes

In traditional programming languages such as C, you often use structure variables within structure definitions to add modularity to a design. There is less motivation to use this kind of nesting in C++ because there are other mechanisms for achieving the same result (specifically, *inheritance*, which is discussed in Chapter 8). However, the simple example of using a class within another class to define variable members of a class to be objects of another class is a readily understood example that underscores the flexibility of the class data type. Listing 3-5 is an example of this simple circumstance.

Listing 3-5. A nested class definition: phone.h.

```
#include <string.h>
#include <iostream.h>
#define SPA " "

struct name  {

  char first[40];
  char mid[40];
  char last[80];
 };

struct phone  {
   char area[4];
   char prefix[4];
   char number[5];
 };
```

```
class p_rec  {
  name name;
  phone phone;

public:
  p_rec(char*,  char*, char*, char*, char*, char*);
  void display_rec();
};

 p_rec::p_rec(char * f, char* m, char* l, char* a, char* p, char* n)
{
 strcpy(name.first, f);
 strcpy(name.mid,  m);
 strcpy(name.last,  l);
 strcpy(phone.area, a);
 strcpy(phone.prefix,  p);
 strcpy(phone.number,  n);

}


void p_rec::display_rec()
{
  cout <<name.first << SPA << name.mid  <<  SPA  << name.last  << "\n";

  cout <<  "("  << phone.area << ")" << SPA << phone.prefix << "-"
<< phone.number << "\n";
}
```

This example defines the class p_rec to contain the name and phone number of an individual. The name is subdivided into the familiar first, middle, and last name. The telephone number is also divided into an area code, prefix, and number. To simplify the design, the name member of the class is itself a class—the structure name. The phone member, too, is predefined in this way. In both cases, the subclasses are groups of character strings. The interface consists of the constructor and the member function display_rec(). The latter function takes no parameters and simply displays the current values of the class. The constructor takes six character strings as its parameters and sets the private part of p_rec accordingly. The use of a struct class as a component for another class is a fairly straightforward operation. The simplicity of the structure—particularly one without member functions—fits many common design situations.

One danger inherent in the ability to define classes is the temptation to create intricate class structures. Often, the complexity that occurs with many nested and interlocking class structures defeats the advantages of using classes in the first place. An important element in the philosophy of C++ programming is that you should not overburden programs with intricate class constructions. Figure 3-2 illustrates the relationship among these classes. For complicated circumstances, there are better ways to combine classes using inheritance, which is covered in Chapter 8.

Another important point to note when you deal with nested structures involves the scope of the class definition. C++ is, at heart, still C, and the degree of data-hiding that you can do is still restricted. To understand this restriction, consider Listing 3-6, which has an alternative definition for the class p_rec in Listing 3-5.

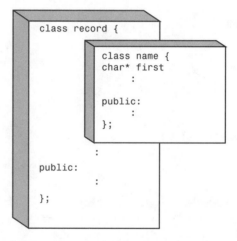

Figure 3-2. The relationship among nested classes.

Listing 3-6. A class with internal class definitions.

```
class p_rec  {
    struct name  {
        char first[40];
        char mid[40];
        char  last[80];
    } name;
```

```
    struct phone  {
        char area[4];
        char prefix[4];
        char number[5];
    } phone;

public:
    p_rec(char*, char*, char*, char*, char*, char*);
    void display_rec();
};
```

**Listing 3-7. A driver program
to illustrate the class p_rec.**

```
main()
{
   p_rec  employee("Jane", "Darwin", "Smith", "415", "555", "1235");

   name x("James", "Jonathan", "Quick");

   employee.display_rec();
   cout <<  x.first << SPA << x.mid << SPA << x.last << "\n";
}
```

Although it might not appear so, this code is equivalent to the earlier definition. Even though the structures are defined in the private part of the class and the definitions seem profoundly hidden, the class definitions actually are not hidden from the rest of the program. The structure name and the structure phone are, in fact, available anywhere else in the program as new data types. You could, for example, declare a variable to be of type name later in the program. Listing 3-7 contains a brief driver program that illustrates this point.

Note, however, that there is no connection between variables that use the class defined in p_rec and p_rec itself. A variable of type name, for example, gives you no special privileges to go into a variable of type p_rec. These are independent objects that are not even of the same type. Because you cannot hide definitions the same way you hide data, you have little motivation to use this form. The original definition is neater and easier to read. The important point to remember is that you have limits to what you can do with data abstraction.

3

The Design Process Using Classes: The *line* Class

Now, let's consider a more ambitious design problem. One of the first steps in the creation of a text-editing program is to devise a strategy for representing the text information in a form that is easy to access and manipulate. There are many ways to view a text file: as a stream of individual characters, as a collection of words, or as a series of lines. Each of these formats has advantages and disadvantages. A stream of characters is the most flexible but also the most complex method. It also is potentially time-consuming as you navigate through a long file. If you treat a text file as a series of lines, it more naturally follows the commonsense notion of a document, but this too, suffers some problems of efficiency and access. Similarly, a long collection of words also might entail inefficiencies.

The plan adopted here is a combination of words and lines. Ultimately, the representation of a text file is as a list of lines. Each line is a list of individual words. This structure offers the maximum flexibility and speed of access. In Chapter 5, I add details to this project and eventually end up with a small but effective class that could be the basis of a text editor. In this chapter, you take the first step by creating a class to represent a line.

To create a line class, let's stop and define some terms that you'll need. We've decided to represent a line as a linked list of words. A word is defined as a character string delimited by a white-space character, a new-line character, or the beginning of a line. You need some way of presenting the line to the class object and then extracting the words from it. By breaking the line into individual words, you can more easily move, insert, and delete words, regardless of how large the file is.

Listing 3-8 contains the code for the line class. Note first the overall structure of the class. You start out with a simple struct-based class, tvalue, the objects of which carry each word in the line. Each tvalue object contains one token or word from the line and a pointer to the next token in the list. This class definition is similar to the struct that might be used in a C program. To simplify the code, there are no member functions.

The line class itself contains a pointer to a tvalue object. This pointer serves as the head of the list of tvalue objects that contain the information on the line. To simplify some of the member function code, the class also contains a length member, len, which indicates how many nodes—and thus words—are on the list. Most of the work of the class is done by the constructor and destructor functions. Additional member functions permit access to the entire list (show_all()), as well as an individual word specified by its offset from the beginning of the line (nth_element()).

The constructor accepts a line as a single character string. This format has advantages in terms of input and output. It certainly makes more sense to store a line of text in a file in a compact format like a single string. Similarly, input from the keyboard is most conveniently accessed in the form of a line or character string, but once you start to alter or manipulate the line, you must convert it to the specified format. The constructor converts the line by using the standard library function strtok(), which accepts a character string and a set of delimiter characters and strips off substrings based on these delimiters until the end of string is reached. In the constructor, each time a new substring is stripped from the line, a new tvalue object is created, initialized with that substring, and placed at the end of the list. Because the tvalue class is defined as a struct, it is public by default, which allows the line class to handle the details of the linked list directly. Also, note the new operator is being used to create a class object. This feature of the operator is explored more fully in Chapter 5.

Listing 3-8. The line class.

```
#include <iostream.h>
#include <stdlib.h>
#include <string.h>
#define SPA "   "

struct tvalue  {
  char* value;
  tvalue* next;
 };

class line  {
  tvalue *toke;
  int size;

public:
  line(char*);
 ~line();
  char* nth_element(int);
  void show_all();
 };

line::line(char* o_line)
{
   char* temp;
```

continues

Listing 3-8. continued

```cpp
    if((temp = strtok(o_line, SPA)) == 0)  {
      cout << "error condition\n";
      size = 0;
      exit(1);
    }
    toke = new tvalue;

    tvalue* cursor = toke;
    cursor->value = new char[strlen(temp) + 1];
    strcpy(cursor->value, temp);
    cursor->next = 0;

    for(int i = 1 ; (temp = strtok(0, SPA)) ; i++) {
      cursor->next = new tvalue;
      cursor = cursor->next;
      cursor->value = new char[strlen(temp) + 1];
      strcpy(cursor->value, temp);
      cursor->next = 0;
    }
    size = i;
}

line::~line()
{
    tvalue *prev, *cursor = toke;

    while(cursor != 0)  {
        prev = cursor;
        cursor = cursor->next;
        delete prev->value;
        delete prev;
    }
}

char* line::nth_element(int num)
{
  tvalue* cursor = toke;
```

```
  for(int i = 1 ; i < num ; i++)
    if(cursor->next != 0)
      cursor = cursor->next;
    else
      return 0;
  return cursor->value;
}


void line::show_all()
{
  tvalue* cursor = toke;

  for(int i = 0 ; i < size ; i++)  {
    cout << "==>" << cursor->value << "\n";
    cursor = cursor->next;
  }
}
```

The destructor is necessary here because of the ultimate purpose of the line class. If it's going to be part of a text editor, you can safely assume that occasionally you will have to delete lines. The destructor assures you that in such an event, the memory resources will be returned to be reused. The design of the destructor may appear a little strange at first. A cursor variable moves through the linked list with a companion class variable, deleting the class object behind it. However, strange as the algorithm is, it's more efficient than doing it in the more orthodox way of deleting the last node and then searching for the new last node.

Show_all() borrows its algorithm from the constructor. It sets up a cursor variable to point to the head of the list, toke, and moves ("walks") to each node in turn. When it is at a node, cursor is used to access and display the word stored there. The address of the next node also is available, allowing cursor to move down the list. The last node is signaled by a next value of 0, which stops the member function.

nth_element() searches for a particular node by number. This number represents the offset from the beginning of the list. Again, variable cursor of type tvalue* is initialized with the value in the member toke. A for loop moves through the list, this time counting the number of nodes to which it has traveled. When it arrives at the desired node, it returns its value through the function. Listing 3-9 contains a small driver program to illustrate the basic operation of the line class.

**Listing 3-9. A brief driver program
to illustrate the line class.**

```
main()
{
  line x("This is only a test");

  x.show_all();
}
```

In subsequent chapters, you learn to modify this class and use it in combination with other classes.

Object-Oriented Design: Encapsulation Within a Class

Before I discuss this important topic of encapsulation, it's necessary to choose some terms that you can apply in a neutral way. In other words, you need to choose terms that do not refer to a single implementation of object-oriented technology. An object, however and wherever it is defined, consists of two parts: the value-holding part, and the methods that manipulate the value. Different object-oriented programming tools interpret these two parts in different ways. It's up to you to find these interpretations. In C++, the value-holding part is implemented by the variable members of the class. Methods are the function members.

One of the key characteristics of object-oriented programming tools is this capability of encapsulating data and methods within a single entity. There must be some way to define a value so that it contains the operations that manipulate and change it. Encapsulation is still a vague concept that is tied closely to a particular programming language and indirectly to the particular philosophy of programming that underlies that language. These differences are most striking in the different relationships that are found among objects.

When you define a class in C++, you usually create two regions within the class. The public part gives access to the class; it allows other parts of the program a controlled entrance to the class and to the class values. The private part of the class is unique to the class and is inaccessible except to members. The public part of the class, which usually consists of function members, represents a highly controlled access. One important advantage of C++ is this high level of control you can exert over the access. A programmer cannot design a program to access the values within the class except through the methods that you create to channel this access.

One important result of the high level of control exerted over access to the class is that the implementation of the class is independent of the rest of the program. The internal details of the class can change, and as long as the interface remains the same, these changes have no effect on the rest of the program. This independence has implications for program maintenance and debugging: A program becomes a collection of autonomous entities. It becomes much easier to make changes or isolate obscure bugs.

Most programming languages, object-oriented or not, allow the creation of more or less strictly autonomous regions. C++ takes this capability one step further with the definition of classes. Compare Listing 3-4 with Listing 3-10 to see the differences. In Listing 3-4, you saw a C++ implementation of a stack data type. In contrast, Listing 3-10 shows a C language version of a stack data type.

Listing 3-10. A stack defined in C.

```c
#define MAX_ELEMENT 10


static double stak[MAX_ELEMENT + 1];
static   top = -1;

static void error_rep(int mes_num)
{
 static char* messages[] = { "NOP",
                             "ERROR: STACK overflow condition",
                             "ERROR: STACK underflow condition"};

 cout << messages[mes_num] << "\n";
}

void push(double x)
{
 if(top < MAX_ELEMENT)
     stak[++top] = x;
else
     error_rep(1);
}
```

continues

83

Listing 3-10. continued

```
double pop()
{
 if(top >= 0)
  return stak[top—];
 else
  error_rep(2);
 return 0;
}
```

The C version of the stack depends on an additional factor that is not clear from the listing. The function definitions and data type declarations must be contained in an independent file separate from the rest of the program. The static modifier for stak[] and top restricts the scope of these variables to that file. They are unaccessible in the rest of the program. Similarly, the error_rep() function is restricted to the containing file. Because the scope of these variables and the function is restricted to the file, the implementation is well-hidden and independent of the rest of the design.

There is one important difference between the C solution and the C++ class. In C, you can define only one stack type with these particular operations. The push() and pop() functions are and need to be globally available in order for the program to work. If you need another stack, you must create a new file with its own set of functions, including different names so that they can be distinguished. You might have cpop() and cpush(), for example. Although it seems as if you're creating a new data type, it's a restricted one: It can be used only to create a single object.

In contrast, the C++ class object easily can create as many or as few objects as are needed in the program. Each one has its own variable and its own space. More importantly, the same member functions are called for each stack.

Summary

This chapter explored many aspects of the C++ class facility. With classes, the programmer can create small autonomous regions within a program. These regions have their own local variables and functions and support the kind of modularization necessary for modern software design. In addition, the C++ class is an ideal medium for implementing the notion of a data object or a structured representation of a complex real-world entity. You can use data objects to further enhance the modularity and structure of a program. A class represents a high-performance, user-defined data type that includes both data storage and data manipulation functions. Furthermore, a class contains a private and a public section. The private section contains variables and functions that can be accessed only by other members of the class. The public section represents the interface to the rest of the program.

Of equal importance are the special member functions: the constructor and destructor. The constructor is a function that is always called when a class object is created, whether through an ordinary declaration or dynamically through a call to new. In either case, the programmer has an opportunity to do a variety of initialization tasks at this point. Similarly, the destructor executes when a class object is destroyed; it offers new possibilities for ensuring the graceful deallocation of such a class object. Both of these special members enhance the capabilities of the C++ program designer.

4

Using Functions in C++

Using Functions in C++

Although the focus of C++ is on the object-oriented features of the class, functions still play an important part in any C++ program. To implement effective class definitions, you need the capability of creating sophisticated member functions. After all, functions do the actual work in a program.

Functions in C++ retain the features of C functions but add some important new abilities. In addition, a new data type modifier, the *reference* type, enables designers to create even more efficient code when they implement a function. In the next few pages, I discuss these new C++ features as well as look at some of the carryover techniques from C that are given new focus in an object-oriented environment.

The Definition of Functions in C++

C++ retains the base elements of function definition and use from C. There are three things to consider when dealing with functions.

- Function declaration
- Function definition
- Function-calling

Each of these works the same as it does in C. A C++ function must be declared before it is used. The only exception is when the function definition occurs before the first use—a rare circumstance in both C and C++. A function declaration must include, in addition to the function identifier, the return type and the number and type of each parameter in the list. A typical declaration is

```
int func(double, int);
```

All the elements are included: the function return value `int`, the identifier `func`, and the parameter list. The latter consists of two arguments: a `double` and an `int`. Some designers use an alternative form for the parameter list declaration. They include a dummy variable name chosen to indicate the meaning of the parameter; such a declaration would look like

```
int func(double primary, int multiplier);
```

In this case, the addition of the names `primary` and `multiplier` is meant to remind you which kinds of values should be sent to the function. It's important to note that these declaration identifiers are optional, and in fact, have no real connection to the subsequent definition. They are used as a form of documentation.

The definition of a C++ function also follows the same standard set that a C function follows. In this case, you need to repeat the declaration as a header to the function. This time, however, you need to include the formal parameters because they are needed in the body of the function.

```
double func(double primary, int multiplier)
{
  double temp;

  temp = primary * multiplier
    :
  return temp;
}
```

A `return` statement is necessary to send a value back to the calling program through the function name. Without a `return`, the function name is set to 0.

Calling a function in C++ is the same as it is in C. A function identifier can either stand alone on a line, as in

```
func(p, q);
```

or it can be part of an expression, as in

```
x = func(p, q);
```

In the former case, the function must perform some activity independently of its return value, because that value is not used in the calling function. The latter case, using the return value, is common not only to C and C++, but also to many programming languages.

To this core of function syntax that carries over from C, C++ adds a number of powerful new features that increase the flexibility of the new programming language.

Providing Parameters with Default Values

Many programs use general-purpose functions. For example, instead of writing two functions, one to square a number and another to cube it, you might design a single function that raises a number to any specified power. This approach produces shorter programs, because rather than three or four functions, only one must be included. Additionally, the programmer doesn't have to juggle different names for more specialized functions.

The problem with using specialized functions is obvious; it leads to a proliferation of functions that might each be too small for efficient design. Rather than `power()`, you might have `square()`, `cube()`, `fourth()`, and so on. The overhead of a function call is more than that of the statements executed. The general-purpose function, however, also has disadvantages. The power function, for example, needs a minimum of two parameters to indicate what needs to be done.

```
double power(double number, int exponent)
```

The function itself is more complicated because it must recognize more than one circumstance and choose alternative code. In addition, a general-purpose function is less readable than specialized functions. There are more details to remember and additional parameters to consider. The trade-off is readability against source code size.

C++ offers a third alternative. When declaring a function, you can specify in the parameter list a default value for one or more of the parameters. This is done by following the parameter declaration with = and the desired value. In

```
int example(int, int =12)
```

the second parameter of the function has a default value of 12. Consider the following code fragment:

```
x=23;

example(x);
```

Because the call to `example()` does not specify a value for the second parameter, the value of the second parameter is set to 12 (the default value specified in the declaration). If the function call had been `example(x, 4)`, the second parameter would have been set to 4, as specified in the call. The example clearly shows the syntax of the default argument specification. In the declaration for each parameter with a default value, you must include an expression of the following form:

```
type = value
```

You can set any or all of the arguments of a function this way. Note that the default specification appears in the declaration of the function `example()` and not in the definition itself. In fact, nothing in the function definition indicates a defined default value; this is evident only when you examine the declaration. The calc2.c program (Listing 4-1) is an example of how to define a general-purpose function and provide defaults for the most commonly used values.

Listing 4-1. A simple calculator program with a function that uses a default parameter value: calc2.c.

```
#include <iostream.h>


#define BLANK ' '

#define STOP 0

main()
{
 double x;
 double y;

 double radd(double,double);
 double rsub(double,double);
 double rmul(double,double);
 double rdiv(double,double);

 double rpow(double, double =2);
char opr = BLANK;

while ( opr != STOP )  {
  cout << "enter expression ";
```

```
  cin >> x >> opr >> y;

  switch (opr)  {
    case '+' : cout << "=" <<  radd(x,y);
               break;
    case '-' : cout << "=" <<  rsub(x,y);
               break;
    case '*' : cout << "=" <<  rmul(x,y);
               break;
    case '/' : cout << "=" <<  rdiv(x,y);
               break;
    case '^' : if(y == 2)
                      cout << "=" <<  rpow(x);
                  else
                  cout << "=" <<  rpow(x,y);
                  break;
    case 'x' : opr = STOP;
               break;
    default  : cout << "not yet implemented!\n";
               break;
    }
  cout << "\n\n";
 }
}

double radd(double a, double b)
{
 return( a + b);
}

double rsub(double a, double b)
{
 return a - b;
}

double rmul(double a, double b)
{
 return a * b;
}}

double rdiv(double a, double b)
{
```

continues

Listing 4-1. continued

```
if(b == 0)
   return 0;
return a / b;
}

double rpow(double a, double e)
{

double t = a;

if(e == 0)
   return 1;

for(double i = 1 ; i < e ; i++)
   t *=a;
return t;
}
```

This program defines a simple calculator and adds a new operator (^) to handle exponentiation. The function that manipulates the operator—rpow()—is declared in the same list as the other functions. However, the parameter list for the declaration of rpow() not only lists each parameter, but also includes a default value for the last parameter. Examine the switch clause that handles the input for this function. If the specified power is 2, rpow() is called with only one parameter, although two are specified in the definition of the function. The default value of 2 automatically is assigned to the second parameter. If you specify a number other than 2, both parameters are included in the call, and the function does not use the default value.

There are some commonsense restrictions for using default arguments. The values you specify must either match the parameter in type or be reasonably compatible. In other words, the implicit conversion from one to the other must make sense. Converting a char value to an int makes sense, because a char is in essence a small integer number. On the other hand, a conversion from a double to an int usually generates an incorrect or unreasonable value. Furthermore, C++ does not provide for defaulting parameters in the middle of an argument list; this operation is purely positional. When you call a function, you can omit all the arguments as long as the declaration specifies all the defaults or the last arguments in the list. But you cannot eliminate only the middle one and expect them to assume default values. For example, in the function declaration

```
double example(int =123, char ='a', double = 1.2);
```

you can call the function with the int and char parameters (using the default of the double), you can call the function with only the int parameter (using the default for both the char and the double), or you can call the function with no parameters (using the defaults for all of the parameters). However, you can't call example() by supplying only the int and the double arguments, because the C++ compiler can't tell whether you intended to omit the second value or the third value.

Call by Reference

There are two ways that values can be passed into a function at the time it is called: *call by value* and *call by reference*. In the former case, a temporary variable of the specified data type is created and the value is copied into this variable. In the case of call by reference, only the address of the value is passed into the function. The difference between these two kinds of value manipulation is illustrated in Figure 4-1.

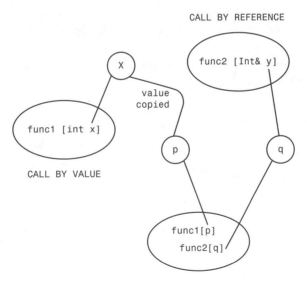

Figure 4-1. Call by value and call by reference.

The consequences of a function call when the parameters are passed by value are an important consideration in designing a program. Take a simple example

```
int func(int x)
{
    x *= 2;
  return x;
}
```

When the function is called, a local, automatic variable of type int is created (x). Whatever value is used to call func(), is copied into this variable. Any changes you make to x are lost as soon as the function terminates, because all local variables are destroyed at this point. Therefore, if you call the function with the sequence of statements

```
int p = 123;
int w;

w = func(p);
```

the value stored in w is two times the value of p, or 246. The value in p, however, is still 123. Refer to Figure 4-1. The relationship between the actual argument p and the parameter x is one of assignment or copying. Although you've changed x, that change does not appear in p. One important consequence of this situation is that with call by value, you can get only one value back from a function—the value of the return statement.

In call by reference, the programmer faces a different situation. Let's redefine the simple function.

```
int func(int* ptr)
{
    *ptr *= 2;
    return *ptr;
}
```

In this case, although the parameter variable ptr is still local and automatic and still disappears at the termination of the function func(), the value that goes into it is the address of a variable back in the calling function. Consider this sequence of statements:

```
int p = 123;
int w;

w = func( &p );
```

ptr contains the address of p. Because the assignment statement in the function definition is an indirect reference using the address of p, what gets the new value is the variable p. The consequence of executing the immediately preceding sequence of statements is that both p and w have the same value.

Call by Reference in C++

In examining the distinction between call by value and call by reference, you have seen the traditional ways of accomplishing these function calls in both C and C++. In both languages, the default for function parameters is call by value. In C, the only way to set up a call by reference situation is to use pointer variables in the function parameter list. This is just what you've been doing in exploring the concept of call by reference.

The use of pointers in a parameter list is still available in C++. In fact, this method is used often, particularly in the case of character strings. C and C++ share another related feature: Array parameters are always call by reference. For example, in the function

```
void func(int x[], int size)
{
  for(int i = 0 ; i < size ; i++)  {
    cout << "=>";
    cin >> x[i];
    }
}
```

an array back in the calling function is being changed interactively. For example, you can call this function within the following context:

```
int p[20];

func(p, 20);

for(int j = 0 ; j < 20 ; j++)
  cout << p[j] << "\n";
```

In this case, the array p[] is filled in the function and is available after the termination of its execution.

Many programming languages recognize that there are two forms of reference when parameters are used with a function call, and those languages allow the designer to specify which kind of access is applied to each parameter. C does not make this kind of distinction. Call by reference is not a built-in mechanism. Its implementation is the responsibility of the programmer. C++, however, parts company with C on this point by making direct provision for call by reference parameters. The mechanism of the call by reference parameter in C++ is the reference data type.

The Declaration of Reference Variables

C++ provides a form of call by reference that is easier to use than pointers. First, let's examine the use of reference variables in C++. Like C, C++ enables you to declare regular variables or pointer variables. In the former case, memory is actually allocated for the variable. In the latter case, a memory location is set aside to hold an address for an object that will be allocated at another time. C++ has a third kind of declaration—the reference type. Like a pointer variable, it refers to another variable location. Like a regular variable, however, it requires no special dereferencing operators (see Figure 4-2).

```
int x = 123;
int& y - x;
```

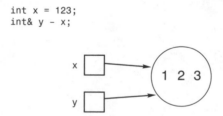

```
Both variables point to the same location in memory.
```

Figure 4-2. The relationship between a reference variable and an ordinary variable.

The syntax of the reference variable is straightforward.

```
int x;
```

```
int& y = x;
```

This example sets up the reference variable y and assigns it to the existing variable x. At this point, the referenced location has two names associated with it— x and y. Because both variables point to the same location in memory, they are, in fact, the same variable. Any assignment made to y is reflected through x; the inverse also is true. Changes to x occur through any access to y. The reference data type creates an alias for a variable.

The reference type has a restriction that serves to distinguish it from a pointer variable, which, after all, does something similar. The value of the reference type must be set at declaration. A reference variable cannot be changed during the run of the program. After you initialize this type in the declaration, it always refers to the same memory location. Thus, any assignments you make to a reference variable change only the data in memory, not the address of the variable itself. In other words, you can think of a reference variable as a pointer to a constant location.

Reference Variables and Pointers

You already know how to use pointers. So why should you use references? Consider the declaration of function parameters. By using a reference type in a parameter declaration, you can create a call by reference without using the cumbersome pointer mechanism discussed earlier. The advantage of using a reference variable inside a function is that the assignment and manipulation of its values are straightforward. They don't need to be dereferenced constantly with the * pointer operator. This constant dereferencing makes the situation fertile for accidental misreferencing. In the following example, the function swap() interchanges the values in its parameters.

```
int value1 = 123;
int value2 = 456;

swap(value1, value2);
    .
    .


void swap(int& x, int& y)
{
  int temp = x;
    x = y;
    y = temp;
}
```

In this case, value1 ends up as 456, whereas value2 is changed to 123. Reference parameters eliminate the need for declaring pointer variables with their attendant dereferencing syntax—*x or *rate—in order to perform a call by reference. Consider the swap() example implemented by using pointers.

```
swap(&value1, &value2);
    .

    .


void swap(int* x, int* y)
{
  int temp = *x;
    *x = *y;
    *y = temp;
}
```

The pointer example is less readable than the earlier version that used reference variables as parameters.

The mean.cpp program (Listing 4-2) demonstrates the use of a reference data type in the parameter list of a function. This simple program calculates the average of any set of real numbers. It consists of three functions: get_value(), mean(), and main(). The get_value() function accepts values from the keyboard and accumulates them in the variable accum. The function's parameter is defined as a reference type in the parameter list and is incremented through the for loop. The special input value of stop ends the operation of this function and returns control to the calling function. The mean() function checks for division by 0 and then calculates the value. The main() function ties the two functions together by calling each one and displaying the results.

Listing 4-2. A program that calculates the mean of a set of numbers and uses a reference parameter: mean.cpp.

```
#include <iostream.h>
#include <string.h>
#include <stdlib.h>

main()
{
 int temp;
 double get_value(int&);
 double  mean(double,int);
 double  accum;

 accum = get_value(temp);
 cout << "mean =" << mean(accum, temp) << "\n";
}
```

```
double get_value(int& t)
{
 char x[50];
 double accum = 0;

 cout << "enter values below:\n";

 for(t = 0 ; ; t++ ) {
   cin >> x;
   if(!strcmp(x,"stop"))
     break;
   accum +=  atof(x);
  }

 return accum;
}

double mean(double x, int total)
{
 if(total == 0)  {
   cout << "error--attempted division by zero!\n";
   return 0;
  }

 return x / total;
}
```

The first few lines of mean.cpp perform the necessary initialization by including the header files string.h and iostream.h from the standard directory. The declarations

```
int temp;
double get_value(int& t);
double mean(double,int);
double accum;
```

set up the functions that get the numbers and calculate the mean.

The int& t parameter in get_value() is a reference parameter. Therefore, changes in the get_value() function are reflected in main(). The accum variable is an ordinary real variable that holds the current total of entered numbers. temp counts the number of entered values.

The heart of `main()` consists of two function calls. The first

```
accum = get_value(temp);
```

retrieves the numeric values from the user through the input function. The second

```
cout << "mean =" << mean(accum, temp) << "\n";
```

displays the result of the calculations based on the two values in `mean()`. Because the parameter of `get_value()` was declared as a reference type, you do not need to use the address-of operator `&`.

The definition of `get_value()` echoes the reference declaration

```
double get_value(int& t)
```

This declares the variable `t` equivalent to any formal argument that calls it and passes all changes to the calling function. The rest of the program is straightforward. After the declarations, the function prompts the user to enter data and uses a loop to accept values from the keyboard.

```
for(t = 0 ; ; t++) {
    cin >> x;
    if(!strcmp(x,"stop"))
        break;

    accum += atof(x);
}
```

The program handles keyboard values as character strings—through the standard input stream `cin` and the input operator `>>`—because they are the most convenient form of input to test. If you had entered the values directly as numbers, it wouldn't be as easy to signal the end of the input loop. Some number would have to serve as a `flag` value. By using character strings, a natural indication (stop in this case) can serve to indicate a halt to the loop. You have available the full range of numbers. Here, the function tests only for the special string `stop`, but you could add more thorough error-checking. If the loop doesn't encounter the exit condition, `get_value()` uses the standard library function `atof()` to convert the character string into its numeric value. It adds this value to the current total and sends the accumulated value to `main()` through the `return` statement. Because the counter `t` is a reference variable, all of the changes that occur in the loop occur also in the originating function. Notice that this function is much more readable than an orthodox C program because it doesn't require pointer dereferencing.

The `mean()` function does calculations based on the two values supplied by `get_value()`. After it tests for division by 0, it performs a simple division and returns the result.

This example is particularly interesting because of the interaction between the parameter t in get_value() and the variable temp, which invokes it from main(). Because t is a reference variable parameter, the calling sequence initializes it to refer to temp. In other words, both variable names are set to point to the same location in memory. Any changes to t (in this case, incrementing by 1) are permanent changes.

There are several reasons why you should use a reference variable as a parameter rather than as a pointer variable. Assignments are direct and do not need to be mediated by an indirection operator. Even more importantly, the calling function does not need to use the & (address-of) operator with the parameter; it uses the variable name directly. Reference types present fewer chances for errors—particularly the mistake of invoking a function with a variable when a pointer variable is expected.

Functions with a Variable Number of Parameters

The same spirit of flexibility in C++ that permits default values for function parameters also lets you specify a variable number of parameters. This feature is needed because the parameter values in a function might not be set until run time. Sometimes even the number of parameters is not known until run time.

A good example of this kind of function is printf(), which occurs in most C programs. Before the ANSI standard, you could use functions with a variable number of parameters in C, primarily because that language did no parameter-checking. You could leave out arguments of a function, and as long as you supplied code to recognize this situation in the function definition, the program would still run. Also, C contains a set of macros that help support functions with no set number of parameters, although printf() is not implemented with them. This facility is available also in C++.

However, when function prototyping (which is a feature of C++ as well as ANSI C) was established, this simple solution became impossible. Now when you declare a function, you must declare also an attendant argument list. Such a declaration checks for proper argument passing, thus preventing you from sending extra variables or failing to supply some arguments. In this case, flexibility was discarded for safety.

However, an easy-to-understand syntax is available for this kind of unspecified function call—without sacrificing the benefits of parameter type-checking. You need only to use an *ellipsis* (...) to indicate a variable number of parameters. The ellipsis causes the type-checking mechanism to skip your undeclared function parameters.

103

4

Specifying a Variable Number of Parameters

A typical use of the ellipsis syntax involves a function declaration in which some set parameters are followed by the variable parameter specifier. For example,

```
int example(int,int,double ...)
```

specifies a function that requires two integer arguments, a double, and a number, which is unknown at compile time, of further parameters. This is a proper declaration of a C++ function, yet it preserves the freedom that pre-ANSI C programmers took for granted—a fluidity of parameter passing. C++ also has an associated set of macros (found in the header file stdarg.h) that collect any actual parameters that you might send to the function. This syntax allows the full C++ parameter-checking for those parameters that are specified. The prntvals.cpp example (Listing 4-3) is a simple program that uses these macros to call a function.

Listing 4-3. A program that illustrates a function that uses a variable number of arguments: prntvals.cpp.

```
#include <iostream.h>
#include <string.h>

#include <stdarg.h>

main()
{
 void print_many(int ...);

 print_many(3,1,2,3);
}

void print_many(int n ...)
{

   va_list ap;

   va_start(ap,n);

   for(int i = 0; i < n; i++)  {
      int temp = va_arg(ap,int);
```

```
      if(temp != 0)
        cout << temp << "\n";
      else
        break;
  }

 va_end(ap);
}
```

In this example, `main()` declares a function called `print_many()`, which takes a variable number of parameters. Note that the header file, stdarg.h, appears at the beginning of the program file. This file contains the macros that support the use of variable numbers of arguments. Because `print_many()` always takes an integer as its first parameter, the program first passes it the argument 3, which indicates the number of items to be printed. Next, the program passes the values to be printed: 1, 2, and 3.

The first statement in `print_many()`

```
va_list ap;
```

declares the argument list ap. The startup macro `va_start()` uses this argument list as its first parameter, and it uses the name of the last parameter specified before the ellipsis as its second argument (the integer n in this example). After `va_list` is set up, the macro `va_arg()` strips off each argument that is passed to the function. The macro

```
va_arg(<va_list object> , <data type>)
```

returns a variable of the same type that it receives as a parameter. In the example, the macro returns an integer type and assigns the value to the variable `temp`. After `cout` displays this value, the last line in the function calls the macro `va_end()` to clean up the `val_list object`.

Inline Expanded Functions in C++

Let's shift the focus of this discussion from improvements in the function call mechanism to the question of whether you should use a function call at all. In traditional C, macros are a convenient way to insert code into a program. Anywhere a macro name occurs in the code, the preprocessor replaces the name with the defined statements. This is a useful device because it improves readability and sometimes helps you avoid the overhead of function calls. The problem with the macro preprocessor is the way it simplemindedly interprets a macro definition, performing a straight textual substitution. For example,

```
#define RATE 1.5
```

causes the character string 1.5 to be substituted for the string RATE. This works fine, but what happens when you use a #define with parameters to produce a function-like syntax? This kind of macro is more powerful because it can generate program code for a variety of situations, but it often can lead to problems. The definition

```
#define tax(x) x*RATE;
```

works for some substitutions but not for others. For example, if you call the macro with an expression rather than a single variable, as in

```
tax(p+2);
```

the macro expansion generates the code

```
p + 2 * RATE;
```

rather than the correct (p + 2) * RATE. C programmers learn to be extremely careful when using the #define in this way.

Other problems with the construction focus on the fact that a macro is not a function. It doesn't have local variables, and it doesn't even define a block. Macros also do not permit parameter-checking when prototypes are used. In short, a #define macro is a series of statements masquerading as a function.

C++ solves the drawbacks of the C macro with a feature called the *inline expanded function.* Inline expanded code gives a programmer the opportunity to use a macro-like facility without any of the problems associated with the #define preprocessor statement.

The inline modifier lets you mark a particular function to be expanded rather than compiled as an ordinary function. Thus, whenever the function is called, it is replaced literally with the statements found in the function definition. (Actually, inline expansion is merely a request to the C++ compiler, which can be ignored if your function is too complicated or too long; in which case, it becomes an ordinary function.) The big advantage that an inline function offers is that it maintains all of the attributes of a true function: It defines a block, it can have local variables, and it permits the same kind of error-checking as an ordinary function. Creating multiline inline functions also presents no special problems.

Another important advantage of using inline functions is that they can help you write well-designed, modular programs that remain efficient at the code level.

For convenience, most programmers divide a program into small, individual functions. When many modules are defined, the program usually is easier to follow and understand and thus is designed better. Ideally, each module should perform a single task. A well-structured program is much easier to update or change also because side effects caused by variables with wide-ranging scope are eliminated and any errors created by new program code can be isolated easily.

However, small functions also can create a problem by being inefficient. A function containing only one line can require more time and resources to set up than it does to actually run. This overhead includes such operations as saving the status of the calling function, copying parameter values to the function, and calling the function. Reloading the original function after the called function executes involves the inverse of this procedure. Thus, the overhead of the function dominates its execution time. Often, the designer can ignore these factors. A program occasionally requires high performance, however, especially if it must perform many repetitive operations. With C++, you can eliminate this type of overhead. Merely use the inline modifier to declare small functions as inline expanded.

Defining an Inline Function

When you use the inline modifier as the first element of the function definition line,

```
inline example(int x)
{
    .
    .
}
```

it requests the compiler to place the following function in the program whenever the program calls the function. With ordinary function calls, value objects are saved and control is passed to a subprogram. With the inline modifier set, the function code is copied into the program at the point of every call. At compilation, there are as many copies as there are calls in the program, and none of them require overhead. Because the code is reproduced many times (thus increasing the size of the object code), however, only small functions benefit from this modification.

The mean2.cpp function in the following example contains the mean() function of a previous example program (Listing 4-2) declared inline. Nothing else in the definition has changed. Actually, the function is a borderline case for inline expansion. It is almost too long to benefit from the treatment. Loading a file with code created from inline functions can cause overhead problems.

```
inline double mean(double x, int total)
{
 if(total == 0)  {
   cout << "error--attempted division by zero!\n";
   return 0;
  }

 return x / total;
}
```

Inline Expanded Member Functions

The use of inline expanded functions finds its most convenient expression in the definitions of class member functions. In this application, it can save time and add clarity of expression to the definition of member functions. Additionally, member functions declared inline are more efficient in just the same way that ordinary non-member functions are.

The line.cpp function in the following example illustrates two types of inline definitions. You use the standard, or explicit, inline definition with member functions the same way as you would with ordinary functions. Here, the function show() is explicitly inline. Note that the member is declared in the class definition, but no reference to how the function is defined is included. Only at the actual definition of the function code itself is the inline member function specified as inline.

You also can define an inline member function implicitly. If you include a function definition with the member declaration in a class, that function is implicitly inline. In the example, the destructor ~line() is an implicit inline function. The implicit form is more commonly used because of its brevity.

```
class line   {
  char* buf;
  int len;

public:
    line(char*);
    ~line()  { delete buf;}
    char* show();
};
```

```
line::line(char* ch)
{
 buf = new char[ (len = strlen(ch)) + 1];
 strcpy(buf, ch);
}

inline char* line::show()
{
 return buf;
}
```

Note that the usage here conforms to good design practice as it applies to `inline` definitions. Only simple (and above all, short) functions should be declared in this way. Because the code that defines an inline function becomes part of each instance of the class, large inline functions waste memory and can slow access to the class. Your request to declare these functions inline is ignored by the compiler.

Versatile Functions Created with Overloading

Often, two functions within a program perform the same operation but on different data types. For example, one function might perform a series of calculations on a set of real numbers, whereas another might handle integers. C programs usually differentiate between these functions with special switching code. For example, in the following program fragment:

```
double z = 1.2;
int w =123;

if( real_flag)
     x = f_std(z);
else
     i = i_std(w);
```

the function `f_std()` performs calculations on real value parameters, whereas `i_std()` performs the same calculations on integers. You must create a separate, unique function for each one.

C++ provides a better solution: You can create a single function name that serves both purposes. The overloading feature handles the differences.

You must approach the technique of function name overloading with a great deal of caution. When you first begin to program in C++, you should restrict yourself to a few carefully considered and obvious examples. During the process of reusing a name, you can easily lose track of which version is being used in any specific context. It is even more difficult for someone reading the program to keep these different contexts straight. Proceed with care! Overloading buys clarity in function-calling at some cost in the complexity of program internals.

Overloading a Function Name

When you declare a function name with the following form:

```
double example(double);
long example(int);
```

you alert the compiler that the program contains more than one set of code referenced by the name `example()`. In this case, `example()` returns a `double` or `long`, depending on the data type of the parameter used when it is called. The only requirement for an overloaded function is that the parameter lists must differ in at least one argument. This is how the compiler selects the proper set of code to honor a function call. The return value of the function is not even considered. The parameter lists must differ in number of parameters, or there must be at least one parameter that is of a different type than the other function definitions.

The "uniqueness" requirement for an overloaded function list of arguments includes some additional restrictions. There must be a clear-cut, unambiguous difference between the parameter lists of overloaded functions. You cannot always rely on the flexible data conversion that C++ does implicitly. To resolve the call of an overloaded function, C++ first tries to match exactly the type of the actual arguments with the type of the appropriate parameters. For example,

```
int example(int,int)
```

matches

```
x = example(1,2);
```

If C++ doesn't find an exact match, it applies a built-in conversion to try to reconcile the actual argument with the formal argument. However, those conversions don't always make sense. For example, `double` to `int` is not carried out by the overloading mechanism, although C++ generally permits such operations to take place. As a last resort, C++ attempts user-defined conversion operations to choose the proper function. (This kind of conversion is discussed in connection with operator overloading in the class data type.)

The mean3.cpp program (Listing 4-4) is an example of an overloaded function name. In this program, the user enters a series of numbers in the following form on the command line:

```
mean 1.2 3.4 6.3 7
```

The program returns the average of these numbers. You can specify either real or integer values. The answer always matches the entered numbers—double for real numbers and long for integer numbers.

Listing 4-4. A program that calculates the mean of a set of numbers and uses function overloading: mean3.cpp.

```cpp
#include <iostream.h>
#include <string.h>
#include <stdlib.h>
double mean(double, char*[], int);
long mean(long, char*[], int);

main(int argc, char* argv[])
{
 if(argc == 1)  {
   cout << "Enter values on command line\n";
   exit(1);
  }

 if(strchr(argv[1],'.') == 0)  {
   long i = atol(argv[1]);
   long x = mean(i,argv,argc);
   cout << "mean = " << x << "\n";
  }
 else  {
   double j = atof(argv[1]);
   double x = mean(j, argv, argc);
   cout << "mean = " << x << "\n";
  }
}

long mean(long x, char* buffer[], int len)
{
 long temp = x;
```

continues

Listing 4-4. continued

```
 for(int i = 2 ; i < len ; i++)
    temp += atol(buffer[i]);

 return temp / (len - 1);
}

double mean(double x, char* buffer[], int len)
{
 double temp = x;

 for(int i = 2 ; i < len ; i++)
    temp += atof(buffer[i]);

 return temp / (len - 1);
}
```

Following the #include statements, the two mean() declarations alert the compiler to the nature of the function.

```
double mean(double, char*[], int);
long mean(long, char*[], int);
```

Note that only the first parameter in each one differs; the rest of the parameter lists are the same. The overloading mechanism uses this first parameter to decide which version to use throughout the course of the program. (The second parameter in each function, char* buffer[], might seem unusual. It passes an array of pointers to character strings.)

Notice that the code in main() which manipulates the arguments is passed through argv[] from the command line; this is a common C convention that carries over to C++. The command line is passed to the program as a series of character strings; the first goes into the character string array argv[1], the second into argv[2], and so on. Argv[0] always contains the name of the program or command that is called. The integer argc contains the total number of arguments supplied when the program is called. In Listing 4-4, if the user runs the program without supplying additional arguments, the following code causes the program to print an error message and end:

```
if(argc == 1)  {
    cout << "Enter values on command line\n";
    exit(1);
 }
```

Remember, a program always has one command-line argument—the program name itself. Thus, if argc is 1, the user entered no numbers on the command line.

Another method of handling incorrect input would be to rewrite the main function to prompt the user for the missing values.

In normal execution, the program checks the first argument to see whether it contains a period. If it does, the argument is a real number. The first argument is converted into a number, and the rest of the arguments—still in the form of character strings—are sent to mean(). Then the program displays the return value. If the function doesn't detect a period, it assumes the value is an integer and converts the first character into a long value. This value and the rest of argv[] are sent to mean(). Because this is a long value, however, the second definition of mean() is called. Again, the program displays the value. The two mean functions differ only in the manner in which they handle the string-to-number conversion.

Let's examine the mechanics of the program in more detail. After the program confirms that the command line contains some arguments, it must decide which function to call. It converts the first argument to the proper numeric value. This is accomplished by sending the first argument in the parameter list to the standard library function strchr(), which checks the digit string for an embedded period. A real number has a decimal point and strchr() tests for this. If no decimal point is found, the program converts the first value into a long value with the standard library function atol(). Otherwise, the program calls atof() to convert the value into a double. In both cases, the resulting value is passed to mean(), and the calculated value is displayed. Note that the variable x is declared as an automatic variable and is initialized by a call to mean(). This declaration is restricted to one of the inner blocks of the if statement. Thus, using the same variables helps make the code more symmetrical.

Both mean() functions have nearly identical code. After execution passes to the appropriate definition header,

```
long mean(long x, char* buffer[], int len)
```

or

```
double mean(double x, char* buffer[], int len)
```

the function handles the command-line arguments by converting each one into a number while simultaneously adding it to the current total. The only difference between the two headers is in the data type of the function. The first parameter makes the choice of the correct definition unambiguous. If it is a double value, double mean() is called. If it is a long value, long mean() is called.

Overloaded Member Function Names

Member function names share the overloading capability of ordinary functions. In fact, programmers use overloading extensively with classes because it can produce highly flexible interface members. To create an overloaded member function, declare more than one definition with the same name.

The date3.cpp example (Listing 4-5) shows an overloaded member function. The member function that lets the user reset the date, new_date(), is overloaded. The user supplies a date to this function by entering three integers—one each for the day, the month, and the year. The user can call new_date() also by passing it a character string with the name of the month first and the day separated from the year by a comma.

This example shows the flexibility of an overloaded function. Because it offers two different methods for initializing this class, it increases the class's generality so that it can be used in more programming contexts. This flexible member makes it easier also for the designer to write the rest of the program and to reuse previously created modules. The reusability of modules is an important design tool. The overloading of member functions increases the likelihood that two classes can be used together regardless of the fact that they were not designed together.

This example also uses a constructor with default values. When you declare a variable of type date, the same three integers required by new_date() must be supplied, or the internal values of the class are set to 0. In fact, the constructor calls this function to do its work. Note that the constructor calls another member function, new_date(), which actually does the work of making the changes to the variable members. This design avoids including redundant code in the class.

Listing 4-5. A date class that uses an overloaded member function: date3.cpp.

```
#include <stdlib.h>
#include <iostream.h>
#include <string.h>
#include <stdio.h>

#define COMMA ","

#define SPACE " "
```

```
const char* mname[]={ "illegal date", "January", "February", "March",
                      "April", "May", "June", "July",
                      "August", "September", "October",
                      "November","December" };

class date  {
  int day;
  int month;
  int year;

public:
  date(int =0,int =0, int =0);
  void new_date(int,int,int);
  void new_date(char *);
  char* give_date();
};

date::date(int d,int m, int y)
{
 new_date(d,m,y);
}

void date::new_date(int d,int m,int y)
{
 if ( (d >= 1 && d <= 31) &&  (m >= 1 && m <= 12) )  {
   day=d;
   month=m;
   year=y;
 }
}

void date::new_date(char* dat)
{
 char *mn,*dy,*yr;

 mn=strtok(dat,SPACE);
 dy=strtok(0,COMMA);
 yr=strtok(0,COMMA);
```

continues

Listing 4-5. continued

```
for(int i=1 ; i <= 12 ; i++)
  if( ! strcmp(mn,mname[i]))
     break;

if(i <= 12)  {
  month=i;
  day=atoi(dy);
  year=atoi(yr);
 }
else
 month=day=year=0;
}

char* date::give_date()
{
 char *buf=new char[80];

 if(day==0 ¦¦ month==0 ¦¦ year==0)
   sprintf(buf,"%s",mname[0]);
 else
   sprintf(buf,"%s %d, %d",mname[month],day,year);

 return buf;
}
```

Although this date class contains a good example of overloaded member functions, you can use overloading even more effectively in another situation. Constructor functions can be, and often are, overloaded to accommodate differing formats for the same data type. To demonstrate this usage, let's expand the date example. Sometimes it is convenient to store a date as a single, positive number, which simplifies comparisons and calculations of time duration. You can store a date as the number of days since some convenient, but not always significant, event. A date of this kind is frequently called a *Julian* date. The problem with these arbitrary values is that they sometimes run counter to the way people think of dates. The problem is one of conversion and how to move back and forth conveniently between two kinds of time representation. The solution is to create a new date class that accommodates different methods of setting the date. The date4.cpp example (Listing 4-6) implements this solution.

Listing 4-6. A `date` class that uses overloaded constructors: date4.cpp.

```
#include <iostream.h>
#include <string.h>
#include <stdlib.h>


const int months[]={0,31,59,90,120,151,181,212,243,273,304,334,365};

const char* mnames[]={"", "January", "February", "March",
                      "April", "May", "June","July",
                      "August", "September", "October",
                      "November","December"};

class julian  {
   int days;

public:
   julian(int, int);
   julian(char*,char*);

   char *current_date();
};

julian::julian(int mon,int day)
{
 days = months[mon-1] + day;
}

julian::julian(char* mon,char* dy)
{

   for(int i=1 ; i <= 13 ; i++)
     if(!strcmp(mnames[i],mon))
        break;
   if(i > 12)
     days=0;
   else if(i == 1)
     days=atoi(dy);
   else
```

continues

Listing 4-6. continued

```
      days=months[i-1]+atoi(dy);
 }

char* julian::current_date()
{
 int mn,dy;

 if(days<=31)  {
   mn=1;
   dy=days;
  }
 else
   for(int i=2; i<=12; i++)
     if(days<=months[i])  {
        mn=i;
        dy=days-months[i-1];
        break;
     }

  char *buffer = new char[20];
  sprintf(buffer,"%s %d",mnames[mn], dy);

  return buffer;
}
```

This example defines a new class called julian. Dates are stored internally in the integer member days. The program interprets a date as the number of days since January 1 of the current year (no provision is made for leap years). Two constructors offer two ways to create an object of type julian. You can supply two integer values that represent the month and day, or you can pass the constructor two character strings, one that contains the name of the month and another one that specifies the day. The only other member function defined is current_date(), which converts the days since January 1 into a character string that consists of the month and day.

The code for the constructor in the julian class is obscure enough to require some elucidation. The constructor

```
julian(int =0, int =0)
```

converts its initial argument into the number of days since January 1. The first parameter represents the number of the month (January is 1, February is 2, and so on). This month identifier then must be converted into the number of days since the beginning of the year. The array months contains this translation information. Each cell in this array contains the Julian day (from January 1) of the last day of each month. For example, the Julian day of January 31 is 31, but the value for June 30 is 181. The current date is calculated by taking the Julian date of the prior month and adding the current day. The Julian day for July 3, for example, is 181 + 3, or 184. The constructor function uses the mon parameter to index the array for the previous month and then adds the other parameter, day. The other form of the constructor uses a similar array, but this one contains the names of the months in the proper order. Examine the character string array mnames. The string "January" occupies cell 1, "February" occupies cell 2, and the rest of the names follow in the appropriate order. This constructor converts the month name to a month number and then uses this value to extract the Julian date in the same manner that the first, simpler constructor did. This matching is done by the following loop:

```
for(int i=1 ; i < 13 ; i++)
    if(!strcmp(mnames[i],mon))
        break;
```

The standard library strcmp() function returns a 0 if the strings match (are equal), so this test for "!strcmp()" is actually a test for equality. Note that the loop goes beyond the number 12 to permit a distinction between "December" and an illegal month name. Later in the code, the if-then-else-if construction tests for this error condition. It sets the variable days to 0 if the user enters an illegal month. Otherwise, the program calculates the Julian day in a way similar to the other constructor.

Being able to create as many constructors as there are conversion formats is obviously a convenient tool for the programmer. However, the overloading capability offers another power that transcends this convenience. For example, you can use the class julian to act as a bridge between as many different date formats as you require. After you add the proper member functions and debug their code, you never have to be concerned with explicit conversion again, because the object does it for you. Conversion software is always tricky, often messy, and sometimes renders a program unreadable. This procedure gives you a method for keeping it under control.

Object-Oriented Design

C++ is a programming language that supports object-oriented design techniques. In Chapter 3, this support was shown in the class data type, which provides the capability of creating an object that contains not only its own values, but also the methods that manipulate those values.

In this chapter, attention has turned to the traditional function definition. C++ offers some important improvements here, but the single most significant difference as it relates to object-oriented techniques is function overloading. This capability, as you've seen demonstrated in some of the examples that you've been considering, meshes with the class definition to offer even more powerful tools for program design.

Function Overloading

The first important component of object-oriented design that I discussed was encapsulation, which is the ability of the designer to compact values and methods—variables and functions—into a well-defined and autonomous object. Furthermore, this object has a well-defined and controllable interface to any program in which it is used. The mechanism of this encapsulation in C++ is the definition of classes and the creation of class objects.

Overloading function names adds a second object-oriented dimension to C++. This capability gives the designer power to draw relationships between similar but distinguishable data types. Functions that perform the same task should use the same name, even if the variables and values they work on are different. A function that calculates the mean of a series of values should use the same name, even if the values are different. Even more importantly, the member functions of a class should share a name, even if they use different external values to manipulate the other members of the class. If a date class can be initialized either by a Julian date or by a character string with the month, day, and year, there should be two functions with the same name, each of which performs one of these initializations.

Polymorphism

Function name overloading partially satisfies a property of object-oriented design called *polymorphism*, which is just a technical term for an important goal—reusability. Objects, if they are properly designed, represent resources that the software designer can use to create systems. Ideally, an object represents a problem that has been solved, which means that the code written for this problem doesn't have to be rewritten. Polymorphism, the use of function names to stand for similar operations, helps realize this goal of seamlessly integrating existing objects into new systems.

An important secondary benefit of this implementation of polymorphism is a more straightforward syntax for function calling. Rather than a complex, spaghetti-like web of conditional statements calling functions with unique, and sometimes less than clear, names, a simple function call suffices to activate more than one set of code, depending on its parameter list. The checking and specific calling are done "behind the scenes" and do not become part of the direct design.

Better examples follow in later chapters as your use of classes becomes more advanced. For right now, however, let's consider a concrete example. Suppose that you want to integrate a complex number class object into a system that includes real and integer values. This integration is much smoother if one function name can be used to manipulate any information in the system. In other words, if you want to find the mean value of a set of values, the program, thanks to function overloading, needs only to call mean(). The compiler can figure out just exactly which version of the function you need. If later you need to expand this capability by an additional data type, as long as you can define a mean() function for this new value, it is easy to integrate into the existing system.

I return to this subject of overloading and polymorphism later.

Summary

In this chapter, I've focussed on the function in C++. Although the key innovation in this language is the class, several improvements have been introduced to the function definition syntax. In addition, you cannot create classes without the ability to define member functions.

The key element in function definition for C++ is function overloading, particularly as it relates to member functions. The ability to have several functions that share the same name is an important consideration when designing programs and systems for an object-oriented environment.

Of lesser but still useful interest is the concept of inline expanded functions. Taking a middle ground between true functions with associated overhead and macro definitions with their simpleminded textual expansion, inline functions offer the designer the low overhead of the latter with the local scope capabilities of the former. Inline expanded functions should be limited to simple pieces of code. The decision to honor the inline modifier is left to the compiler.

An important innovation in C++ that does not relate directly to the object-oriented nature of the language is the reference data type. This allows the programmer to set up a function parameter to be called by reference rather than by value, as is the default. Furthermore, this call by reference does not use the traditional pointer for a C program. Reference variables add to the readability of a program.

Default argument values for function parameters and functions with a variable number of parameters provide welcome flexibility for designing and implementing functions.

5

Creating Complex Classes

Creating Complex Classes

Beyond the basic definition of a class object is the difficult task of designing useful classes. It is easy at this point to use C++ as a kind of "supercharged C" and continue to create function-dominated programming designs rather than take advantage of the new possibilities inherent in object-oriented techniques. This chapter emphasizes using classes to design objects, rather than the earlier focus on the syntax of classes.

Global Constructors and Destructors

When an object is created from a class definition, several mechanisms are put into play. These mechanisms are necessary to the functioning of the class object as well as its integration into the system as a whole, but their utility goes beyond this simple task. These mechanisms—constructors and destructors—are elements that can be used also to create new and powerful software systems. This section explores the way these features can be utilized in the design process.

Chapter 3 introduced the mechanism of constructors and destructors for class objects. You recall that these are special member functions called automatically at specific key points in the program: The constructor is called when the object is created, whereas the destructor is called when the object is destroyed. The principal use of the constructor is for initializing members of the class object. Similarly, the destructor is seen primarily as a deallocation mechanism for these user-defined data types. When you explore the relationship between these special member functions and scope and storage classes, however, a new world of utility opens before you.

In C, the relationship between variables and the other components of a program are complex. The simplest layer of this relationship is the basic notion of *scope*. Scope refers to the accessibility of a variable—where in the program it can be used and where it is not available. A global variable is available anywhere in the program. It must be defined outside a block, which usually means the declaration is outside any function. In contrast, a variable of local scope is restricted to the block or function in which it finds itself. These relationships are illustrated by Figure 5-1.

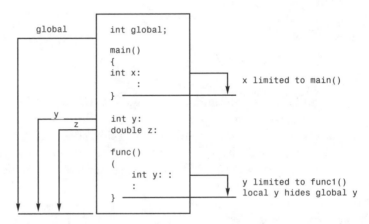

Figure 5-1. Global and local scope.

Note in Figure 5-1 that the variable global has as its scope the entire program, including the functions main() and func1(). The scope of a variable actually is from the point of its declaration to the end of the file. Thus, the scope of y covers only the function func1() and is unknown to main(). The same is true of z. The variable x in main() is an example of a local variable with a scope limited to that function. The same is true of the y declared inside func1(), but here there is an additional point to note. The local y hides (or masks) the global one. Therefore, accessing this global variable inside the function is not possible.

To the traditional notions of scope, C adds the related concept of the *storage class*, which refers to where a variable is actually placed in memory and how long it persists. Global variables defined outside of a function have storage class `extern` and persist until the program execution is terminated. Variables local to a function have the `automatic` storage class. Such variables are created when a program enters a function and are destroyed when it leaves the function. Some local variables can have a storage class of `static`. These variables persist and maintain their value between function calls, even though they are local to a function. Global variables also can be declared `static`, but here the effect is actually to limit their scope. This effect occurs only when a program is created using more than one file.

Global variables are initialized before the program starts to run, which is true also of static variables, even if they have a scope local to a function. Even if no explicit initialization is given, they are set to the value zero (this is an ASCII zero and not the digit '0'). Automatic variables are initialized each time the function in which they are declared is called. An automatic variable without an explicit initialization is undefined; no default value is provided by the compiler.

Both C and C++ share these twin concepts of scope and storage class. The mechanisms for initialization and the duration of both these variable types is identical. This is the same for class variables as it is for variables of built-in types. With a class declaration, however, a new mechanism takes hold. If a class variable has a constructor, the constructor is called when the variable is allocated. A defined destructor is called when the variable is destroyed. For an automatic class variable, the constructor and destructor are called each time the function in which they are found is called. However, a global or static class variable is created before the program starts to execute and persists until the program is terminated. If you make a class declaration before the `main()` function, the constructor for that class executes before the program begins and the destructor executes after `main()` exits; therefore, the destructor is the last code executed in the program.

The C++ class is an object that contains both value storage and the methods or functions to access and manipulate that storage. Declaring a class variable creates an object in this expanded sense and expands the notion of initialization. You can use this expansion, coupled with the control of variables borrowed from the traditional C syntax, to use a constructor to create a module that will be the first code executed in a program. A destructor can be used to specify code that will be the last code executed in a program. In a portable and high-level format, the program designer has limited access to the run-time environment.

Listing 5-1 is a simple example of the mechanism of the global constructor. The definition of the class `global` is straightforward, consisting of a simple integer variable to hold a value and a constructor which serves to put a value into this member. A simple `show()` member function displays the contents. The destructor does nothing more than announce its own operation.

Listing 5-1. The use of a global constructor and destructor.

```
#include <iostream.h>
class global  {
   int x;

public:
   global(int p)  { cout << "Executing The Constructor...\n"; x = p;  }
 ~global()           { cout << "Executing The Destructor.....\n"; }
    void show()  { cout << "x = " << x << "\n";}
};


global glob(3);

main()
{
  cout << "Entering Main Function\n";
   glob.show();
  cout << "Exiting main() Function\n";
}
```

The interest of this example is in where the class object is created. A declaration above main() ensures that the object is created at the time the program loads and runs and before main() is called. The definition of main() offers two bracketing I/O statements and a call to the member function show() to put the constructor and destructor calls in perspective. The output of Listing 5-1 would be

```
Executing The Constructor...
Entering Main Function
x = 3
Exiting main() Function
Executing The Destructor.....
```

The execution of the constructor and destructor bracket the execution of the main() function.

This ability to run a function before the start of a program and after a program executes gives you a greater degree of control than is possible with C over the execution cycle of a program. The designer can create a set-up routine, for example, that executes before any other part of the program. Equally important is the ability to guarantee that code will be executed after the program is exited. For example, a

global destructor could ensure the graceful shutdown of the program, closing files and deallocating resources. Moreover, you exert this control, not with some low-level access to the machine or the operating system, but with a straightforward programming construction. This adds portability to the code you produce. As a somewhat more ambitious example, consider the class definition in Listing 5-2.

Listing 5-2. A keymap table to illustrate global constructors.

```
#include <iostream.h>
#include <io.h>
#include <fcntl.h>

struct key_map  {
    char key_value;
    char mapped_value[20];
};

class table  {
  key_map value[26];

public:
  table(char*);
 ~table()  { cout << "Exiting Program\n"; }
  char* get_value(char key);
};

table::table(char* fname)
{
  int fd = open(fname, O_RDONLY);

  cout << "Loading table values....\n";

  for(int i = 0 ; i < 26 ; i++)
      read(fd, (key_map*)&value[i], sizeof(key_map));

  close(fd);
}

char* table::get_value(char key)
{
  for(int i = 0 ; i < 26 ; i++)
      if(key == value[i].key_value)
```

continues

Listing 5-2. continued

```
            return value[i].mapped_value;

  return 0;
}

table x("table.dat");

main()
{
 char ch;
 for(;;)  {
     cin >> ch;
     if(ch == '*')
       break;
     cout << x.get_value(ch);
  }
}
```

The example in Listing 5-2 defines a class table that contains a set of mapping to the keyboard. The values of this mapping are stored in a file, table.dat. The constructor takes a file name, opens the associated file, and reads the values into the key_map array value[]. The simple key_map class associates a value with a character. This example uses only the letters A through Z. The class table contains a member function, get_value(), which acts as a filter to convert letters into their associated values. Although the definition of table is simplified, it could be expanded and used to define a key macro facility like that found in many text editors. Whether or not such a table needs to be loaded into memory ahead of everything else in the program depends on the nature of the program design. C++, however, offers this capability in a portable form—one that easily can be made to work on different implementations.

Unions and Bit Fields in C++

Just like C, C++ has two derivative data structure mechanisms: *bit fields* and *unions*. Although the syntax of these two mechanisms is similar in both languages, C++ adds flexibility to their operation.

The bit field syntax allows the programmer to work with odd-sized data types that are smaller than the basic unit of address (the byte), or that are not an even multiple of this basic unit. Often a flag's value is binary—either on or off—and requires only a 0 or a 1 to indicate its state. In another context, you may have a quantity that easily fits into three bits. Using an entire byte for a value that needs less than eight bits seems wasteful. One way to deal with this waste is to pack several of these small quantities into a larger data type. The bit field mechanism is an alternative to using the bitwise operators.

Bit fields are defined using one or more data members of a class. A member declaration is followed by a colon and the number of bits to be allocated for that member: `member_name : num_bits`. For example,

```
struct bclass   {
    unsigned  flag1 : 1;
    unsigned  flag2 : 1;
    unsigned  flag3 : 2;
  };
```

defines three data members. The first two, `flag1` and `flag2`, are allocated one bit each. The third member, `flag3`, uses two bits. Access to these member functions is through the usual class mechanism. Thus,

```
bclass sample;
```

```
sample.flag3 = 3;
```

would define a variable of type `bclass` and initialize the third field, `flag3`.

There are restrictions to the use of bit fields that result from the way they are implemented. Bit fields must be defined using one of the basic integral data types. Each bit field member uses whatever number of bits it requires to satisfy its format. Succeeding members use additional bits. One important restriction is that no field can span across two basic types. In other words, if the basic type is a 32-bit integer, there are only three bits left, and the next bit field member requires six bits, a new integer is allocated. Because bit field members are packed into basic types, there can be no address taken of the member—although you still can take the address of a class object as a whole. Figure 5-2 illustrates how this packing might be accomplished. The exact mechanism is implementation-dependent.

The following code contains an example of a class that has defined bit fields as members. Three members, each of which is one bit wide, are defined in the class `bit_test`.

```
class  bit_test  {
  unsigned b1 : 1;
  unsigned b2 : 1;
  unsigned b3 : 1;
public:
  bit_test()  { b1 = b2 = b3 = 0; }
  void toggle_bit(int);
  void show_bit(int);
};

void bit_test::toggle_bit(int bit_idx)
{
 switch(bit_idx)  {
     case 1 : b1 = !b1;
                    break;
     case 2 : b2 = !b2;
                    break;
     case 3 : b3 = !b3;
                    break;
     default: cout << "No Such Bit Field\n";
 }
}

void bit_test::show_bit(int bit_idx)
{
 switch (bit_idx)  {
     case 0 : cout << (b1 ? "TRUE" : "FALSE") << "\n";
                    cout << (b2 ? "TRUE" : "FALSE") << "\n";
                    cout << (b3 ? "TRUE" : "FALSE") << "\n";
                    break;
     case 1 : cout << (b1 ? "TRUE" : "FALSE") << "\n";
                    break;
     case 2 : cout << (b2 ? "TRUE" : "FALSE") << "\n";
                    break;
     case 3 : cout << (b3 ? "TRUE" : "FALSE") << "\n";
                    break;
  }
}
```

```
struct bclass {
    unsigned flag1 : 1;
    unsigned flag2 : 1;
    unsigned flag3 : 2;
} ;
```

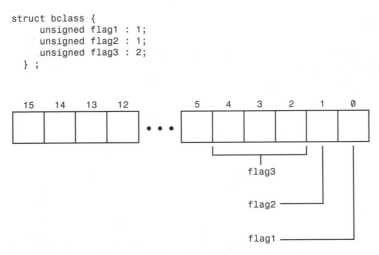

Figure 5-2. Bit field members packed into basic data types.

The constructor and two member functions in the public section of the class offer initialization as well as access to the bit fields. The constructor offers a minimum initialization, setting each member to 0. The show_bit() member function produces a pattern of FALSE and TRUE based on the value of the individual bit field members. This function takes as a parameter a number to indicate which bit field is to be displayed. A 0 causes the function to display patterns for all three bit field members. The use of the conditional operator ? simplifies the code. If b1 is 0, the conditional evaluates as false and returns the second value FALSE. Otherwise the first value, TRUE, is sent to cout. The same is true for the value of b2 and b3. Finally, toggle_bit() accepts also an integer parameter to indicate a bit field. This member converts the specified bit field into its complement: If the value is 0, it becomes 1, and 1 becomes 0.

There is some controversy concerning the value of the bit field mechanism. The efficiency of the code depends on factors outside the programmer's control: the machine architecture and the implementation strategy chosen by the compiler writer. The direct manipulation of the bits using bitwise manipulation operators such as the right shift operator (>>) and the and operator (&) always produce code that is at least as efficient as the bit field access. This is true because the operators are directly linked with machine-level instructions. The worth of the bit field mechanism is in its simplicity of expression and obviousness. If you need to produce fast and compact code, you probably should avoid using bit fields.

The union data type is a variation on the class that allows the overlaying of two different data formats on the same class object. These variations are mutually exclusive and have no direct communication with each other. When a union object is created, enough space is allocated so that either variation can be assigned to the object. The following code illustrates a simple example of a union definition:

133

```
union u1  {
  int i;
  double f;

  u1(int x)  { i = x; }
  u1(double p) { f = p; }
  void show_int()  { cout << "i=" << i << "\n";}
  void show_real() { cout << "f=" << f << "\n";}
};
```

This example is a variation on the simple C union, which is meant to show the important differences between the two programming languages. Union u1 has two formats: It stores either an integer value, i, or a real number, the double value f. Because this is a class definition, there are member functions. In this case, one constructor sets the integer value and another initializes the double value. Remember, it is this assignment that determines which format of the union is used. Similarly, there is a display member function for each possibility: show_int() if the integer value is in force, and show_real() if the double value has been initialized.

The use of overloaded constructors adds a new dimension of flexibility for a union type. There also is less danger of accidently changing the value of the object after it is created, particularly if no member function can alter the value after this point. This is tempered by the fact that there can be no private section in a union. In fact, the modifiers public and private cannot be used at all within a union. The other two members, however, exist in either form of the union. The program still has to have some way to decide which of these functions gives a true value and which returns an undefined value.

The following example shows a more ambitious union definition. This code tackles the problem of defining an address record for two kinds of students: an on-campus student who lives in a particular room in a particular dormitory, and an off-campus student with a more orthodox address. Use a union to ensure that one of these choices is activated.

```
class address1  {
  char street[80];
  char city[80];
  char state[80];
  char zip[80];
public:
  void set_address(char*, char*, char*, char*);
  void show();
};
```

```
void address1::set_address(char* str, char* cty, char* st, char* zp)
{
  strcpy(street, str);
  strcpy(city, cty);
  strcpy(state, st);
  strcpy(zip, zp);
}

void address1::show()
{
  cout << street << "\n";
  cout << city << ", " << state << "  " << zip << "\n";
}

class address2  {
  char dormitory[80];
  char room[80];
public:
  void set_address(char*, char*);
  void show();
};

void address2::set_address(char* dm, char* rm)
{
  strcpy(dormitory, dm);
  strcpy(room, rm);
}

void address2::show()
{
  cout << "Dormitory: " << dormitory << "\n";
  cout << "Room:      " << room << "\n";
}

union address  {
  address1 off_campus;
  address2 on_campus;

  address(char*, char*, char*, char*);
  address(char*, char*);
  void show_on_campus();
  void show_off_campus();
};
```

```
address::address(char* dm, char* rm)
{
  on_campus.set_address(dm, rm);
}

address::address(char* str, char* cty, char* st, char* zp)
{
 off_campus.set_address(str, cty, st, zp);
}

void address::show_on_campus()
{
  on_campus.show();
}

void address::show_off_campus()
{
  off_campus.show();
}
```

Each kind of address is defined as an independent class complete with the member functions to access and manipulate it. Of course, this union is not an efficient way to use memory. If you declare an on_campus variable, enough memory is allocated to cover the bigger requirements of the off_campus type. Note the absence of any constructors for these two classes. Constructors and destructors pose some problems in contexts such as a union. A little later in this section, you explore this difficulty.

The union itself combines one or the other of the two address formats: address1 for students living off campus and address2 for those in a dormitory. The union itself has a pair of overloaded constructors. The first constructor has four parameters and is responsible for activating the off_campus member. The remaining constructor with its two parameters ensures that the on_campus member is the one being used. Two member functions, show_on_campus() and show_off_campus(), are responsible for displaying the content of the class in the appropriate format. Note that in both cases, the show member calls a similarly named member function in the address class: show_off_campus() calls show() in address1, and show_on_campus() calls show() in address2.

The use of the constructor to activate as well as initialize a member function adds a new vitality to the union type. In C, the programmer has to know too much about the union's structure to be able to use it effectively. To a lesser degree, that's still true. You have to call the correct member function to get a reasonable value. Even so, the programmer can choose the proper format by calling the correct constructor and ignoring the internal construction of the class. For example, just by writing

```
address x("Morrison Hall",  "102")
```

the on_campus format is chosen. An expression of the form

```
address y("22 Castro", "Mountain View", "CA", "94022")
```

chooses the off_campus member. The focus has shifted from the mechanics of the union to the content of the data. This is a significant improvement.

One notable attribute of this last example is the lack of a constructor for either address1 or address2. The member function set_address(), found in different forms in both address1 and address2, performs the kind of initialization that usually is done by a constructor. In the context in which you are using these classes, however, it would be impossible to call a constructor and pass it arguments. The declaration of the class object is a member of another class—in this case, the union. Arguments are not legal in such declarations. After the member class object is created, it's no problem for the union's constructor to call individual member functions of this class. There are two solutions to the problem of calling constructors for class objects that are declared in another class. The preferred option is to use derived classes, which is discussed in subsequent chapters. Another way around this problem is to use pointers and dynamic memory allocation, as in the following example:

```
class name  {
  char first[80];
  char mid[80];
  char last[80];
public:
  void set_name(char*, char*, char*);
  void show();
};

void name::set_name(char* f, char* m, char* l)
{
 strcpy(first, f);
 strcpy(mid, m);
 strcpy(last, l);
}
```

```
void name::show()
{
  cout << first << " " << mid << " " << last << "\n";
}

class record  {
  name nm;
  address* x;
public:
  record(char*, char*, char*, char*, char*, char*, char*);
  record(char*, char*, char*, char*, char*);
  void show_on_campus();
  void show_off_campus();
};

record::record(char* f, char* m, char* l,  char* str, char* c, char* st,
char* z)
{
 x = new address(str, c, st, z);
 nm.set_name(f, m, l);
}

record::record(char* f, char* m, char* l, char* d, char* r)
{
 x = new address(d,r);
 nm.set_name(f,m, l);
}

void record::show_on_campus()
{
 nm.show();
 x->show_on_campus();
}

void record::show_off_campus()
{
 nm.show();
 x->show_off_campus();
}
```

The example starts with an ordinary name class definition; this is a straightforward class that is well understood from previous examples. The record class contains as data members a variable of type name, but also a pointer to an object of type `address`. By using the address, you can call the constructor for `address` directly through the `new` operator. The following example shows a simple driver program:

```
#include <iostream.h>
#include <string.h>
main()
{
 record student1("John", "Thomas", "Berry",
                          "Morrison Hall", "123");

 student1.show_on_campus();
}
```

The union class is not as controversial as the use of bitfields, which raises some real questions about efficiency and code size. The union is a more straightforward construction. I should point out, however, that many of the design problems that can be solved by the use of a union can be solved also by using derived classes. The union mechanism is simpler, but derived classes offer more powerful features. The trade-off has to be judged for each individual project.

Linked Data Structures Using Classes

The ubiquitous linked data structure is an important challenge for the programmer because it taxes the resources of the implementing language. This data type ranges from common constructions, such as binary trees, to more exotic multilink networks. Linked lists are used to implement text editors and compilers, in the interface to database, and even order-entry systems. The C++ class has special features that simplify the creation of the code that manages these linked types.

The basic linked data structure consists of nodes that can be stored anywhere in the system's memory. Each node contains the data associated with the node and the address of the next node. Figure 5-3 shows the logical structure of such a data type.

The key advantages of a linked list center on its dynamic nature. Each time a new node is required, it is allocated from available memory. When a node is no longer needed, its memory is released back to the operating system. A linked list is an efficient way of relating values to one another. Also, any operation on a particular node takes about the same amount of time as the same operation on any other node. There are two important variations on the way you can implement a linked list in C++: using a static class member and using container classes.

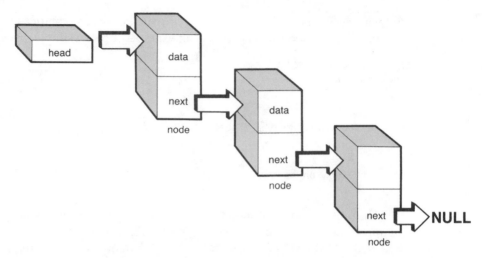

Figure 5-3. A linked list data type.

Implementation Using a Static Class Member

Two features of C++ help simplify the creation of linked list nodes: *static class members* and the *this* pointer. Each one is important to the implementation of this data type.

The variable members of a class have a scope that is restricted to objects of that class. The private members can be accessed only by member or friend functions. Each time you create a class object—either through a declaration or by dynamic allocation with the new operator—a complete set of class members is created for that particular object. Each variable of a class type has its own private set of values. If you use the static modifier in a member declaration, however, that member behaves in a different way: It becomes common to all the objects of that class type. A static member can serve as a bridge to each individual object of the class. Figure 5-4 diagrams the relationship between a static class member and the actual objects of that class.

Another important feature of a class and its associated class object is the ability of the object to access not only its own members but also itself—a kind of self-reference. Each object contains an implicit self-reference pointer contained in a special variable called this. The this pointer contains the address of the object that is calling it. The self-referential relationship is difficult to visualize. Figure 5-5 indicates the nature of the this pointer.

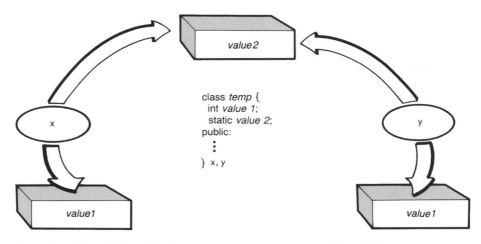

Figure 5-4. The relationship between a static *member and class objects.*

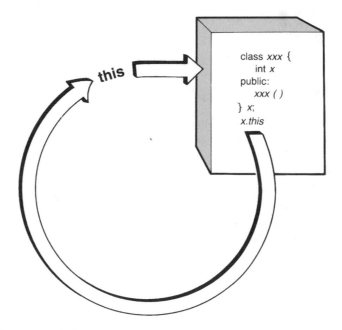

Figure 5-5. The this *pointer.*

You can use both of these features to create a linked list of classes. The example in Listing 5-3 illustrates their use. The heart of the list is a defined *node class.* Each time you must expand the list, merely create a new object of this class and attach it to the end of the existing list. The static pointer head, which is part of the private section, maintains the unity of the list. (There is only one copy of this member for all of the class objects.)

Listing 5-3. A simple linked list class.

```
#include <iostream.h>
#include <string.h>

class node  {
  static node *head;
  node *next;
  char *info;

public:
  node(char* =0);
  void display_all();

};

node::node(char* ptr)
{
    if(ptr != 0)    {
       info=new char[strlen(ptr)+1];
       strcpy(info,ptr);
       next=0;
       node *cursor=head;
       while(cursor->next != 0)
        cursor=cursor->next;
       cursor->next = this;
      }
   else  {
     info = new char[strlen("root")+1];
     strcpy(info,"root");
     next = 0;
     head = this;
    }}
}

void node::display_all()
{
   node *cursor=head;
   for( ; cursor ; cursor = cursor->next)
        cout << "*" << cursor->info << "\n";
 }
```

Each time you create a new node object, the class constructor starts at the member head. Because this member is `static`, its scope is common to the entire class of objects; therefore, it points to the first node, not to the currently created one. As a result, any navigation of this list moves from the first member to the last member. Had you declared the member head as an ordinary member, its reference would be restricted to the current node, thus making the creation of the list impossible. The `this` pointer is used to refer to the current node and attach it to the end of the list.

Using a `static` member as the head of a linked list is a simple and attractive solution to the problem of creating a linked list of class objects. There are some drawbacks, however. The most important one is that with this implementation design, you can create only one list for each class. For a large number of applications, one list would be perfectly adequate. What you often really need, however, is the ability to create many different lists based on the same class. You need to find an alternative method of list creation.

Container Classes

An important variation on the previously described linked list is the container class. Basically, a container class is a data type that consists of a dynamic collection of values—a traditional data table, for example. Although creating and using these types is an important part of all programming, the C++ class type makes their implementation particularly simple.

In Chapter 3, I defined a linked list class. The contain.cpp example (Listing 5-4) defines a token class or more correctly, a *tokenizing* class that is a more developed version of that earlier design. In creating an object of this type, the constructor accepts a character string as a parameter. The class `token` holds a linked list of the *tokens* that comprise its initializing character string. In this case, a token is defined as one or more contiguous characters separated by blank spaces, the beginning of the line, or the end of the line. The list of tokens could represent an English sentence or a command and its parameters. The primary interface is through the member function `nth_token()`. This function takes an ordinal number and returns the appropriate token in the list.

Listing 5-4. An example of a container class: contain.cpp.

```
#include <iostream.h>
#include <stdlib.h>
#include <string.h>
#define SPA " "
```

continues

Listing 5-4. continued

```
class tvalue  {
  char* value;
  tvalue* next;
public:
  tvalue(char*);
 ~tvalue();
  void put_next(tvalue*);
  tvalue* get_next();
  char* show_value();
 };

tvalue::tvalue(char* data)
{
  value = new char[strlen(data) + 1];
  strcpy(value, data);
  next = 0;
}

tvalue::~tvalue()
{
  delete value;
}

void tvalue::put_next(tvalue* tnode)
{
 next = tnode;
}

tvalue* tvalue::get_next()
{
  return next;
}

char* tvalue::show_value()
{
  return value;
}


class token  {
  tvalue *toke;
  int size;
```

```
public:
  token(char*);
 ~token();
  char* nth_token(int);
  void show_all();
 };

token::token(char* x)
{
 char* temp;

 if((temp = strtok(x, SPA)) == 0)  {
   cout << "error condition\n";
   size = 0;
   exit(1);
  }
 toke = new tvalue(temp);

 tvalue* cursor = toke;

 for(int i = 1 ; (temp = strtok(0, SPA)) ; i++) {
  cursor->put_next(new tvalue(temp));
  cursor = cursor->get_next();
 }
 size = i;
}

token::~token()
{
 tvalue *prev;
 tvalue *cursor = toke;

 while(cursor != 0)  {
  prev = cursor;
  cursor = cursor->get_next();
  delete prev;
 }
}

char* token::nth_token(int num)
{
 tvalue* cursor = toke;
```

continues

Listing 5-4. continued

```
for(int i = 1 ; i < num ; i++)
 if(cursor != 0)
     cursor = cursor->get_next();
 else
   return 0;
 return cursor->show_value();
}


void token::show_all()
{
 tvalue* cursor = toke;
 for(int i = 0 ; i < size ; i++)  {
     cout << "==>" << cursor->show_value() << "\n";
     cursor = cursor->get_next();
 }
}

main()
{
 token x("This is only a test line");

 x.show_all();
 cout << "Show the 3rd token: " << x.nth_token(3) << "\n";
}
```

The only private member of the class token is the pointer to the list of tvalues. Most of the work of this class is done by the single constructor, which takes a character string as an initializing variable—token x("this is only a test"). If you do not supply this character string in the declaration, an error condition results, and no data object is created. If a correctly formatted character string is sent to token(), the member function creates a linked list, each node of which is a word from the string. The standard library function strtok() does the parsing (although you easily could write a customized function like strtok() in C++).

The initial call to the strtok() function is done in the conditional construction that tests for the presence of a string.

```
if((temp=strtok(x,SPA)) == 0)  {
```

Note that the first node on the list is created and filled independently of the loop that strips the other words from the list. This is done primarily because by doing the test, the program already has grabbed the first token. The subsequent words are put into nodes by repeated calls to strtok().

```
for(int i = 1 ; (temp = strtok(0, SPA)) ; i++) {
 cursor->put_next(new tvalue(temp));
 cursor = cursor->get_next();
}
```

These calls in the loop continue until the function returns a 0 to indicate the end of the string. The execution of the constructor leaves the data object of type token with a value that consists of the linked list of tokens.

The member function nth_token() returns the value of the specified node on the linked list. Thus, a call to nth_token(3) returns the value of the third word in the list. A simple for loop moves through the linked list until it finds the requested node. If nth_tok() is called with too high a number, it returns an end-of-string marker ('\0') to indicate this failure. The destructor for the token class is straightforward, but it's somewhat unwieldy. It steps through the linked list and deallocates each node. If you examine it closely, you notice that it removes nodes behind itself. This practice is a little strange, but it's reasonably efficient.

In contrast to the example in Listing 5-3, this class consists of two nested classes. One class, tvalue, defines a simple linked list. This list is wholly contained in the containing class, token. The differences between this class and the earlier one define the notion of a container class. In a traditional linked list, each node is an instance of the class. In a container class, however, the entire list is contained in one class object. By creating a class that wholly contains a linked list, you can have as many different lists using just one class in a program as are necessary. In contrast, when you use a static member to create a linked list, you can define only one list per class.

Case Study: The *doc* Class

At this point, you need a long example to tie together the various threads I have discussed in this chapter. Not only does such an example illustrate the use of the class and its features, but it also offers insight into designing with the class. Using the container class I defined in Listing 5-4, you build, in stages, a document class. This document class allows you to store and manipulate several lines of words. Figure 5-6 illustrates the plan for a document class and the relationships between its various parts.

Listing 5-5 contains the definition of a word class, which is a modification of the tvalue class defined in Listing 5-4. It's a simple class that contains, besides the member functions that allow the manipulation of the class object within a linked list, two more specialized member functions: update() and get(). The update()

function allows the alteration of the wd member in the object, which is necessary because of one of the important actions that is performed within the document class: changing the value of an individual word. Get() returns the value of the particular object. The only other necessary action at this level is the removal or deletion of a word, which is covered by the class destructor.

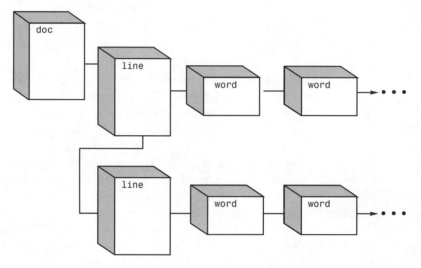

Figure 5-6. A document class.

Listing 5-5. A **word** class.

```
#include <iostream.h>
#include <string.h>
#include <stdio.h>

#define SPA " "

class word   {
  char* wd;
  word* next;
public:
  word(char*);
 ~word()                                   { delete wd; }
  void put_next(word* w)  { next = w; }
  word* get_next()              { return next; }
  void update(char*);
```

```
   char* get()                              { return wd; }
};

word::word(char* v)
{
  wd = new char[strlen(v) + 1];
  strcpy(wd, v);
  next = 0;
}

void word::update(char* v)
{
  delete wd;
  wd = new char[strlen(v) + 1];
  strcpy(wd, v);
}
```

Objects of the class word are put together in a linked list to form a sentence or a line. This linked list is contained within another list, line, which builds and manipulates a single line of words. This class is shown in Listing 5-6. As with the word class, its relationship to the earlier example of a container class is obvious. A member, first, points to the linked list of type word. As with the earlier example, the constructor accepts a character string and parses it into tokens based on the space as a delimiter. Each of these words is packed into a word object and placed at the end of the linked list.

Listing 5-6. A line class.

```
class line  {
  word* first;
  line* next;

public:
  line(char*);
  ~line();
  void put_next(line* n)      { next = n; }
  line* get_next()                { return next; }
  void erase(char*);
  void insert(char*, char*);
  int search_replace(char*, char*);
  char* show_line();
```

continues

Listing 5-6. continued

```
};

line::line(char* l)
{
  char* temp = strtok(l, " ");

  word* cursor = first = new word(temp);

  for(; (temp = strtok(0, " ")) ; cursor = cursor->get_next())
      cursor->put_next(new word(temp));
  next = 0;
}

line::~line()
{
  word* cursor = first;
  word* prev;

  while(cursor)  {
      prev = cursor;
      cursor = cursor->get_next();
      delete prev;
  }
}

void line::erase(char* key)
{
  word* cursor = first;
  word* prev;

  for(; cursor ; cursor = cursor->get_next())  {
      if(!strncmp(cursor->get(), key, strlen(key)))  {
          prev->put_next(cursor->get_next());
          delete cursor;
       }
      prev = cursor;
  }
}
```

```
void line::insert(char* key, char* value)
{
  word* cursor = first;
  word* prev;

  for(; cursor ; cursor = cursor->get_next())  {
      if(!strncmp(cursor->get(), key, strlen(key)))  {
          prev->put_next(new word(value));
      prev->get_next()->put_next(cursor);
       }
      prev = cursor;
  }
}


char* line::show_line()
{
    char* buffer = new char[81];
    word* cursor = first;
    strcpy(buffer, cursor->get());
    cursor = cursor->get_next();

    for( ; cursor ; cursor = cursor->get_next())  {
    strcat(buffer, SPA);
      strcat(buffer, cursor->get());
  }

    return buffer;
}

int line::search_replace(char* key, char* replace)
{
 word* cursor = first;

 for(; cursor ; cursor = cursor->get_next())
     if(!strncmp(key, cursor->get(), strlen(key)))  {
       cursor->update(replace);
       return 1;
      }
     return 0;
}
```

In addition to the basic container class functions, the line class also has two sets of members. One set supports the creation of another linked list. In this example, it is a linked list of lines. The set of members includes line* and the member functions get_next() and put_next(), which are almost identical to the functions found in the word class. The other set of members defines the interface to the line itself. Included here are basic editing functions that also interact with the two manipulation members found in the word class.

Aside from the creation of the line, which is handled by the constructor, the actions to be performed on a given line are erase(), insert(), and search_replace(). These actions are not a minimal set, but they do define a workable interface. Erase() simply removes a word from the list. Insert() performs the complementary function; it inserts a new word into the linked list in front of the specified node. Search_replace() searches through the line's linked list looking for a match to its key value. When that key value is found, it is replaced with the new value. Search and replace is a powerful operation that is found in most editing programs.

One member function to take note of is show_line(). This function does the inverse of the constructor: It reconstructs the line as a character string. An important compromise was made here to keep the code simple enough for an example. An 80-character line is assumed. Show_line() builds the character string by walking through the linked list and concatenating the value of each word object. Note the essential introduction of spaces between each concatenation.

At this point in the example, you have a container class, line, which allows the manipulation of a single line of text. Sufficient functionality is built into the class to allow you to perform typical editing operations. These operations create a well-behaved interface to a single line. Certainly you could expand this interface by creating different kinds of insertions. For example, you could create an append or add support for storing this information in a disk file. Whether or not this is necessary, you do have a coherent and complete example.

If words make up a line, lines make up a document. The next step in the example is to create a class that contains a linked list of lines. In this way, you can define a document. The definition for this class is found in Listing 5-7.

Listing 5-7. A document class.

```
class doc   {
  line* lne;
  line* search(int);

public:
  doc();
  int search_replace(int, char*, char*);
```

```
  int erase(int, char*);
  int insert(int, char*, char*);
  void show();

};

doc::doc()
{
  cout << "Entering Insert Mode..." << "\n";

  char* buffer = new char[80];

  cout << "~";
  gets(buffer);

  line* cursor = lne = new line(buffer);
  cursor->put_next(0);

  for(;;  )  {
      cout << "~";
    gets(buffer);

      if(!strncmp(buffer, ".", strlen(buffer)))
          break;
      cursor->put_next(new line(buffer));
      cursor = cursor->get_next();
  }
}

line* doc::search(int line_num)
{
 line* cursor = lne;

  for(int i = 1  ; (i < line_num) && cursor ; i++)
      cursor = cursor->get_next();
  return cursor;
}

int doc::search_replace(int line_num, char* key, char* value)
{
  line* cursor = search(line_num);
```

continues

Listing 5-7. continued

```
  if(!cursor)
      return 0;

  cursor->search_replace(key, value);
  cout << cursor->show_line() << "\n";
  return 1;


}

int doc::erase(int line_num, char* key)
{
  line* cursor = search(line_num);

  if(!cursor)
      return 0;

  cursor->erase(key);
  cout << cursor->show_line() << "\n";
  return 1;
}

int doc::insert(int line_num, char* key, char* value)
{
 line* cursor = search(line_num);

 if(!cursor)
     return 0;

  cursor->insert(key, value);
  cout << cursor->show_line() << "\n";
  return 1;
}

void doc::show()
{
  line* cursor = lne;

  for( ; cursor ; cursor = cursor->get_next())
      cout << cursor->show_line() << "\n";
}
```

```
main()
{
  doc x;

  cout << "\nOriginal Document:\n\n";
  x.show();

  x.search_replace(2, "nothing", "everything");

  cout << "\nChanged document:\n\n";
  x.show();

  x.insert(2, "wrong", "right");

  cout << "\nAfter and insert:\n\n";
  x.show();

  x.erase(2, "wrong");

  cout << "\nAfter an erase:\n\n";
  x.show();
}
```

Like the line class, which contains a linked list of words, the doc class contains a linked list of line objects. The construction of this linked list, however, is different from the earlier class. Note also that there is a similar public interface: search_replace(), erase(), insert(), and show().

The constructor for the doc class creates its list interactively. Whenever a doc object is created, the constructor calls on the user to add text to the object until done. This particular implementation has an editor-like interface: It prompts for each line. A single period or just a carriage return at the beginning of a line causes the function to stop. Of course, after a string of characters has been entered, a line object is created and placed at the end of the linked list. One important advantage to using an object-oriented programming language is that the details of managing the line itself are taken care of by the constructor of the line class. This set of details is removed from the current constructor, making it much simpler and easier to follow. This is possible only because each object contains methods to take care of its own manipulation.

The other member functions—`search_replace()`, `erase()`, `insert()`, and `show()`—share in this design philosophy. In each case, the only responsibility of the member is to find the current line. When that is accomplished, the object that was found is given a message to perform the appropriate operation on itself. For example, if `search_replace()` is called, the `doc` member function positions a local variable, `cursor` of type `line*`, by walking through the linked list. Thus, cursor is used to call the line version of `search_replace()` and makes the substitution. Similarly, `show()` walks through the linked list, displaying each line through a call to `show_line()`. Listing 5-7 also shows a driver program to test these class definitions.

If you look back through the definitions in the `doc` class, you can see that this is a complicated programming situation. Yet at each level, you need to concentrate on only a small number of the operations. You leave some of the details at each level and replace them with the public interfaces defined in each class. This is a kind of modularization that is difficult to achieve in C or any other language that is not object-oriented. Yet in C++, it's a straightforward implementation.

Summary

This chapter explored some of the more complicated aspects of the C++ class facility. Added to the basic definition outlined in Chapter 3 and Chapter 4 were global constructors and destructors, the creation of bit field classes, and the use of the union class. All these offer designers more options when they are creating a program to solve a particular problem.

Perhaps most importantly of all, you have seen how a group of difficult programming problems can be solved in a simpler and more elegant way by using the new class data type. Linked lists are easily created by defining a node class. The more complex container class, which you can use to create tables, lists, and so on, also is much easier to implement. The case study of the `doc` class shows just how well the use of class objects can help the designer deal with the control of complexity and detail.

6

Friend Functions and the Class

6

Friend Functions and the Class

Accessing the Class Space

The essence of a class object is that it represents an area or "space" within the program that is accessible only through the deliberate interface of its public section. Even accessing the class object in this controlled way requires that a specific object be indicated. The private section is available only to other class members; it is not available to any other part of the program.

Using a class object effectively requires a specialized access to its features and methods. Designing an effective object is a trade-off between allowing sufficient access to the class and maintaining control over the object.

The Public Section Interface

The nature of access to the class puts the burden on the designer to create an effective interface, one which contains just enough access to the class without opening it up to tampering from outside of its space. The struct keyword was quickly abandoned because it produced classes that were completely open to other parts of the program. Even when using class to define objects, there is always a tension between access and privacy.

There is no data representation problem that cannot be solved through the use of a class. This is not to say, however, that the nature of any particular solution is obvious or necessarily simple. C++ is guaranteed by its designers not to be a less efficient language than C on the objective code level. This kind of efficiency, however, does not necessarily translate into simplicity of source code.

Because all access must go through the public section of the class (and this access is through member functions), it's rare, but not impossible, that a data member is found in a public section. In certain circumstances, a simple access can be seen as less than optimal. This is particularly true when the interaction is between two classes.

Non-Member Access Through a Friend Declaration

One solution to the class designer's dilemma is to allow a mechanism to expand access to the private part of the class. This mechanism gives a selected group of non-member functions the ability to manipulate data members directly or to call function members that are not part of the public interface.

The C++ syntax contains also a mechanism that allows a non-member function to access the private part of a class. When you declare a function as a friend to the class, the function gains the same privileges as a member of that class. The integrity of the class is maintained because it still has a restricted and declared interface; however, now you can permit entry to selected outsiders. Of course, you must be careful not to declare so many friend functions that you compromise the privacy of a class. Every time you grant friend access you decrease the level of encapsulation that the class type offers. Used sparingly, however, this capability provides an important programming tool for creating easy-to-access software.

Creating a Friend Function

The `friend` keyword is a function declaration modifier. It takes the general form

```
friend return_type function_name(parameters);
```

Additionally, a friend declaration is legal only within a class definition. A typical friend declaration would look like the following:

```
class simple {
    int value;

    friend int access(simple, int);

public:
    simple(int x)  { value = x; }
    int show() { return value; }
      };
```

This declaration creates a new class type, simple, but it also gives private access to the access() function, which is not part of the class. This latter feature is brought home by the fact that one of the function's parameters must be either a variable of the class type or a pointer to the class type. Although access() is able to alter the member value, it must be given an object of class simple so that there is a value to alter. Additionally, the friend declaration is unaffected by its location in the class. Putting it in the private section or the public section has no effect on its functionality.

One way to look at a friend declaration is that the class gives rights of access to specific functions. In this way, although the interface is widened, the designer still can control it. Only the declaration of the class can give these rights. You still know just exactly how the internal part of the class can be reached. No one can get into it without using one of those access paths.

The timedat1.cpp example (Listing 6-1) shows the syntax of a friend declaration. This example defines two simple classes—tme and dte—and includes a simple driver function that lets you explore their use. Each class has a constructor and a single friend function: gtime() for tme, and gdate() for dte. Each friend function formats and displays the values currently held by the class: tme uses the *hours:minutes* format, whereas dte uses the *day/date/year* format. Note that both friend functions require a parameter of the appropriate class type.

**Listing 6-1. A program that illustrates
the use of a friend function: timedat1.cpp.**

```
#include <iostream.h>
#include <stdio.h>
#include <stdlib.h>
#include <string.h>
#define COLON ":"

class tme {
  long secs;
  friend char* gtime(tme);
```

continues

Listing 6-1. continued

```
public:
 tme(char*);
 };

tme::tme(char* tm)
{
 char *hr, *mn;

 hr = strtok(tm, COLON);
 mn = strtok(0, COLON);
 secs = (atol(hr) * 3600) + (atol(mn) * 60);
}

class dte  {
 int month;
 int day;
 int year;
 friend char* gdate(dte);

public:
    dte(int m, int d, int y)  { month = m; day = d; year = y;}
};

main()
{
 tme x("10:30");
 dte d(10, 31,1989);
 char* gtime(tme);
 char* gdate(dte);

 cout << gtime(x) << "\n";
 cout << gdate(d) << "\n";
}

char* gtime(tme x)
{
 char *buffer = new char[10];

 int h = x.secs / 3600,
     m = (x.secs % 3600) / 60;
```

```
 sprintf(buffer, "%02d:%02d", h, m);
 return buffer;
}


char* gdate(dte x)
{
 char* buffer = new char[15];

 sprintf(buffer, "%2d-%2d-%4d", x.month, x.day, x.year);
 return buffer;
}
```

This example shows other differences between friend and member functions. Declaring a class declares all the members of that class. Because friend functions are independent, however, you must declare them as you would any other function. In the example, both such functions return a character string and are declared together. The dot notation used by member functions is not available to friends; you must explicitly pass them class objects. This simple example explores the syntax of a friend declaration and definition. In both classes, however, this formatting and display function could have been handled better by a member function. Let's look at some more practical uses for friend functions.

Friends as Bridges Between Classes

One important function that a friend can perform is to act as a bridge between two dissimilar classes. In this case, it serves as a link between classes that are not otherwise connected. Although other methods for linking classes are available (later you'll see that derived classes permit the creation of class hierarchies), in many cases, friend functions offer a secure and clean connection. A simple example of this kind of "friend bridge" is shown in timedat2.cpp (Listing 6-2).

Listing 6-2. A program that illustrates a friend function used to bridge two classes: timedat2.cpp.

```
#include <iostream.h>
#include <string.h>
#include <stdlib.h>
```

continues

Listing 6-2. continued

```c
#include <stdio.h>

#define COLON ":"

class dte;

class tme {
  long secs;
  friend char* time_date(tme, dte);

public:
 tme(char*);
 };

tme::tme(char* tm)
{
 char *hr, *mn;

 hr = strtok(tm, COLON);
 mn = strtok(0, COLON);
 secs = (atol(hr) * 3600) + (atol(mn) * 60);
}

class dte  {
 int month,
     day,
     year;
 friend char* time_date(tme, dte);

public:
 dte(int m, int d, int y)  { month = m; day = d; year = y;}
};


main()
{
 tme x("10:30");
 dte d(10, 31,1989);

 char* time_date(tme, dte);
```

```
 cout << time_date(x, d) << "\n";
}

char* time_date(tme t, dte d)
{
 int h = t.secs/3600,
     m = (t.secs % 60) / 60;

 char* buf = new char[50];
 sprintf(buf, "time: %02d:%02d\ndate: %2d-%2d-
     %2d",h,m,d.month,d.day,d.year);
 return buf;
}
```

This example declares the function time_date() as a friend to the time class and the date class. This "super friend" function formats a display string that contains both time of day and date information and returns it for display. The only way it can do this is to access the private parts of both classes. Although each class operates independently from the other and uses its own constructor and internal storage strategy, this friend function temporarily bridges them for a single purpose. You could accomplish this task also by creating a regular function that has a time parameter and a date parameter. In that case, however, you would need to pass two class objects to the function. Access to their internal values would require the overhead of a call to a member function. Clearly, the friend function approach is a more efficient method.

This example has another interesting facet. Note that you must declare the name dte as a class before you actually define it. If you fail to do this, the declaration of time_date() in the tme class fails because one of its parameters—namely, dte— is undefined. This kind of predeclaration of class types is a relatively obscure concept, and one that is easy to overlook. Another way to avoid this problem is to use the void* data type. Recall that this type is compatible with a pointer to any data type. The timedat3.cpp example (Listing 6-3) illustrates this approach. It has no undefined reference problem because the parameter is declared as a pointer to a void. Later, in the definition of the time_date() function, the parameter is cast back to dte*. By then, however, the dte class has been defined and is no longer an unknown quantity. Unless you feel comfortable with manipulating a void*, this approach may appear even more obscure than using a forward declaration.

Listing 6-3. A bridge function
without a forward declaration: timedat3.cpp.

```cpp
#include <iostream.h>
#include <stdio.h>
#include <stdlib.h>
#include <string.h>
#define COLON ":"

class tme {
  long secs;
  friend char* time_date(tme*,void*);

public:
 tme(char*);
 };

tme::tme(char* tm)
{
 char *hr, *mn;

 hr = strtok(tm, COLON);
 mn = strtok(0, COLON);
 secs = (atol(hr) * 3600) + (atol(mn) * 60);
}

class dte  {
 int month,
     day,
     year;
 friend char* time_date(tme*, void*);

public:
 dte(int m, int d, int y)  { month = m; day = d; year = y;}
};

main()
{
 tme x("10:30");
 dte d(10, 31,1989);
```

```
char* time_date(tme*, void*);

cout << time_date(&x, &d) << "\n";
}


char* time_date(tme* t, void* v)
{
 dte *d = (dte *) v;

 int h = t->secs/3600,
     m = (t->secs % 60) / 60;

 char* buf = new char[50];
 sprintf(buf, "time: %02d:%02d\ndate: %2d-%2d-%2d",h,m,d->month,d->day,
               d->year);
 return buf;
}
```

Member Functions as Friends to Other Functions

All of the previous examples declared independent functions as friends to one or more classes, thus offering outside links to the internal structure of these classes. Friends are not, however, restricted to these ordinary functions. The member functions of one class can become the friends of another. In fact, you can declare all of the functions of one class to be friends to another class. In this case, just as with the more ordinary case of an independently defined function, special access is granted to the member functions. The difference is, of course, that these functions have access also to the private part of their own class.

The timedat4.cpp program (Listing 6-4) demonstrates the usefulness of this procedure. Here, both gdate(), which gives the current date, and gtime(), which returns the current hour and minute, are members of the dte class, although there is a separate tme class. By defining the entire dte class to be a friend to the tme class, you guarantee that gtime() has adequate access to the private part of the needed tme class. Of course, you could include also an entire set of member functions in one class to stand in the friend relation to another class. You are not restricted to only one such function.

Listing 6-4. A program that illustrates the use of friend classes: timedat4.cpp.

```cpp
#include <iostream.h>
#include <stdio.h>
#include <stdlib.h>
#include <string.h>
#define COLON ":"

class dte;

class tme {
  long secs;
  friend class dte;

public:
 tme(char*);
 };

tme::tme(char* tm)
{
 char *hr, *mn;

 hr = strtok(tm, COLON);
 mn = strtok(0, COLON);
 secs = (atol(hr) * 3600) + (atol(mn) * 60);
}

class dte  {
 int month,
     day,
     year;
 friend char* time_date(tme, dte);

public:
 dte(int m, int d, int y)  { month = m; day = d; year = y;}
 char* gdate();
 char* gtime(tme);
};

char* dte::gdate()
{
```

```
 char* buffer = new char[15];
 sprintf(buffer, "%2d-%2d-%4d", month, day, year);
 return buffer;
}

char* dte::gtime(tme x)
{
 char* buffer = new char[10];
 int h = x.secs/3600,
     m = (x.secs % 3600)/60;
 sprintf(buffer,"%02d:%02d", h, m);
 return buffer;
}

main()
{
 tme x("10:30");
 dte d(10, 31,1989);

 cout << d.gtime(x) << "\n";
 cout << d.gdate() << "\n";

}
```

The special declaration

```
friend class dte;
```

gives this special status potentially to any of the member functions of the class tme. Potential is not actual. You must provide a dte parameter to a tme member function if you want the latter to access this other class.

Friendly Cautions

Although friend functions rarely are essential to a C++ program, they do serve to produce code that is more efficient than that which is produced by relying solely on class member functions. This efficiency is particularly obvious when you consider the run-time overhead. Through their ability to access the private part of another class directly, friend functions often let you save the overhead that another member function would incur. This increased efficiency is particularly important if your program must change continually or update the private part of the class. Even with this advantage, you should use friend functions sparingly. From the standpoint of C++ philosophy, member functions that define the interface to a class still are preferred.

Many C++ programmers feel uneasy about the use of friend declarations. Certainly a case can be made for moving cautiously. In particular, declaring an entire class as a friend to another class as you did in Listing 6-4 is something to consider deliberately before committing yourself to it. Let's consider some of the possible trade-offs in using friend functions.

In Chapter 5, I defined a simple container class (Listing 5-4), which consisted of a small value or node class, tvalue. This class was used as the building block for a linked list that was contained in another class, token. The definition of tvalue and token are reproduced in Listing 6-5.

Listing 6-5. The `tvalue` class definition from Listing 5-4.

```
class tvalue  {
  char* value;
  tvalue* next;
public:
  tvalue(char*);
 ~tvalue() { delete value; }
  void put_next(tvalue* tnode)  { next = tnode;}
  tvalue* get_next()  { return next; }
  char* show_value() { return value; }
 };

class token  {
  tvalue *toke;
  int size;

public:
  token(char*);
 ~token();
  char* nth_token(int);
  void show_all();
 };
```

Recall that the token class constructor takes as a parameter a character string of text—words surrounded by white-space characters—and creates a linked list in which each node is of type tvalue and contains one word from the line. The code to accomplish this "tokenizing" is reproduced in Listing 6-6.

Listing 6-6. The constructor for the `token` class.

```
token::token(char* x)
{
 char* temp;

 if((temp = strtok(x, SPA)) == 0)  {
   cout << "error condition\n";
   size = 0;
   exit(1);
  }
 toke = new tvalue(temp);

 tvalue* cursor = toke;

 for(int i = 1 ; (temp = strtok(0, SPA)) ; i++) {
  cursor->put_next(new tvalue(temp));
  cursor = cursor->get_next();
 }
 size = i;
}
```

The algorithm for `token()` is straightforward. It strips words from the character string one by one until it comes to the end. Each time it picks up a new word it creates a `tvalue` node, copies the word into it, and attaches the node at the end of the list. In order to accomplish this latter task, `token()` must have access to the next field of each `tvalue` object. Because `tvalue` is a class and the next member is in the private part, you must give the `tvalue` class two public member functions that can access this member. This is done in `put_next()` and `get_next()`.

An alternative would be to use the friend mechanism to grant privileged access to the `tvalue` class from `token`. Listing 6-7 shows the container redefined using this alternative declaration.

**Listing 6-7. A new version of the container class
that relies on a friend declaration.**

```
#include <iostream.h>
#include <stdlib.h>
#include <string.h>
#define SPA " "
```

continues

Listing 6-7. continued

```
class tvalue  {
  char* value;
  tvalue* next;
  friend class token;
public:
  tvalue(char*);
 ~tvalue()    { delete value; }
 };

tvalue::tvalue(char* data)
{
  value = new char[strlen(data) + 1];
  strcpy(value, data);
  next = 0;
}

class token  {
  tvalue *toke;
  int size;

public:
  token(char*);
 ~token();
  char* nth_token(int);
  void show_all();
 };

token::token(char* x)
{
 char* temp;

 if((temp = strtok(x, SPA)) == 0)  {
   cout << "error condition\n";
   size = 0;
   exit(1);
  }
 toke = new tvalue(temp);

 tvalue* cursor = toke;
```

```
 for(int i = 1 ; (temp = strtok(0, SPA)) ; i++) {
  cursor->next = new tvalue(temp);
  cursor = cursor->next;
 }
 size = i;
}

token::~token()
{
 tvalue *prev;
 tvalue *cursor = toke;

 while(cursor != 0)  {
  prev = cursor;
  cursor = cursor->next;
  delete prev;
 }
}

char* token::nth_token(int num)
{
 tvalue* cursor = toke;

 for(int i = 1 ; i < num ; i++)
  if(cursor != 0)
      cursor = cursor->next;
  else
    return 0;
  return cursor->value;
}


void token::show_all()
{
 tvalue* cursor = toke;
 for(int i = 0 ; i < size ; i++)  {
     cout << "==>" << cursor->value << "\n";
     cursor = cursor->next;
  }

}
```

continues

6

Listing 6-7. continued

```
main()
{
 token x("This is only a test line");

 x.show_all();
 cout << "Show the 3rd token: " << x.nth_token(3) << "\n";
}
```

Because I've declared the `token` class as a friend to `tvalue`, this latter class can be much simpler. It shrinks to only a constructor and a destructor. The tasks performed by the other functions—`get_next()`, `put_next()`, and `show_value()`—are now done directly by the containing class `token`.

Changes to the `token` class are minimal. The same algorithm you found in the earlier one, with nearly identical code, is used in this alternative version. The only significant difference is in the way `token`'s member functions access the values in the linked list. The access now is direct. In the `token` constructor, for example, instead of referring to the `tvalue` next field through a `tvalue` member function

```
cursor->put_next(new tvalue(temp))
```

it does it directly

```
cursor->next = new tvalue(temp)
```

The next field is referred to similarly in the other token member functions.

What have you gained by using friend functions instead of the more orthodox access through the public section of a class? Unfortunately, not much. In the present case, the member functions that you replaced already were inline expanded, so you cannot expect a dramatic improvement in efficiency on that score. If these members had been true functions with a concomitant overhead, using friend function access might have saved some execution. Whether or not this would be a significant saving is tied to the particular circumstance. You do have a slightly less complex algorithm with which to deal. The program designer has to decide on a case-by-case basis whether or not to use friend functions and classes.

The Dangers of a Friend Declaration

So far in this chapter I've focused on the mechanics of friend declarations, with a little discussion about their ultimate value. The conclusion is that they are certainly not the kind of constructions that you would use in everyday programming. The experienced programmer reserves these constructions for a few special cases in which their small efficiencies might be appreciated. Up to this point, however, I haven't discussed the danger that is inherent in the friend mechanism.

When you declare a friend function in a class, you open a door to the usually closed part of that class. The door that you open is potentially wider than you might realize. Although it's true that you have control of the format of the function declaration that becomes the friend to your class, you may have no real control over the code that defines that function. The declaration gives a function name access to the entire class—nothing more than the name, not a particular piece, but any function that has that name. The following code contains the definition of an example class with a friend declaration:

```
class simple  {
  char* value;

  friend void funky(simple);

public:
  simple(char*);
 ~simple()  { delete value; }
  char* show()  { return value; }
};
```

The class has a character string variable that is initialized by the constructor. The only other member functions are a destructor and a simple display function, show(). The source code for the constructor of this class follows. Assume that you compile this file into an object file.

```
#include <string.h>
#include "simple.h"

simple::simple(char* info)
{
  value = new char[strlen(info) + 1];
  strcpy(value, info);
}
```

When you have an object file implementing the member functions of the class, as well as the definition in a header file, you can use it in a variety of programs. This is one of the major advantages of object-oriented programming. Ordinarily, you would have control over access to this class. The public section defines the interface. For example, with the current class, there is no provision to change the value of the class after it has been initialized. By exercising this access control, you can alter or change the implementation of the class. As long as you maintain the same public section, you can be confident that you are not destroying any code that uses this class.

You cannot be so confident in the present case, however, because you've defined a friend function that gives a user carte blanche to access anything in the class, whether it's in the public section or the private part. The access is granted to the function name and its format—in other words, the return value and the parameter list—and not to any particular function. This function can be written long after the class is compiled. Different programs can use different parts of the function, as long as the name and the format stay the same.

Listing 6-8 contains a program built on this "class library." The function funky() defined in this file gives you more access to simple than the public section of that class allows. You can change the value of the class even after it has been initialized. This power comes in spite of the fact that the program in Listing 6-8 has no access to the source code that implements simple and cannot, in fact, recompile it. This illustrates dramatically the fact that the friend mechanism tends to diminish the power of the class to encapsulate values and control methods.

Listing 6-8. A program using the simple class library.

```
#include <iostream.h>
#include "simple.h"
#include <string.h>

main()
{
  void funky(simple);

  simple x("This is only a test");

  cout << "original version: " << x.show() << "\n";

  funky(x);
  cout << "altered version: " << x.show() << "\n";
}

void funky(simple p)
{
  delete p.value;
  p.value = new char[strlen("Ha Ha I Changed It") + 1];
  strcpy(p.value, "Ha Ha I Changed It");
}
```

The situation is even worse with the declaration of a friend class; here you give up even the minimal control you have over the format of the friend function. Within a friend class, all you have to do to access the private sections of another class is to allocate a class variable as a member. Consider the program outlined in Listing 6-9 through Listing 6-11.

Listing 6-9. A class definition that contains a class friend declaration: simple2.h.

```
class simple2  {
  char* value;

  friend class whoops;

public:
  simple2(char*);
 ~simple2()  { delete value; }
  char* show()  { return value; }
};
```

Listing 6-10. The implementation of the class library.

```
#include <string.h>
#include "simple2.h"

simple2::simple2(char* info)
{
  value = new char[strlen(info) + 1];
  strcpy(value, info);
}
```

Listing 6-11. A program that takes advantage of the friend class.

```
#include <iostream.h>
#include "simple2.h"
#include <string.h>

class whoops  {
  simple2* access;
```

continues

Listing 6-11. continued

```
public:
  whoops(char* info)  { access = new simple2(info); }
  void change_it(char*);
  char* show()  { return access->value; }
};

void whoops::change_it(char* info)
{
  delete access->value;
  access->value = new char[strlen(info) + 1];
  strcpy(access->value, info);
}

main()
{
 whoops x("this is only a test");

 cout << " The original: " << x.show() << "\n";

 x.change_it("This is a different string");

 cout << " The altered value: " << x.show() << "\n";
}
```

Because any class named whoops is given access to the simple2 class, you have wide latitude to attack the latter's encapsulation more aggressively. When it was a single function, you had to abide by the given parameter list. In this case, every function potentially can access the simple2 class, because the doorway into this is a pointer variable that happens to be a member of the whoops class. In this example, you have effectively cancelled the access control that is a part of the syntax of the C++ class.

Where Does it Make Sense to Use Friends?

Rather than enhancing the object-oriented nature of C++, the friend mechanism represents a retreat back into more traditional forms of programming style. Used to extreme, as you have seen, it can cancel completely some of the aspects of C++

that make it an object-oriented programming vehicle. Because of this danger, you must approach the use of friend functions and, particularly, friend classes, with careful consideration.

It's easy to see where you should not use the friend mechanism. If your goal is to create a library of reusable classes (classes that serve in a variety of circumstances), you should avoid friend functions and friend classes. Only if you can exercise complete control over both the source code and the object code is it advisable to consider using a friend declaration.

If you compare the cautions to the meager advantages that the friend syntax offers, only a few specialized circumstances can justify its use. In day-to-day programming, friend functions probably are best avoided.

Summary

In this chapter you have explored the friend mechanism. `friend` is a modifier that can give to a function that is not a member of that class access to a class's private sections. Moreover, you can declare a class to be a friend to another class. This first class then has access to every part of the second class. Each of its member functions potentially can share in this privilege.

Two important considerations, however, tend to diminish the utility of the friend mechanism. First, the advantages offered by the friend mechanism do not yield dramatically improved code or more efficient operation. Advantages tend to be specific to particular problems. Secondly, and more importantly, there are real dangers in using these declarations. Whenever a friend declaration is made, it opens an access to the class that is much wider than is desirable in an object-oriented programming environment. A friend class can all but destroy the advantages of the class data type.

In conclusion, the use of friend function declarations must be approached on a case-by-case basis. You must weigh the benefits against the real dangers. Friend functions are not the stuff of day-to-day programming.

7

Overloading Operators

7

Overloading Operators

It should be clear to you now that the C++ class is more than an enhanced version of the C structure. The class sets up an environment in which the software designer not only can create objects that contain their own methods (in the form of member functions), but also can exercise almost total control over the access of class implementations. This object-oriented environment extends even further to include the use of traditional operator symbols in conjunction with class objects.

One weakness of traditional programming languages occurs when the languages must handle higher-level constructions, such as structures. Because these new data types are created by the programmer, they can't be manipulated with the same operators that work with the built-in types. For example, in C you can't add two structures together, even if the operation is legitimate, as it would be in the case of structures that define complex numbers. You can define an equivalent function that performs addition on particular structures, but you can't magically attach that function to the + operator. Thus, to perform the operation you must use the function call mechanism rather than the simpler syntax of operators. For example, suppose you have defined the following complex number type in C:

```
struct complex  {
   double  real;
   double imag;
 } x , y, z;
```

In order to give the program the capability of adding two complex numbers, for example, you need to define a function, such as `addcplx()`. The actual addition might look like this:

```
z = addcplx( x , y);
```

Most programmers are accustomed to this kind of circumlocution. Consider, however, how much more clearly the code would perform its task if it merely read as follows:

```
z = x + y;
```

As you might expect, C++ addresses this shortcoming of C. It gives your programs added flexibility by letting you redefine the existing operators so that they work also with class objects. Not only can you give unique new characteristics to standard symbols such as +, *, and +=, you can redefine the subscripting symbol (`[]`) and the function call operator (`()`). Because overloading of the `new` and `delete` operators for memory management also is possible, you gain the ability to create class-specific memory allocation and deallocation routines.

For overloading to be effective, the actions associated with the object must have the same intimate relationship to the value as do the actions of the built-in data types. For example, when you add two integers using the + operator, the code that implements that addition operation knows how an integer is stored and how to manipulate it. You don't have to write code that accomplishes this task bit by bit. C++ gives the same flexibility to programmer-created data types. The aim of the operator overloading mechanism is to short-circuit the external connection between data and action that is found in traditional programming languages, thus forming a more intimate connection between these two aspects of the object.

This chapter explores the operator overloading capability of C++ by offering practical and illustrative examples of useful techniques. For example, the programs in this chapter show you how to use overloaded operators to simplify the manipulation of

- Complex numbers

- Character strings

- A circle class

- A rational number type

Each example demonstrates how to replace the more cumbersome function call syntax with a simple and obvious operator.

A Review of Overloading

The mechanism for connecting class objects with operators is another form of overloading. There are important restrictions on what can be done. Moreover, as with the use of friend functions, caution is advisable. As you see shortly, some classes lend themselves more naturally to operator overloading than others do.

You're already familiar with one kind of overloading: function name overloading. Although there are significant differences, some of the same design issues apply to both mechanisms.

Function Overloading

Before discussing operator overloading, let's briefly review the mechanics of overloading. The same function name can represent several different pieces of code. For example, one mean() function might manipulate double values, whereas another—also called mean()—might calculate the average of integer values. The program decides which of these functions is specified by a particular function call by matching the actual argument type with the two function definitions. For example, as a simple solution to a perennial problem, you can specify two mean() functions—one for long values and one for double values.

```
long mean(long);
double mean(double);
```

Each version of mean() must have a different definition, so that the program can choose the correct code. In this case, the selection is based on the data types of the parameters passed to the function. In the following code fragment:

```
int x, m;
double y, rm;
    .
    .
m = mean(x);
rm = mean(y);
```

the long version of the mean() function fills the variable m because the parameter x is long. Similarly, rm accesses the appropriate function code for a double because y is a double.

You gain important advantages from using overloaded functions. First, you can dispense with the sometimes awkward code that is needed to choose one implementation of a function over another. Second, you no longer need to give functions unnatural names such as `fmean()` and `imean()` and place them in an `if` statement that uses a complicated conditional expression to choose one or the other. Third, your program source listings become clean and easy to read because you can replace the circuitous meanderings of complex conditional expressions with more straightforward code.

Extending Overloading to Operators

In a way analogous to function overloading, operator overloading lets the programmer give new meanings to the operator symbols that already exist in C++. For example, you can construct your own implementation of + or -, the increment and decrement operators (++ and --), or even the memory allocation operators `new` and `delete`. Remember, too, that when you perform overloading, the existing functionality of the C++ operators is preserved. For example, ++ still always increments an integer as expected.

Operator overloading—giving multiple meanings to the same symbol—is not as unusual as it first seems. Every programming language uses the procedure to some extent; however, because the overloading is built-in, you might not even realize it has been done. For example, the + that adds two integer values is not really the same as the + that adds two `double` values. In both C and C++, many basic operators also are redefined to perform completely different functions than arithmetic calculations. For example, the * operator, depending on the context, can be a multiplication operator or represent the dereferencing of a pointer variable, letting you obtain the data from the address pointed to. What is new in C++ is that this overloading capability extends to user-defined data types—class types—and it is made accessible to the designer.

There are some restrictions to operator overloading, however. Redefinition is confined to existing operator symbols—you can't make up a totally new operator syntax. Operators can be overloaded only in the context of class definitions—you cannot, for example, redefine + for integers or any other built-in data type. You also cannot change the place that the operator holds in the table of precedence or change it from a binary to a unary operator or vice versa (this is explored more fully later in the chapter). Finally, the capability for defining new operators for pointers is limited. Even with these restrictions, however, operator overloading is a powerful tool for program structuring.

Advantages of Operator Overloading

The principal advantage of being able to define new operators to work with classes is that it helps establish class types as fully functioning parts of the C++ programming language. Operator overloading permits C++ to become an extensible language in an even more profound sense: The program designer can add to the language specialized data types that promote better data representation, afford modularity, and yet are as easy to use as the basic built-in operators.

By removing the distinction between user-defined types and the traditional types, C++ also opens the door to more efficient code. Now you can extend natural operations to handle similar, but not identical, situations. For example, you can redefine the + operator—used traditionally to indicate the addition of numbers—to concatenate character strings. In C, you can carry out this concatenation only by using a function from the standard library.

```
static char  s1[10] = "ABC";
static char  s2[10] = "DEF";
char  s3[20];

s3 = strcat(s1,s2);
```

Here the concatenation is performed by the function call, so you must be careful that the receiving string variable has sufficient space to store both string values. In C++, by contrast, you can redefine the + operator to represent this same operation.

```
static char s1[10] = "ABC";
static char s2[10] = "DEF";
string s3[20];

s3 = s1 + s2;
```

This code can perform the same work; however, the operator syntax is clearer and unambiguous. More importantly, the function of the code is more obvious. Concatenation, in a broad sense, is similar to the arithmetic concept of addition. Most programmers seeing the operator used in this context would understand almost instinctively the meaning of the operation.

Operator overloading thus lets you create programming "metaphors" like the concatenation operator. Figure 7-1 illustrates this concept. A metaphor is simply an extension of the operational concept of one data type to a different, but analogous, type. In the case of concatenation, the notion of numeric addition is given a similar meaning in the context of character strings. Note that this extension of the meaning of addition is not merely a mechanical procedure—the operation of adding two numbers is distinct from the merging of two strings. Therefore, a programming metaphor lets the programmer shift perspectives and see data types, particularly complex ones, in a new light.

Additions: "adding two numbers"

Concatenation: "adding two strings"

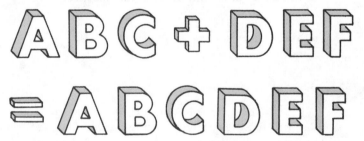

Figure 7-1. Programming metaphors.

Many C++ designers are disillusioned with operator overloading. They feel strongly that it is a technique that can be abused easily. Some even feel that the specification and implementation of this part of the language needs to be improved. Without taking sides in the issue, it is certainly true that the beginning C++ programmer must approach operator overloading carefully. It is as powerful as it looks but not as well behaved or controllable as it seems, which is a dangerous combination. Even more than with function overloading, the beginner quickly can produce code that is obscure to the point of being opaque—not only to the outside reader but to the author as well.

Even the experienced programmer is at risk. The uses and meaning of these operators can become so ingrained that if the meaning of one is switched in one part

of a program, it can lead to a confusion of meaning in another. For example, the use of the > to signify a string concatenation operation in

```
string x("This is a dangerous precedent");
string y("Attach the string here");
x > y;
```

could be confusing to all but the individual who designed the class.

The safest use of operator overloading is with numeric objects. Defining complex numbers as a class and overloading the usual arithmetic operators is a common, well-behaved example of a clear and balanced use of this facility. Not every possible overloading situation is as useful, however. You could redefine the % to signal string concatenation, for example—which is possible but not useful. Keep this in mind as you design your C++ programs.

The Mechanics of Operator Overloading

Before delving into the applications of operator overloading, let's examine the mechanism in C++ that permits you to use this procedure. The key to operator overloading is a special built-in C++ function that lets the programmer substitute a user-defined function for one of the existing operators. The general form of this function is

```
type operator op (parameter list);
```

First, *type* identifies the class type with which the new operator works. *op* represents the operator you want to overload (spaces around the operator symbol in the declaration are optional). *parameter list* is a (possibly empty) list of arguments to be passed to the new operator overloading function. For example, the declaration of an addition operator for complex numbers might look like the following:

```
complex operator + (complex);
```

Although this example takes only one argument, the parameter list is not restricted to a single variable. Remember, the declaration of a new operator must be followed by its definition. The definition syntax of an operator function is the same as it is for any other class member function: A header identifies the class and the particular member and is followed by the appropriate code. For example:

```
complex::complex operator+(complex x)
```

After this function definition is compiled, whenever the program references the specified operator, a call to the `operator+` function executes these statements. For example, the following code:

```
main()
{
    complex x(2,3);
    complex y(4,6);
    complex z;

    z = x+y;
}
```

leaves the variable z with a real value of 6 and an imaginary value of 9. The cmplx.cpp example (Listing 7-1) illustrates how to redefine an operator. This definition of a complex number type includes a constructor, an addition operator, and a display function. (Because the focus here is on the operator definition, the example omits the destructor and other potentially useful member functions.) Recall that each complex number consists of two parts: a real part and an imaginary part. Each of these parts is represented by a `double` value stored in the private section of the complex class. The addition of complex numbers involves adding the real parts and the imaginary parts independently to produce a new two-part value. In the example, you must initialize a data object of type `complex` with a value in the form `mm + nni` (you can substitute any numbers in this expression). Figure 7-2 illustrates the form of a complex number.

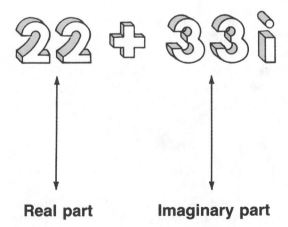

Real part   **Imaginary part**

Figure 7-2. A complex number.

Note that for convenience, the initializing expression is a character string that the program converts to the appropriate numeric values using character string functions from the standard library. Specifically, strtok() divides the string expression into two parts at the + character. The program assumes that the real part is to the left of this operator and that the imaginary part is to the right. As a further check, the program calls strtok() again to search for the i character, which traditionally indicates the imaginary part of a complex number. The program then uses the library function atof() to convert both strings into numbers.

Listing 7-1. A complex number class that uses an overloaded operator: cmplx.cpp.

```cpp
#include <string.h>

class complex  {
  double real;
  double imaginary;

public:
  complex() {real=imaginary=(double)0;}
  complex(char*);
  complex operator+(complex);
  char* display();
};

complex::complex(char* cnum)
{
    real=atof(strtok(cnum,"+"));

    imaginary=atof(strtok(0,"i"));
}

complex complex::operator+(complex cnum)
{
 complex temp;

 temp.real = real + cnum.real;

 temp.imaginary = imaginary + cnum.imaginary;

 return temp;
}
```

continues

Listing 7-1. continued

```
char* complex::display()
{

 char* temp = new char[10];

 sprintf(temp,"%f + %fi",real,imaginary);

 return temp;
}
```

This example focuses on the operator function, which is declared to redefine the + symbol to handle the addition of two complex quantities. This redefinition is quite simple. The complex number that is passed as a parameter is added, component by component, to the complex class that calls it.

The action of this operator function is implemented by the following statements in its definition:

```
temp.real = real + cnum.real;
temp.imaginary = imaginary + cnum.imaginary;
```

One of the complex numbers is passed to the function as the parameter cnum. The private part of the first class supplies the other value. This class is the calling class, although its position is obscured by the syntax. The program adds the two real sections before adding the two imaginary ones. In both cases, the result is stored in the variable temp. At the end of the operation, this temporary value is returned to the caller.

Note that the redefined symbol, +, is appended to the keyword operator and is outside of the parentheses that enclose the list of arguments to the function. This is because the symbol is part of the name of the function and not a function parameter. In the example, the parameter is another complex number to be added to the value of the current complex object, the object that contains operator+() as a member. Because the operator function returns the result, the function must be declared as type complex.

Let's clear up one potentially confusing issue: Remember that the redefinition of the operator—in this case +—takes place only in the context of the class in which the overloading occurs. That is why you can use the standard meaning of the + symbol inside the function definition itself. The values being added here are ordinary double values. You cannot overload operators as they apply to built-in data types, because new operator meanings can be created only for user-defined types (classes). The cmplx.cpp program (Listing 7-2) is a simple driver that illustrates how you could use the `complex` class. This program uses the member function `display()` to produce readable and formatted output.

**Listing 7-2. A driver program that
tests the `complex` class type: cmplx.cpp.**

```
#include <iostream.h>
#include "cmplx.cpp"

main()
{
 complex x("22 + 2i");
 complex y("11 + 3i");
 complex z;

 z=x+y;

 cout <<  "z= " << z.display() << "\n";
}
```

Overloading Binary Operators

In addition to the general restrictions mentioned earlier, there are also restrictions on the way a particular overloaded operator can work. Some of these restrictions arise from the original definition of the operator symbol. First, you must respect the original functional "template" of the operator. For example, you cannot change a binary operator—one that works on two operands, such as the division operator /— to create a unary operator, which works with a single operand. In the same way, you can't convert a unary operator to perform binary operations. You must maintain also the general form of the operator's syntax, although you might change what the operator does and the objects on which it works. Of course, when you overload operators that can perform either binary or unary functions (such as + and -), you can use them in either context. C++ recognizes the difference.

Another restriction related to the operator's "template" concerns precedence. Recall that precedence controls the order in which operations are performed when two or more operators are embedded in an expression. For example, in the integer expression x + y / 2, the division is performed before the addition because it has a higher precedence. C++ has an explicit and complex set of precedence rules (see the "Precedence of Operators" box). You can change an operator's definition, but you cannot change its precedence. An overloaded operator always retains its place in this list.

Precedence of Operators

`++ -- sizeof (`*type*`) new delete` *evaluates right to left*

`*` (indirection) `&` (address-of) `+` (unary) `-` (unary)

`* / %`

`+ -`

`<< >>` ‘

`< <= > >=`

`== !=`

`&` (bitwise and) *evaluation order not guaranteed*

`^` (bitwise exclusive or) *evaluation order not guaranteed*

`¦` (bitwise or) *evaluation order not guaranteed*

`&&`

`¦¦`

`?` (conditional operator) *evaluates right to left*

`= += -= *= /= %= >>= <<= &= ^= ¦=`

`,` (comma)

Let's look at a complete set of overloaded operators. Complex numbers are popular examples. Almost every C++ implementation contains a library of well-developed objects implementing this important numeric type. Instead let's look at an implementation of a rational number type. A rational number expresses the ratio between a numerator and a denominator. Listing 7-3 implements a rational number using a simple class definition.

Listing 7-3. A rational number class with overloaded operators: rational.cpp.

```cpp
#include <iostream.h>
#include <stdio.h>
#include <stdlib.h>
#include <string.h>

class rat {
    int nmr;
    int dnm;

public:
  rat() { nmr = 0; dnm = 1; }
  rat(int n, int d) { nmr = n; dnm = d; }

  rat operator + (rat);
  rat operator - (rat);
  rat operator * (rat);
  rat operator / (rat);

  char* show();
  };

rat rat::operator+(rat x)
{
 rat temp;

 temp.nmr = (nmr * x.dnm) + (x.nmr * dnm);
 temp.dnm = dnm * x.dnm;
 return temp;
}

rat rat::operator-(rat x)
{
 rat temp;

 temp.nmr = (nmr * x.dnm) - (x.nmr * dnm);
 temp.dnm = dnm * x.dnm;
 return temp;
}
```

continues

Listing 7-3. continued

```
rat rat::operator*(rat x)
{
 rat temp;

 nmr = nmr * x.nmr;
 dnm = dnm * x.dnm;
 return temp;
}

rat rat::operator/(rat x)
{
 rat temp;

 nmr = nmr * x.dnm;
 dnm = dnm * x.nmr;
 return temp;
}

char* rat::show()
{
  char *buffer = new char[40];

  sprintf(buffer, "%4d\n------\n%4d", nmr, dnm);
  return buffer;
}
```

In the rational number class, you store the numerator and denominator as integer members in the private part. You have two constructors. The default constructor—without any parameters—sets the two numeric members to values that are chosen more for their harmlessness than for any mathematical reason. The four common arithmetic operators are overloaded to work with this class. Each one implements the proper algorithm for performing the operation on a rational number. The "Rational Number Algorithms" box briefly summarizes the algorithms that are implemented in the member functions.

Rational Number Algorithms

Addition:
```
n1/d1 + n2/d2 =     ((n1 * d2) + (n2 * d1)) / (d1 * d2)
```

Subtraction:
```
n1/d1 - n2/d2 =     ((n1 * d2) - (n2 * d1)) / (d1 * d2)
```

Multiplication:
```
n1/d1 * n2/d2 = (n1 * n2) / (d1 * d2)
```

Division:
```
(n1/d1) / (n2/d2)  =  (n1 *  d2) / (d1 * n2)
```

Note that each operator function has the class type rat as a return value. This is to maintain a consistency in the arithmetic operators. For example, you expect that when you add two numbers, you will get a number as the result—a number that subsequently can be assigned to another numeric variable. This is an important design consideration when you use overloaded operators. The new use of an operator should mirror as closely as possible the way other data types use that same operation.

Before you can use this rational number class seriously, however, some improvements must be included to correct awkwardness in the design. For example, the class does not factor the number to its lowest term. But it can serve to indicate how you would go about designing a successful class that uses overloaded operators. Listing 7-4 contains a driver program to illustrate the operations of rational.cpp.

**Listing 7-4. A driver program to exercise
the function of the rational number class.**

```
main()
{
 rat x(1, 2);
 rat y(3, 4);
 rat z;

 cout << "\n\nz = x + y:\n";
```

continues

Listing 7-4. continued

```
z = x + y;
cout << z.show() << "\n";

cout << "\n\nz = x * y:\n";
z = x * y;
cout << z.show() << "\n";
}
```

Extending Operator Overloading to Non-Numeric Classes

Operator overloading is used most successfully in classes that implement mathematical entities—particularly numeric ones. The examples are easy to understand, the interface is clean and well behaved, and, above all, the redefined operators do not stray too far from their traditional uses. Although caution is strongly advised, you can apply operators to nonmathematical classes successfully. Listing 7-5, string.cpp, contains a class defined to implement a character string type.

**Listing 7-5. A character string class
with overloaded operators: string.cpp.**

```
#include <iostream.h>
#include <string.h>

class string  {
  char *v;
  int len;
public:
  string()    { len = 0; v = (char*)0; }
  string(char*);
 ~string() { delete v; }

  string operator + (string);

  char* show() { return v; }
};
```

```
string::string(char* s)
{
 v = new char[(len = strlen(s))];
 strcpy(v,s);
}

string string::operator + (string p)
{
   string temp;

   temp.v = new char[ (temp.len = len + strlen(p.v) + 1) ];
   strcpy(temp.v, v);
   strcat(temp.v, p.v);
   return temp;
}
```

In the `string` class you overload the + operator so that it can be used to concatenate two strings. As with the earlier rational number class, the operator returns a type of string so that you can use this concatenation in an assignment expression. The algorithm expressed in the `operator + ()` function is easy to understand. A `temp` variable of type `string` is set to take `char*` values from both the calling class and the class variable that's passed in as a parameter. When the temporary variable is filled, it's returned through the operator function.

In this class, I am stretching the meaning usually associated with +. Sticking two strings together to make a longer one is not the same as adding two numbers. But does this example stretch the meaning too far? This question has no easy answer. In this example, the intent and the implementation are clear enough that there is little chance for confusion. In other more complicated cases, judgment has to be reserved for the context of the design.

You can take this string design a step further. Another kind of concatenation that you might want to perform on a string variable is to extend the single variable itself rather than concatenating two string objects and storing the result in a third one. One natural choice for this is the += operator. You can add this operator to the string class easily, as in the following example:

```
class string  {
  char *v;
  int len;
public:
  string()    { len = 0; v = (char*)0; }
  string(char*);
 ~string() { delete v; }
```

```
 string operator + (string);
 void string::operator += (string);

 char* show() { return v; }
};

void string::operator += (string p)
{
 char* temp = new char[ strlen(v) + strlen(p.v) + 1];
 strcpy(temp, v);
 delete v;
 v = new char[ len = ( len + p.len +1 )];
 strcpy(v, temp);
 strcat(v, p.v);
 delete temp;
}
```

The operator += () function in string executes an algorithm similar to that of the operator + (). In this case, however, it is the v member of the calling class object that is altered rather than a third, temporary variable. The value of v is copied to a buffer created for the purpose. An application of the delete operator returns v's current memory allocation to the operating system. A new allocation is made that gives v enough room to contain both strings. They are copied and concatenated from the buffer and the parameter respectively. Because the operator is meant to alter one of its operands directly, no value is returned and the function is declared with type void. Listing 7-6 contains a main() function that acts as a driver to test the two operator functions that were defined for the string class: = and +=.

Listing 7-6. A driver program for string.cpp.

```
main()
{
 string s("this is only a test");
 string t(" Nothing can go wrong");
 string u("...go wrong...");
 string v;

 v = s + t;
 cout << "v = " << v.show() << "\n";

 v += u;
 cout << "v = " << v.show() << "\n";
}
```

Operators with Multiple Overloadings

Just as with overloaded function names, operator functions themselves can be overloaded. It's possible to have more than one definition for any particular operator. The mechanism is the same as for any other function: Each function that serves the same operator must be distinguished in its parameter list, either by the number of parameters or their type.

One important motivation for overloading operator functions is to deal with the order of operands for a redefined operator. After all, most operations performed on built-in data types are commutative—they work in both directions. With mixed mode operations—those with an integer and a `double`, for example—you safely can ignore the difference because you know that the compiler converts the integer to a `double` value before it performs any operations. When you create your own classes and their associated operations, you must choose explicitly the order of the operands. If more than one order is permissible, you must supply more than one operator function. Fortunately, as with overloaded functions, you can use multiple overloaded operators in a class, as long as their argument lists are different.

The string2.cpp example (Listing 7-7) illustrates a program that contains two formats for the + operator—defined as a concatenation. Both

```
string = string + string
```

and

```
string = string + char*
```

are possible uses of this symbol. I've expanded the notion of not only the + operator, but also the definition of concatenation. This expansion, however, seems reasonable and well behaved.

Listing 7-7. A class that contains an overloaded operator function: string2.cpp.

```
#include <iostream.h>
#include <string.h>
class string  {
  char *v;
  int len;
public:
  string()    { len = 0; v = (char*)0;}
  string(char*);
```

continues

Listing 7-7. continued

```
~string() { delete v; }

  string operator + (string);
  string operator + (char*);

  void string::operator += (string );

  char* show() { return v; }
};

string string::operator + (string p)
{
  string temp;

  temp.v = new char[ (temp.len = len + strlen(p.v) + 1) ];
  strcpy(temp.v, v);
  strcat(temp.v, p.v);
  return temp;
}

string string::operator + (char* ptr)
{
  string temp;

  temp.v = new char[  (temp.len = len + strlen(ptr) + 1) ];

  strcpy(temp.v, v);
  strcat(temp.v, ptr);
  return temp;
}

main()
{
  string s("This is only a test");
  string t(" Nothing can go wrong");
  string u;
  string v;

  u = s + t;
  cout << "u = " << u.show() << "\n";
```

```
    v = u + "...go wrong...";
    cout << "v = " << v.show() << "\n";
}
```

The `main()` function provided in the example illustrates both formats that are now possible thanks to the overloading of the function `operator + ()`. Any time you want to accommodate a different set of values for a particular operation, you must supply a new form of the function.

Using Friend Operator Functions for Flexibility

The examples that you've seen up to this point show the function that redefines the operator as a member of the same class as the new operator. In this case, the left argument is always implicit, and the class "owns" the function. This is, however, not the only way to produce a new operator. You can redefine an operator also by using friend functions. The rational.cpp program (Listing 7-8) is a rewrite of the rational number class first defined in Listing 7-3.

Listing 7-8. Operator overloading implemented using friend functions: rational.cpp.

```
#include <iostream.h>
#include <stdio.h>

class rat {
   int nmr,
       dnm;

public:
  rat() { nmr = dnm = 0; }
  rat(int n, int d) { nmr = n; dnm = d; }

  friend rat operator+(rat, rat);
  friend rat operator-(rat, rat);
  friend rat operator*(rat, rat);
  friend rat operator/(rat, rat);
  char* show();

};
```

continues

Listing 7-8. continued

```
char* rat::show()
{
  char *buffer = new char[40];

  sprintf(buffer, "%4d\n------\n%4d", nmr, dnm);
  return buffer;
}

main()
{
 rat x(1, 2);
 rat y(3, 4);
 rat z;

 z = x + y;
 cout << "z = \n" << z.show() << "\n";

 z = x * y;
 cout << "z = \n" << z.show() << "\n";
}

rat operator+(rat x, rat y)
{
 rat temp;
 temp.nmr = (x.nmr * y.dnm) + (y.nmr * x.dnm);
 temp.dnm = x.dnm * y.dnm;
 return temp;
}

rat operator-(rat x, rat y)
{
 rat temp;
 temp.nmr = (x.nmr * y.dnm) - (y.nmr * x.dnm);
 temp.dnm = x.dnm * y.dnm;
 return temp;
}

rat operator*(rat x, rat y)
{
 rat temp;
```

```
  temp.nmr = x.nmr * y.nmr;
  temp.dnm = x.dnm * y.dnm;
  return temp;
}

rat operator/(rat x, rat y)
{
 rat temp;
 temp.nmr = x.nmr * y.dnm;
 temp.dnm = x.dnm * y.nmr;
 return temp;
}
```

In the case of the new rat class operator functions, the algorithm for each function is the same as the comparable member function in the earlier example. The difference is that these are friend functions that are not members of any other class. In the earlier example, the required class operand was supplied by the enclosing class. In this example, that class object is supplied values by the first parameter in each of the operator functions. For example, in

```
rat operator / (rat x, rat y)
```

the x parameter supplies the required object operand and takes the place of the calling or enclosing object in the earlier example.

One restriction on operator overloading becomes apparent when you use friend functions to create new operators: An operator function must have at least one class object as a parameter. Prior to the current example, this requirement was satisfied by the this argument that was implicit in the class of which the operator redefinition function was a member. Listing 7-7, which concatenates a character array onto a string object, demonstrated that an operator function can have a non-class argument. You cannot, however, use an operator redefinition function that has only nonclass arguments, even if you declare it as a friend to a class so that it has privileges to access the private area of the class. At least one parameter must always be a class object.

You've seen the "how" of operator overloading using friend functions. The "why" is more difficult to explain. For one thing, the caveats mentioned in Chapter 6 apply equally to friend operator functions: You diminish the force of encapsulation by declaring a friend function. In some circumstances, however, a friend operator function might be considered. For example, if you are designing a class that has to accommodate many different data types throughout its life, it makes sense to create a friend function that can be customized to new kinds of values long after the original class has been defined (in Chapter 10, you will see something like this in the customization of the << and >> operators).

Creating Unary Operators

Because you must respect the basic "calling template" of an operator symbol, some symbols can be used only for creating unary operators, which have only one operand. A few operators support both single- and dual-operand calling sequences. The "Unary, Binary, and Binary-Unary" box lists all of the C++ operators that are available for overloading.

Unary, Binary, and Binary-Unary Operators

Unary:	++	--	!	
	~	sizeof		
Binary:	/	%	()	[]
	new	delete	+=	-=
	*=	/=	|	^
	||	&&	<	<=
	>	>=	<<	>>
	|=	^=	&=	<<=
	>>=	==	!=	->
	=	%=	,	->*
Unary or Binary:	+	-	*	&

Redefining a unary operator is similar to redefining a binary one. You use a symbol with the operator function to create an operator that is unique to a particular class. Either a member or a friend function serves the purpose.

The circinc1.cpp example (Listing 7-9) illustrates a unary operator defined as a member function. This program defines a `circle` class that includes both the current value for the radius of a circle and an increment that increases its size. Member functions for both area and circumference also are defined. The focus of the example, however, is on the ++ operator. This operator has been redefined to work with this new figure, although it retains the essence of the increment operator as it applies to built-in data types. Because the member function operator++() is a unary operator, it can take no arguments other than the implied this parameter. The private value incr increases the size of the radius.

Listing 7-9. A unary operator redefinition: circinc1.cpp.

```cpp
#include <iostream.h>

const double pi = 3.1415;

class circle  {
  double radius;
  int incr;
public:
  circle()                { radius = 0; incr = 1; }
  circle(double r, int i) { radius = r; incr = i;}
  double area()           { return pi * radius * radius; }
  double cir()            { return pi * 2 * radius; }
  void operator++();
};

void circle::operator++()
{
 radius += incr;
}

main()
{
 circle x(35, 2);

 for(int i = 0 ; i < 10 ; i++ )  {
     cout << "area = " << x.area() << "\n";
     cout << "circumference = " << x.cir() << "\n";
     x++;
  }
}
```

The driver function main() illustrates how the new ++ operator works. Note that in the context of an overloaded operator, ++x and x++ perform identical operations. The differences between these two forms that occur when the object is an integer type do not translate to its new definition.

Special Problems with Overloading

Nearly all of the C++ operators can be overloaded. This includes some symbols that might be considered unlikely candidates for such treatment: (), =, and the [ ]. Each of these symbols can have a definition specific to a class. Each, as well, poses some special problems for the software designer.

With the basic arithmetic operators, it's easy to come up with cognate operations to be associated with a particular operator symbol. Complex numbers and addition, for example, mesh neatly with the + symbol. Even when you strayed from numeric examples and defined a string class with a + and a += symbol (standing for two different kinds of concatenation), you could see the connection—even if it was stretched. The redefinition of ++ in the circle class also made sense, although it was a bit more arbitrary (++ could have moved the center of the circle rather than changing its radius). The special symbols I've mentioned each pose a different conceptual problem for the programmer. It is not as obvious which operations should be associated with any one of these symbols. I discuss each one in turn.

In fact, there are three additional special operator symbols that do not require additional discussion. These are the new and delete operators and the -> pointer symbol. The circumstances under which it makes sense to make these new definitions are even more limited in the case of these symbols.

Overloading the = Operator

Until now, you've been using the assignment operator = with its built-in operation. Whenever, an assignment is made in an expression, a copying operation is performed. For example,

```
int x = 123;
int y = 24;
int z;

z= x + y;
```

leaves the variable z with a copy of the number that results from evaluating the expression on the right side of the operator. This operation holds true even for classes. Using the string class defined in Listing 7-7, the code fragment

```
string s("This is only a test  ");
string t("Nothing can go wrong");
string u;

u = s + t;
```

causes u to contain a copy of the class that is returned by the operation of the addition operator applied to the string class objects. This copy is an uninterpreted or "bitwise" copy. The assignment operator knows nothing about the structure of the class and is just copying bit values from one memory location to another.

In many cases, this bitwise copying is perfectly adequate, and might be the most effective way to use an overloaded operator. In some contexts, however, it is necessary to give a new and class-specific meaning to the assignment operator. You can turn to the operator overloading mechanism to accommodate the change.

It's difficult to list circumstances under which overloading the assignment operator makes sense. It may be impossible to come up with an effective and foolproof rule. In general terms, anytime an assignment needs to know about the internal architecture of a class object, it is appropriate to redefine. If the bitwise copy is adequate to the task, it's best not to redefine the operator.

Listing 7-10 shows the string class with an overloaded assignment operator. In this case, the redefined operator allows the assignment of a traditional C++ character string (char*) directly to an object of a string class.

Listing 7-10. A string class with an overloaded = operator: string4.cpp.

```
#include <iostream.h>
#include <string.h>
class string  {
  char *v;
  int len;
public:
  string()    { len = 0; v = (char*)0; }
  string(char*);
 ~string() { delete v; }

  string operator + (string);
  string operator + (char*);
```

continues

Listing 7-10. continued

```
  void operator += (string);

  void operator = (char*);
char* show() { return v; }
 };

void string::operator = (char* str)
{
 delete v;
 v = new char[ strlen(str) + 1 ];
 strcpy(v, str);
}

main()
{
 string u("this is only a test");

 u = "This is not a test";

 cout << "u = " << u.show() << "\n";
}
```

Is the redefined assignment operator in string performing the tasks associated traditionally with this operator? If you consider what these traditional tasks involve, you can see an almost one-to-one correspondence. Certainly the right value is being copied over to the object on the left side. Additionally, the process of making this copy includes a data type conversion. This, too, is something that you expect from this operator—in numeric assignments, for example, mixed mode expressions always are accommodated.

I should point out that the default bitwise assignment is still available for those circumstances that do not satisfy the overloading conditions of the operator = () function. The main() function attached to the listing shows the usage of this operator.

New Definitions for []

A more radical change is effected by the redefinition of the [] operator in the class definition found in Listing 7-11. These brackets usually are used to indicate an array-addressing operation. An integer index is used as an offset into a set of contiguous memory locations. In this example, the string class still honors this idea of an offset; however, instead of an integer index, a character string (char*) is used. (The other member functions of this example are defined in Listing 7-7.)

Listing 7-11. A string class with a redefined [] operator: string5.cpp.

```cpp
#include <iostream.h>
#include <string.h>
class string  {
  char *v;
  int len;
public:
  string()    { len = 0; v = (char*)0; }
  string(char*);
 ~string() { delete v; }

  string operator + (string);
  string operator + (char*);

  void operator += (string);
  void operator = (char*);

  char* operator [] (char*);

  char* show() { return v; }
 };

char* string::operator [] (char* key)
{
 for(int i = 0 ; v[i + strlen(key)] ; i++)
     if( !strncmp(&v[i], key, strlen(key)) )
          return (char*)&v[i];
 return (char*)0;
}

main()
{
  string s("This is only a test.  Nothing can go wrong.");

  cout << "s[test] = " << s["test"] << "\n";
}
```

The operator[]() function takes advantage of the fact that the brackets [] are an operator that is applied to an address. In this case, the member variable, v, is a pointer to a string of characters. By using the brackets with v, you can address this string character-by-character. The function loops through the string character-by-character. Each time the loop is incremented, you have a new string that is one character shorter. Each loop compares this processed string to the key value until either a match is made or you reach the end of the string. Note also that the search needs to continue only as long as the remaining string associated with v is shorter than the key string.

If the operator[]() function finds a match, it returns the address of the substring of v that begins with the key value, which includes the key value. The main() function attached shows how this new operation works. In this case, the value ultimately displayed on the screen is

```
test.  Nothing can go wrong.
```

Of course, a different key value yields a different result. If a proposed key is not a substring of the class value, a 0 is returned. The 0 is a good choice because it is compatible with the address that is expected, and yet it never is associated with an actual location.

Redefining the () Symbol

Perhaps the most unusual operator overloading involves the () operator, which often is associated with a function call. Choosing a reasonable redefinition for this particular operator is difficult. You really can't approach the function call syntax in as close a manner as you did with the simple arithmetic operators +, -, *, /, or even with the [] and =. Caution is advisable here. Let's look at a reasonable example.

The following example shows a variation on the earlier rational number example. The parentheses operator, (), is redefined to allow the reinitialization of the class object using two integers. This use is far removed from the notion of a function call. It is, however, close to the operation associated with the declaration and initialization of a class object. The code is simple enough to be defined as an inline expanded function.

```
class rat {
    int nmr;
    int dnm;

public:
    rat() { nmr = 0; dnm = 1; }
    rat(int n, int d) { nmr = n; dnm = d; }
```

```
   rat operator + (rat);
   rat operator - (rat);
   rat operator * (rat);
   rat operator / (rat);

   void operator () (int p, int q) { nmr = p; dnm = q; }

   char* show();
 };
```

Listing 7-12 contains a follow-up example. Here I define another format for reinitializing the class object using the () operator. A character string of the form

`"3/27"`

is translated into two integer values, a numerator and a denominator. The implementation of this new operator uses the `strtok()` library function to strip out the individual numbers. `Atol()` is used to convert the resulting substrings into integers. The `main()` function defined in Listing 7-12 illustrates the use of both versions of the overloaded operator functions.

Listing 7-12. A rational number class
with two overloaded () operator functions: ratnl3.cpp.

```
#include <iostream.h>
#include <string.h>
class rat {
   int nmr;
   int dnm;

public:
  rat() { nmr = 0; dnm = 1; }
  rat(int n, int d) { nmr = n; dnm = d; }

  rat operator + (rat);
  rat operator - (rat);
  rat operator * (rat);
  rat operator / (rat);

  void operator () (int p, int q) { nmr = p; dnm = q; }
  void operator () (char*);
```

continues

Listing 7-12. continued

```
 char* show();
};

void rat::operator () (char* str)
{
 nmr = atol(strtok(str, "/"));
 dnm = atol(strtok(0, "/"));
}

main()
{
 rat z;

 cout << "\n\nUsing the Overloaded (int,int): \n";

 z(5,6);
 cout << z.show() << "\n";

 cout << "\n\nUsing the Overloaded (char*): \n";

 z("12/24");
 cout << z.show() << "\n";
}
```

Object-Oriented Design

How does operator overloading fit into the overall picture of object-oriented design? The answer is complex and not easy to answer. Many factors enter into the equation, including programming style and even issues relating to specific applications.

Polymorphism and Operator Overloading

The most direct connection between object-oriented programming and operator overloading is the issue of polymorphism. You've seen how function name overloading added this new dimension to design: Functions that perform similar actions should share a common name. It's easy to extend this idea of similar actions to operators. For example, the + operator should be used to add two complex or rational numbers, although the operation of adding these values is more complicated than the cognate operation on simple values.

In some ways, operator overloading is an even more striking implementation of the characteristic polymorphism associated with object-oriented design. Operators stand for the most basic tasks within the syntax of a programming language. They often relate directly to basic machine instructions. Such elementary actions should be common to all parts of the programming system, including the special data types that are created to solve particular problems.

Being Cautious with Operator Overloading

Having made the case for operator overloading as helping to fulfill the promise of extendibility offered by OOP technology, it is important, also, to set the context of this overloading. You always must keep in mind that C++ is evolved from the C programming language, a high-level language with basic access to the lowest level of the machine. C++ maintains some of these low-level features; however, just like C, it has a bare minimum of internal checks and gives a great deal of freedom to the individual designer. The operator overloading mechanism, for example, gives the ability to change the actions associated with an operator. It puts no limits on what can replace the traditional algorithms.

The fact that a minimum amount of checking is done on an overloaded function puts the responsibility on the designer to choose actions that complement the traditional uses of the operator symbols. This task has been accomplished in the examples in this chapter by carefully choosing designs that could be construed as noncontroversial: for example, redefining arithmetic operators to fit different kinds of numbers—in this case, complex and rational. It's important that the programmer and software designer understand the limits of this overloading technique and some of the factors that might surround "gray area" choices for new operator functions.

Sensible Overloading Examples

As a rule of thumb, good uses of operator overloading are those which tend to increase the readability and the modularization of the program. You need to review your class designs to see if any of the interactions—either among class objects or between them and other values—is just another form of one of the traditional existing operations or is at least strongly analogous. For example, in the string class (Listing 7-10), the operator function

```
operator = (char*)
```

performs the same kind of operation that is routinely done in any mixed-type arithmetic assignment. Creating this new operator in this context does not create any confusion for anyone who understands the use of the = operator.

Questionable Uses of Overloading

An egregious misuse of the operator-overloading capability is not likely—for example, substituting + for subtraction and - for addition—at least among professional programmers. It's important to realize, however, that less dramatic redefinitions could cause trouble, too. These less flagrant abuses are more difficult to define.

The important point to remember always is that any programming technique, including object-oriented design techniques, is not something that is necesary to the computer. The technique is aimed, rather, at the programmer. With this in mind, a good rule of thumb for choosing operator overloading is to ask yourself if the new definition will make sense to another designer. The program must make sense to someone reading it. This can include the designer if a sufficient amount of time has passed. Part of this readability is a quality that could be called *obviousness*, which can be illustrated best with a simple comparison. The use of the = to indicate the assignment of one string object to another or even a char* value to a string object is an obvious extension of the use of this operator. If instead you had set aside the < operator to stand for this situation, the program reader would have to strain to understand it. In other words, for three string objects (see Listing 7-10)

```
z = s + t;
```

makes more sense than

```
z < s + t;
```

No sharp dividing line delineates the obvious and successful overloadings from the unsuccessful ones. There is large gray area of controversy that is difficult to manage. For example, some designers would object to the use of "+=" to stand for string concatenation (as in Listing 7-10). Some would object also to any overloading of the () operator. Some individuals even feel that the wisest course is avoid any operator overloading at all.

The Psychology of Polymorphic Design

As noted previously, object-oriented design has a strong psychological component. An important component of that psychology is the abstraction of patterns and their subsequent application to other elements in the design. This ability to identify and apply patterns is the hallmark of the accomplished designer. The principle of polymorphism is a recognition that this component should be part of a design strategy.

A simple example of this is the addition operation. The code that adds two integers together is different from the code that adds real numbers (`doubles` or `floats`). Yet both are bound to the + symbol. C++ gives you the ability to continue this pattern, matching another level by reusing the same symbol with a user-defined numeric type: a complex number, perhaps. The basic pattern or concept, addition, is manifested at different parts of the design and even at different levels of the design—a basic built-in type and an object. You can take it a step further and redefine + to stand for some nonmathematical operation. In this chapter, you have used it for the concatenation of character strings.

Because you're able to use the same symbol (or, in the case of functions, the same name) for many different kinds of values, you can make a claim about similarity and underscore the connections between these disparate entities. This kind of relationship helps to enhance the readability of the design by making it more obvious and, perhaps, more coherent. The similarity wouldn't have been as obvious if each participant had a unique name. The design certainly wouldn't appear as unified as it does.

There are less abstract benefits as well. For example, one important consequence of the object-oriented programming paradigm is the control of complexity. Using objects and overloading function names and operators enhances your ability not only to hide details, but also to deal with them at each level in a simple way and then combine these levels through well-understood interfaces.

Summary

In this chapter you've explored the controversial techniques of operator overloading. The overloading mechanism allows the use of existing operator symbols such as + and = to be redefined within the context of a class definition. After this has been done, the symbol has a different meaning for objects of the class than it does for other values in the program.

7

You've seen that when you stick to numeric classes such as those that implement complex or rational numbers, operator overloading is straightforward, easy to understand, and helpful in the creation of compound programs. It's when you leave the realm of numbers that the issues become more clouded and controversial.

In overloading non-numeric objects, you are extending—some might say stretching—the everyday means of the familiar set of operator symbols. You must exercise caution to make sure that these extensions are true to the spirit of the traditional usage. Above all, you want this technique to enhance the design rather than make it more obscure.

8

Introduction to Class Inheritance

8

Introduction to Class Inheritance

Before examining class inheritance relationships, let's briefly review the class data type. This structure contains all the elements that make up a programming object: the members that store data items and the member functions that manipulate the data and communicate with the rest of the program. The most important of the class functions are the constructors, which are called when a class object is created. These member functions can perform complex and extensive initializations and other startup actions that complicated classes sometimes require.

Classes are especially important because they help implement models that enable computer programs to simulate complex real-world situations. Classes efficiently manage the complexity of large programs through *encapsulation.* Each class contains a public part and a private part. Members (both variables and functions) declared in the private part of a class are hidden from the rest of the program. The public section is the interface that connects the objects to the rest of the software environment. This connection enables you to solve the details of a program's implementation piece by piece. As you successfully complete each section, you can hide all of the details of the implementation from the rest of the program, so that only the small public interface can affect—or be affected by—other modules.

The class alone, however, is not enough to support object-oriented programming and design. You need a way also to relate disparate classes to one another. Earlier examples used nested classes. Nested classes are, however, only a partial solution because nested classes don't have the required characteristics to fully relate one class to another. What you need is a mechanism for creating hierarchies of classes in which class *A* is a cognate of class *B,* but with added features. C++ has a mechanism for creating such a hierarchy—the *derived class.* The process of deriving classes is called *inheritance.* Inheritance is one of the distinguishing characteristics of object-oriented languages.

Inheritance and Object-Oriented Programming

One of the key defining points of an object-oriented programming language is that it allows for the creation of hierarchies: A class object is used as the basis for defining other classes; these classes in turn can be used as the basis for another level of objects. A name class can give rise to an address object or a bank account object. The process is illustrated in Figure 8-1.

The relationship of classes illustrated in Figure 8-1 is called *inheritance*, which is the third defining characteristic of an object-oriented programming environment. The other two characteristics are encapsulation and polymorphism.

The mechanism for implementing inheritance in C++ is the derived class. Any class can serve as the base. From this base, additional classes can be derived. These derived classes have the characteristics of their base but also have their own unique characteristics. The "base-derived" class relationship is another tool in the repertoire of the C++ programmer, who can use the relationship to good effect to create libraries of reusable class objects.

Besides creating these one-dimensional hierarchies of related classes, C++ supports also the derivation of classes from more than one base class (*multiple inheritance*). The use of multiple bases opens up an entirely new realm of design possibilities. I discuss multiple inheritance in Chapter 9.

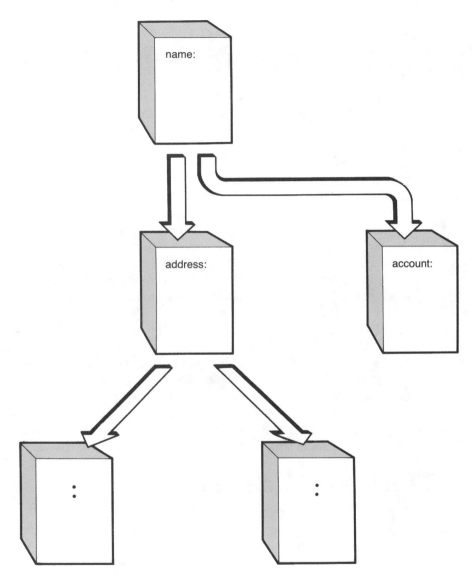

Figure 8-1. A hierarchical class structure.

8

Derived Classes
Enhance Efficiency

Using derived classes also enhances efficiency. You no longer need to create repetitive code. At each level, you can group the details of the lower levels with any necessary processing. You no longer need to create a series of independent and redundant data structures to handle every possible variation of data organization used in a program. For example, if an accounting program must keep track of individuals with multiple accounts, you don't have to add code to link the common identification information with a series of unique data structures, one for each kind of account. In C++, you can create the same structure by using a series of derived classes. You maintain the identification information in the base class and put the details of the kind of account in the appropriate derived class. The customer's name and other identification data still are available, but now they are retained within the account data type itself. This gives you two immediate advantages: You don't need to create a complex structure of conditionals to link one set of values to another, nor do you need to include the customer's name whenever you think the program might need it.

Thus, derived classes save the programmer a great deal of effort because blocks of redundant information don't need to be maintained. Using traditional data structures, each time a field or member is repeated, the memory allocation grows, and access time correspondingly slows. Programs also require more time to evaluate Boolean expressions and to work through complex sets of conditionals to access the desired set of data. In C++, the derivation of classes arranges the hierarchy of data in a highly optimized and transparent manner.

Derived Classes
as a Development Tool

One of the most remarkable features of C++ is the way it enables you to build classes on one another. After you define a class, you can use it as the base of an entire family of related, or derived, classes. For example, in a graphics library, you might define a rectangle class. When you need to define a new kind of rectangle, such as one with rounded corners, you can use the basic features of the rectangle class and then add some unique properties to derive a new class of rectangles (see Figure 8-2).

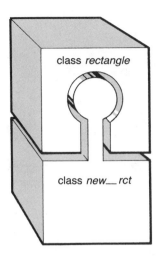

Figure 8-2. Deriving a new rectangle class.

As a more practical example, consider a financial program in which an accounts class contains the identification of a customer as its basic class and adds as derived classes information specific to various kinds of accounts. In the derived classes, the original object is preserved. It is merely replicated so that all of its information is available to each derived class. This mechanism helps you produce more efficient and elegant programs by avoiding redundant storage (see Figure 8-3). These examples suggest how inheritance enables you to model more easily real-world objects and their interwoven relationships without having to use the obscuring conditional statements and branches found in the traditional C approach.

In addition to its use as a means of reconciling the common features and specialized aspects of different data structures, class derivation is also a tool for modularization. For example, a programmer can define a derived class based on an existing class that was produced and compiled outside the current program—perhaps by a different programmer. A designer can create a library of useful classes also by putting the compiled code in a library file and the interface requirements in one or more header files. This "library" of classes then could form the nucleus of many programs, yet the details of implementation need not be published. The integrity of the base class is preserved, yet you can customize C++ for a given project to more closely match the application area (see Figure 8-4).

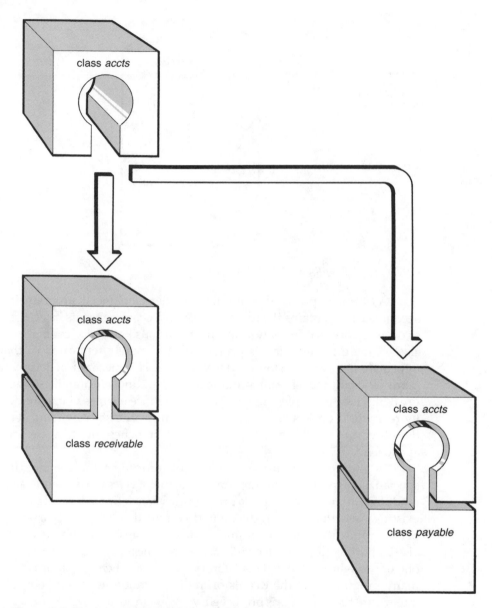

Figure 8-3. Deriving specialized classes for accounting.

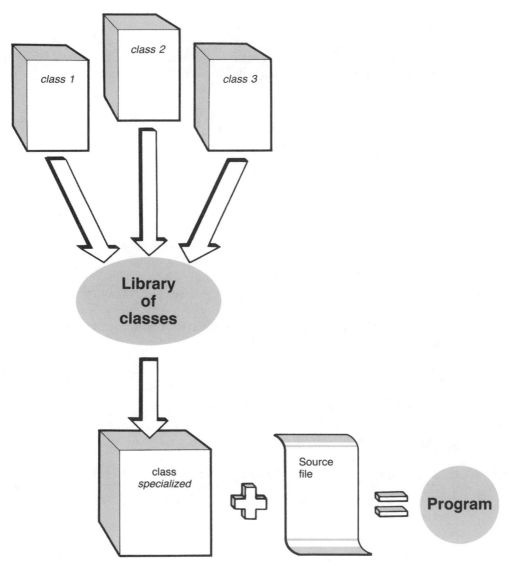

Figure 8-4. Using a library of classes.

The user of a precompiled class can use the contents of a class library to create derived classes. It always is possible to add members to a derived class. Although you don't have a comparable "delete" facility, you can ignore base class members that you don't need. One great advantage to this procedure is that the derived classes don't alter the base class in any way, and therefore you do not need to recompile it. The base class represents a layer of usable code that no longer needs to be modified. Metaphorically, it underlies and supports the new layer of software. Thus, a derived class is truly a medium of modularization.

The Creation of a Derived Class

Now that you understand the advantages of using class derivation in C++, let's examine the actual mechanics of declaring and using derived classes.

Each derived class must refer to a previously declared base class. This base can be precompiled, or it can be defined in the same program in which the derived class is created. If you do not define the base class before the derived class, you must at least declare the name of the base class first, which is a *forward reference.* Nothing is syntactically special, however, about the base class. In fact, nothing distinguishes the base class from any other class definition. Any class can serve as a base.

In contrast, there is a defining mark in the definition of a derived class, which is found in the header of the definition:

```
class derived1 : base1  {
          :
```

The colon following the name of the class indicates that the next word on the line is the name of the base class from which the current definition inherits. Listing 8-1 contains a simple example of a base and its derived class.

Listing 8-1. An example of a simple derived class: bio.cpp.

```
#include <iostream.h>
#include <string.h>

class name  {
  char first[80];
  char mid[80];
  char last[80];

public:
  name()  { first[0] = mid[0] = last[0] = '\0'; }
  void set_name(char*, char*, char*);
```

```
  char* show();
};

void name::set_name(char* f, char* m, char* l)
{
  strcpy(first, f);
  strcpy(mid, m);
  strcpy(last, l);
}

char* name::show()
{
 char* temp = new char[80];

 strcpy(temp, first);
 strcat(temp, " ");   // add a space
 strcat(temp, mid);
 strcat(temp, " ");
 strcat(temp, last);
 return temp;
}

class address : name   {
  char street[80];
  char city[80];
  char state[80];
  char zip[10];

public:
  address() { street[0] = city[0] = state[0] = zip[0] = '\0'; }
  void new_address(char*, char*, char*, char*);
  void new_name(char*, char*, char*);
  char* show_info();
};

void address::new_address(char* s, char* c, char* st, char* z)
{
 strcpy(street, s);
 strcpy(city, c);
 strcpy(state, st);
 strcpy(zip, z);
}
```

continues

Listing 8-1. continued

```
void address::new_name(char* f, char* m, char* l)
{
  set_name(f, m, l);
}


char* address::show_info()
{
 char* temp = show();
 strcat(temp, "\n");
 strcat(temp, street);
 strcat(temp, "\n");
 strcat(temp, city);
 strcat(temp, ", ");
 strcat(temp, state);
 strcat(temp, "  ");
 strcat(temp, zip);

 return temp;
}


main()
{
 address x;

 x.new_address("1234 Pearl Street", "Santa Cruz", "CA", "94080");
 x.new_name("Joseph", "Henry", "Green");

 cout << "** " << x.show_info() << "\n";
}
```

The example consists of two simple classes. name is a straightforward class that contains the first, middle, and last name of an individual. To keep the example simple, it contains a simple constructor and only two additional member functions: set_name(), which gives values to the variable members of the class, and show(), which offers a display string. The constructor could perform the same task as set_name(). For the simplicity of this example, however, you don't need such a well-developed definition. The short driver program defined in main() shows how the class member functions can be used.

The derived class, address, takes the information that is provided in name and adds to it the number and street, city, state, and ZIP code. Moreover, this new class has access also to the public functions of the base. One important way to look at the connection between the base class and the derived class is that the latter is a specialization of the former. The remainder of this chapter spells out in detail the ramifications of this connection.

Access to the Base Class

Now, let's examine the relationship between the base class and a derived class. The class address includes all of the information that is contained in its base, name, but (and this is an important consideration) it has no special access to the private part of the base class. In this sense, there is no magic to the inheritance relationship. Common sense explains why it's necessary to keep the private section of the base class private. Any class can become a base long after it has been designed and compiled. The designer may not have been thinking of derived classes at the time the design was finalized. Thus, the "internals" of the base class must by default be "tamper-proof."

There is something special, however, in the relationship between the base class and the derived class. The base class members are part of the derived class. The public members of the base can be accessed directly without reference to a separate base class object. In the previous example (Listing 8-1), the member function new_name() directly calls the base class member set_name(). No further identification of this function is needed—it really is a part of the new class.

The process of deriving a class ends up making a composite class. Objects of the derived type contain both sets of members. These important points set C++ apart from other object-oriented programming languages in which objects are always distinct and inheritance is just another relationship between independent entities. An important consequence of the composite nature of the derived class is that the base class does not maintain a separate existence inside the derived class. You cannot recapture the base class from outside by using the derived object. Any access to base class members must be mediated by the public part of the derived class object.

Explicit Reference to Members

Listing 8-2 is an alternative definition of the derived class address. In this version, a member function (set_name()) has the same name as a member in the base class. This name conflict will cause a run-time error. The program will compile but will be unable to execute the set_name() member function because it won't know which one to use.

Listing 8-2. A derived class using
explicit base member access: bio1.cpp.

```
class address : name  {
  char street[80];
  char city[80];
  char state[80];
  char zip[10];

public:
  address() { street[0] = city[0] = state[0] = zip[0] = '\0'; }
  void new_address(char*, char*, char*, char*);
  void set_name(char* f, char* m, char* l);
  char* show_info();
};

void address::set_name(char* f, char* m, char* l)
{
    set_name(f, m, l);
}
```

An alternative construction that allows access to any member function regardless of its name uses the C++ scope reference operator (::) to create an explicit reference to a particular member. The class definition found in bio2.cpp (Listing 8-3) uses this procedure. Here, the base name is followed by :: and the member name, set_name(), which solves the name conflict. When using predefined (and often precompiled) class definitions, you aren't always completely free to choose names for variables, so it is useful to have a mechanism that allows you to select a name outside of the present scope.

Listing 8-3. A derived class using
explicit base member access: bio2.cpp.

```
class address : name  {
  char street[80];
  char city[80];
  char state[80];
  char zip[10];

public:
  address() { street[0] = city[0] = state[0] = zip[0] = '\0'; }
```

```
  void new_address(char*, char*, char*, char*);
  void set_name(char* f, char* m, char* l);
  char* show_info();
};


void address::set_name(char* f, char* m, char* l)
{
  name::set_name(f, m, l);
}
```

Derived Classes with Constructors and Destructors

Specifying a constructor for a class often is appropriate—and sometimes it is necessary. Class objects usually are too large and complicated for a simple initialization, and the constructor member function lets you execute as much startup code as you need when you create an object. For example, if a class opens a file and prepares it for writing, a constructor might include code that does garbage collection (the freeing of memory used by objects that are no longer needed) every time a new object is created. This is only one of many other possibilities. (Chapter 3 discussed the use of constructors in the context of a single class definition.) Similarly, the destructor member, if properly designed, can efficiently deallocate a class object (it is good programming practice to return resources that are no longer needed). You also can extend the tasks of the destructor beyond simple deallocation to the performance of a variety of shutdown activities, some only indirectly related to the class of which the destructor is a part. Such uses might include closing files, flushing buffers, or even reinitializing blocks of memory.

A derived class is no less of a class than a base class is. A derived class can have both constructors and destructors. With a derived class, however, you have the additional problem that the base class also can have both of these specialized member functions. Some provision must be made to execute the base constructor and destructor within the framework of a derived class object.

Coordinating Base Classes and Derived Classes

Constructors and destructors also can be a part of a derived class. A few minor differences in syntax, however, reflect the more complicated situation of one class being dependent on another. For example, a constructor or destructor defined for the base class must be coordinated with those found in a derived class. Equally important is the movement of values from the members in the derived class to those members found in the base. In particular, you must consider how the base class constructor receives values from the derived class to create the complete object.

The first issue, *coordination*, is resolved by a policy decision of the C++ language definition. If a constructor is defined for both the base class and the derived class, C++ calls the base constructor first. After the base constructor finishes its tasks, C++ executes the derived constructor. The commonsense nature of this policy makes it easy to remember: You create the base class first, therefore C++ calls its constructor first. The order of execution of the destructor is equally straightforward. The derived class destructor executes first. After it performs its deallocation and cleanup duties, C++ calls the base class destructor to finish the job. In other words, the last class created is the first class destroyed.

Using the Base Class Constructor

One question remains: How do the values that are created in the derived class get to the base class constructor? The answer is not as obvious as the coordination between constructors was. The derived class must explicitly supply the initial values for the base class. This is accomplished by appending the values to the definition of the constructor function of the derived class. The syntax is simple. For example, if the ex_class is derived from a base class named ex_base, the header line from the definition of the constructor for this derived class might look like this:

```
ex_class(int x, int y, int z) : ex_base(x,y);
```

The variables in the parentheses that follow the colon are the values that the base class constructor needs to create the base class. They serve the same purpose as calling the base class constructor and passing it these values. Note that if the base class constructor does not require initializing parameters, you do not need to call it explicitly from the derived class constructor. The compiler invokes the base class constructor automatically.

The bio3.cpp example (Listing 8-4) contains a revised version of the name/ address class hierarchy. Both the base class and derived classes have been rewritten to use constructor and destructor member functions. Note, too, that the variable members have been changed from the statically allocated character arrays to character string pointers that are allocated dynamically. This allows a greater efficiency in storage space because you need to allocate only enough space for each value. The example contains a small driver program in main() to show how the derived class works with actual values.

**Listing 8-4. Base class and derived classes
with constructors and destructors: bio3.cpp.**

```
#include <iostream.h>
#include <string.h>

class name  {
  char* first;
  char* mid;
  char* last;

public:
  name(char*, char*, char*);
 ~name() { delete first; delete mid; delete last; }
  char* show();
};

name::name(char* f, char* m, char* l)
{
  first = new char[strlen(f) + 1 ];
  mid = new char[strlen(m) + 1 ];
  last = new char[strlen(l) + 1];
  strcpy(first, f);
  strcpy(mid, m);
  strcpy(last, l);
}

char* name::show()
{
 char* temp = new char[80];

 strcpy(temp, first);
 strcat(temp, " ");   // add a space
 strcat(temp, mid);
 strcat(temp, " ");
```

continues

235

Listing 8-4. continued

```
 strcat(temp, last);
 return temp;
}

class address : name  {
  char* street;
  char* city;
  char* state;
  char* zip;

public:
  address(char*, char*, char*, char*, char*, char*, char* );
 ~address();
  char* show();
};

address::address(char* f, char* m, char* l, char* s, char* c,
                             char*st, char* z) : name(f, m, l)
{
 street = new char[strlen(s) + 1 ];
 city = new char[ strlen(c) + 1 ];
 state = new char[ strlen(st) + 1 ];
 zip = new char[ strlen(z) + 1 ];

 strcpy(street, s);
 strcpy(city, c);
 strcpy(state, st);
 strcpy(zip, z);
}

address::~address()
{
 delete street;
 delete city;
 delete state;
 delete zip;
}

char* address::show()
{
 char* temp = name::show();
```

```
    strcat(temp, "\n");  // add a new line
    strcat(temp, street);
    strcat(temp, "\n");// new line for city/state/zip
    strcat(temp, city);
    strcat(temp, ", "); // separate city/state with a comma
    strcat(temp, state);
    strcat(temp, "  ");  //add two spaces for zip
    strcat(temp, zip);

    return temp;
}

main()
{
  address x("John", "Jacob", "Smith","1234 Pearl Street",
                 "Santa Cruz", "CA", "94080");

  cout << "** " << x.show() << "\n";
}
```

The name class constructor initializes the three variable members of the base class. It allocates sufficient memory for each member and copies the values from the parameters. Similarly, the constructor for the address class allocates and copies values into the four members in the private part of the derived class. This latter constructor is responsible also for collecting the values that are passed to the name constructor. These values are passed immediately to the base constructor, even before the code of the address constructor is executed.

Calling the Base Class Destructor

By definition, a class destructor takes no parameters. Therefore, coordinating destructors for base classes and derived classes is less of a problem. No explicit call from the derived class to the base class is required. C++ is responsible for coordinating these member functions. Merely remember that the derived class destructor always is executed before the base class destructor.

In the example from Listing 8-4, each class contains a destructor to deallocate the data members used by the variable members of that class. In this case, the order in which these member variables are deleted makes no difference, so no direct evidence indicates this order. The base class members are deallocated first, however.

Private and Public Base Classes

In the creation of derived classes, you haven't been concerned until now with any difference in the way the base class and the derived class are connected. You have been relying on common sense and the definition defaults to set this parameter. Classes can be related in two different ways, however. You can define either public or private base classes.

Private base classes give the designer even more control over access to all parts of the derived class. With private derivation, the only way to access anything is through the public section in the derived class. In contrast, a public base class joins its public section to that of the derived class. Any member in either public section is a member of the composite derived class. This relationship is illustrated in Figure 8-5.

It's not always obvious which designs require a private base class and which work with a public one. Private base classes are most appropriate when the derived class uses services provided by the base, but they really define a new kind of object. A record class might be derived from a base that supplies access to a disk file. In this case, the details of the base class would add nothing to the derived class interface. A public base class, in contrast, should be used if the derived class provides some additional capability to that which already is supplied by the base. If a record class was derived from a name class, for example, the public declaration of name would allow the incorporation of the name public members directly into the derived class.

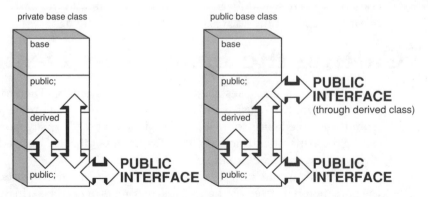

Figure 8-5. Private and public base classes.

Class Members in Private Base Classes

The default relationship between a derived class and its base might be a little surprising. The base is private to the derived class. Thus, the public members of the base class are treated as if they were private members of the derived class: They are available to the derived class and its members but not to outside classes. For example, consider the following class definition:

```
class base  {
    int x;

public:
    base(int);
    int display();
};
```

and the following derived class:

```
class derived : base  {
    int y;

public:
    derived(int,int);
    do_it();
};
```

Any member of the derived class can access the member function `display()` in the public part of class base. The same `display()` function is not available, however, to other classes through the derived class—it's not a public member of `derived` —although the two classes have a tight, dependent relationship. In this respect, the member function `display()` is no different from the variable member y—both are hidden in the private part of the class. Of course, you can access `display()` if you create an object of type base. Such an object, however, would have no connection to any object of the derived class.

The same relationship holds true if the derived class declares the base as private explicitly. Thus,

```
class derived : private base  {
    int y;

public:
    derived(int,int);
    do_it();
};
```

operates in the same way as before. It should be noted that it's more in the spirit of object-oriented design to explicitly declare a private base class rather than depending on the default.

Class Members in Public Base Classes

You can alter the previous default situation, however, by declaring the base class to be public. As a result, the public part of the base becomes a public part of the derived class as well.

You accomplish this declaration by preceding the name of the base class with the reserved word public. Let's alter the simple example of the last section to reflect this new situation.

```
class derived : public base   {
    int y;

public:
    derived(int,int);
    do_it();
};
```

Note that the list of member functions for the derived class includes not only do_it() but also display(). In fact, an object of the derived class can access display(), although display() is not defined as a member of the derived class.

Listing 8-5 is an example of a class, course, derived from a public base, student. The student class contains the name and identification code of an individual. The only member function of this class, aside from the constructor, is show_student(), which displays the stored information on the screen. The class course adds these things to the information from the student class: a course identification, a description of the course, and the grade earned. It has two member functions in addition to the constructor: set_grade() and show_grade(). set_grade() assigns an appropriate value to the grade member, whereas show_grade() displays course and grade information on the screen.

Listing 8-5. A derived class with a public base: grade.cpp.

```
#include <iostream.h>
#include <string.h>

class student   {
  char first[80];
```

```
  char mid[80];
  char last[80];
  char id[10];

public:
  student(char*, char*, char*, char*);
  void show_student();
};

student::student(char* f, char* m, char* l, char* i)
{
  strcpy(first, f);
  strcpy(mid, m);
  strcpy(last, l);
  strcpy(id, i);
}

void student::show_student()
{
  cout << "Name:\n";
  cout << "\t" << first << " " << mid << " " << last << "\n";
  cout << "Identification:\n";
  cout << "\t" << id << "\n";
}

class course : public student  {
  char c_id[10];
  char description[128];
  char grade;

public:
  course(char*, char*, char*, char*, char*, char*);
  void set_grade(char g)  { grade = g; }
  void show_grade();
};

course::course(char* f, char* m, char* l,char* si,
          char* ci, char* cd) : student(f, m, l, si)
{
  strcpy(c_id, ci);
  strcpy(description, cd);
}
```

continues

Listing 8-5. continued

```
void course::show_grade()
{
  cout << "Course identification: " << c_id << "\n";
  cout << "=========================================\n";
  cout << description << "\n";
}

main()
{
  course x("Jane", "Alice", "Oustin","012349876",
          "CIS 25C","Programming in C++");

  x.set_grade('A');
  x.show_student(); // "borrowed" from the base class
  x.show_grade();
}
```

The simple driver program defined in main() illustrates the main point of this section. Note how the member function show_student() is used. It's treated just as if it were a member function. The variable x accesses it without any further dereferencing. You cannot determine from this code that the function is, in fact, a member of the base class; this is the payoff for the use of a public base class.

The Creation of a Base Class with a Protected Section

Although the relationship between a derived class and its base is a special one, you can access any public part of the base class with a member function of the derived class. The private section of the base class, however, remains locked to the members of the derived class. In this regard, the derived class members are no different than the rest of the program. No direct access is permitted.

This "lockout" of the base class's private section can lead to awkwardly constructed code and, in a few cases, can even work against the kind of data abstraction that C++ was designed to provide. This latter issue is an obvious problem. To access any part of the base class's private section, you must include some public member in the definition of the base class. The same public member that allows the derived class access also grants it to the rest of the program; there is no facility for restricting it. In a sense, the more you need data abstraction (for performing delicate operations "inside" a data type), the less protection is afforded. If you need to manipulate directly the internal structure of a class type, the only mechanism available seems to open that internal structure to the entire program, either by putting it into the public section or by declaring a friend function.

There is, however, a solution to the problem of private versus public access to the base class. C++ has a mechanism that lets you define a third level of security for base classes and derived classes. A base class can have a *protected* section. This part of the code is treated exactly like the private section of the class as far as access from the rest of the program is concerned; however, it is available to any classes derived from this base. You define a protected section by placing the keyword `protected:` on a line by itself. The scope of this section continues until another label—`public:`, for example—is specified or you insert the brace that ends the class definition. For example, consider the following definition of a simple base class:

```
class base   {
     int x;

protected:
     int y;

public:
     base(int);
     show_x_y();
};
```

and the following class derived from it:

```
class derived : private base   {
     int z;

public:
     derived(int,int,int);
     show_it();
};
```

Here, any member function of the derived class can access directly its own private variable z and the protected variable member of the base, y. The (by default `private`) x member still is unavailable, however.

You now can define three levels of abstraction in a set of classes. Access to the private section of a class is restricted to the immediate members of that class. The protected section is available only to the members of a class and to member functions in its derived classes. Finally, the public section, as always, is available to the rest of the program and defines an interface between it and the class.

Listing 8-6 has a statement class that is derived from a base class that contains basic information about a business—its name, address, phone number, and so on. The base class is defined with the members that contain the basic business information in a protected section. As a result, they are available for a direct access from the derived class.

Listing 8-6. A derived class with a protected section: invoice.cpp.

```cpp
#include <iostream.h>
#include <string.h>


class business_info  {
  char contact[80];
  char credit[80];

protected:
  char firm[80];
  char street[80];
  char city[80];
  char state[80];
  char zip[10];
  char phone[20];
public:
  business_info(char*, char*, char*, char*, char*, char*);
  void set_credit(char* crate) { strcpy(credit, crate); }
  void set_contact(char* cname) { strcpy(contact, cname); }
  char* report_credit() { return credit; }
  void show_address();
};

business_info::business_info(char* fr, char* s, char* c, char* st,
                                  char* z, char* ph)
{
 credit[0] = '\0';
 contact[0] = '\0';
 strcpy(firm, fr);
 strcpy(street, s);
 strcpy(city, c);
 strcpy(state, st);
 strcpy(zip, z);
```

```
  strcpy(phone, ph);
}

void business_info::show_address()
{
  cout << "--------------------------------------------\n";
  cout << firm << "\n" << street << "\n";
  cout << city << ", " << state << "  " << zip << "\n";
  cout << phone << "\n";
  cout << "--------------------------------------------\n";
  cout << "ATTN. " << contact << "\n";
  cout << "--------------------------------------------\n";
}

class statement : private business_info {
  char date[80];
  double pastdue;
  double current;

public:
  statement(char*, char*, char*, char*,char*, char*,
            char*, double,double);
  void show_statement();
};

statement::statement(char* fr, char* s, char* c, char* st, char* z,
            char* ph, char* dt, double bal,
            double cur) : business_info(fr, s, c, st, z, ph)
{
 strcpy(date, dt);
 pastdue = bal;
 current = cur;
}

void statement::show_statement()
{
  cout << "Firm:\n" << firm << "\n";
  cout << "Address:\n" << street << "\n";
  cout << city << ", " << state << "  " << zip << "\n";
  cout << "========================================\n";
  cout << "Past due balance:  $" << pastdue << "\n";
  cout << "Current charges:   $" << current << "\n";
```

continues

Listing 8-6. continued

```
  cout << "------------------------------------------\n";
  cout << "Total Due:          $" << pastdue + current << "\n";
}

main()
{
 statement x("Acme Widget", "102 Get Rich Quick Alley",
            "Plain Dealing", "KS", "50606", "332 232-1234",
            "June 2, 1991", 1234, 324);

 x.show_statement();
}
```

The derived class operates in a manner similar to the earlier examples. The constructor takes as a parameter not only the information necessary to fill its own variable members, but also the necessary values for the base class constructor. These latter values are passed immediately to the base class. The difference is in the member function show_statement(). The information to be displayed is found either in the private section of the derived class or the protected section of the base class. In either case, it can be addressed directly without the necessity of a dereferencing operator (::).

Virtual Functions

Another important feature of derived classes is the *virtual member* function. Sometimes when you derive a group of classes from a base class, certain member functions that are analogous in purpose need to operate differently in each class. For example, the display() function that shows the values of the base class might need to display different values if it was called from a derived class. Perhaps some of the derived classes could use the display() function as defined in the base, whereas others might require additional items or even completely new formatting. The virtual function mechanism lets you effectively accommodate these kinds of changes.

You could give different names to each display member function in each different class. For example, the base class member could be display(), whereas the derived class would have a corresponding member called show(). Although this solution is workable, it is far from ideal. The need to create many unique names for member functions disrupts a unified design and makes the resulting code more difficult to read and use. This technique of uniquely naming members also is opposed to C++'s philosophy of overloading names that perform similar functions.

A better solution is to overload the function member name. You could, for example, create the member function `display()` in both the base class and the derived class. Then you could use the scope dereferencing operator (`::`) to refer to the base class member. This construction uses overloading the way it was intended: The same name represents two different, but similar, operations. This solution is adequate for a simple set of classes. In a system with many interlocking classes, however, the details of reference easily become buried in a "spaghetti code" tangle of references. The best solution is to identify those member functions in the base class that you might need to customize for use in derived classes and then declare them as virtual functions. This declaration gives you a simple mechanism for redefining the members in any derived class and has an important advantage over the simple overloading procedure discussed previously: When you use a virtual function, if a particular member function is not defined in a derived class, but is called through a derived object, the earlier (base) definition is used. Therefore, the base class definition of the function forms a default definition that the program uses whenever a customized member is not needed or is unavailable.

To declare a virtual function, precede a member function declaration with the keyword `virtual`. You must do this in the declaration line for the function in the base class, before you mention the data type. For example, the following line:

```
virtual char* display()
```

defines a virtual display function in the context of a base class definition. Note that you do not use the keyword `virtual` in the derived class definition. You merely declare the member as you would any other member function.

If you define a virtual function in the base class, any classes derived from that base that do not redefine the member have a default function on which to fall back. You may or may not define new versions of the virtual function in subsequent derived classes, although you can declare them in any class. Because it must be defined in the base class, a program always can access the virtual member function through a base class object—assuming that it is a public member of the class. Any redefinition of the virtual function in a particular derived class causes the original definition to be replaced with the new one whenever the function is used in that class. This change is done at run-time, and not during the compilation process. Thus, the definition in the object accessing the function is the one that is used. Only if no new definition exists does the system resort to the original definition. This relationship is illustrated in Figure 8-6.

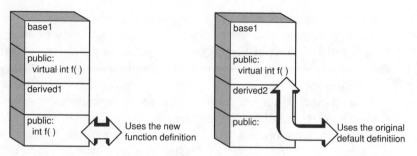

Figure 8-6. The virtual functions and derived classes.

Redefining Base Member Functions

Listing 8-7 has a simple base class, `address`, which contains a name and several `address` members. What's new in this definition is the declaration of the member function `show_address()` as a virtual function—in other words, it is a function that you can redefine in a subsequent derived class. The two derived classes, `off_campus` and `on_campus`, show two different ways you can use this virtual function.

`off_campus` is a derived class that uses the `address` members in the base class as well as the `name` member. This derived class is the same as many of the earlier examples. The definition of `show_address()` as defined in the base class is sufficient for the purposes of the derived class.

In contrast, `on_campus` models a different situation. Here you have a simpler address consisting of only a room and a dormitory name. The base class is still used to store the name of the student, but the address members are not needed. Instead, the local members `dorm` and `room` are pressed into service to store this information. Because you do not use `street`, `city`, and so on from the `address` class, you no longer can use the base class `show_address()`. It is necessary to redefine this member function to reflect the new situation.

The program defined in `main()` illustrates how these two classes are used.

Listing 8-7. A set of derived classes with a virtual function: student.cpp.

```
#include <iostream.h>
#include <string.h>
#include <stdio.h>
```

```
class address  {
    char street[80];
    char city[80];
    char state[3];
    char zip[10];

protected:
    char* name;

public:
    address(char* nm);
    address(char*, char*, char*, char*, char*);
    virtual char* show_address();
    char* show_name()  { return name; }
};

address::address(char* nm)
{
  strcpy(name,nm);
  street[0] = city[0] = state[0] = zip[0] = '\0';
}

address::address(char* nm, char* s, char* c, char* st, char* z)
{
 strcpy(name, nm);
 strcpy(street, s);
 strcpy(city, c);
 strcpy(state, st);
 strcpy(zip, z);
}

char* address::show_address()
{
 char* buffer = new char[strlen(street)+strlen(city)+10];

 sprintf(buffer,"%s\n%s, %s  %s", street, city, state, zip);
 return buffer;
}

class off_campus : public address {
  char status[80];
```

continues

Listing 8-7. continued

```
public:
  off_campus(char*, char*, char*, char*, char*, char*);
  char* show_status()  { return status; }
};

off_campus::off_campus(char* nm, char* s, char* c, char* st,
                       char* z, char* stt) : address(nm,s,c,st,z)
                       {
  strcpy(status, stt);
}

class on_campus : public address {
  char room[10];
  char dorm[80];
  char status[40];

public:
  on_campus(char*, char*, char*, char*);
  char* show_address();
  char* show_status()  { return status; }
};

on_campus::on_campus(char* nm, char* rm, char* dm, char* st) : address(nm)
{
  strcpy(room, rm);
  strcpy(dorm, dm);
  strcpy(status, st);
}

char* on_campus::show_address()
{
 char* buffer = new char[80];

 sprintf(buffer, "%s\nRoom: %s", dorm, room);
 return buffer;
}


main()
```

```
{
  off_campus st1("Joseph Green","12 El Monte Rd",
              "Los Altos Hills",  "CA","94022", "Sophomore");
  on_campus st2("Jane Brown", "231", "Morrison Hall", "Junior");

  cout << "Off Campus Student:\n";
  cout << st1.show_name() << "\n" << st1.show_address() << "\n";
  cout << st1.show_status() << "\n";

  cout << "On Campus Student:\n";
  cout << st2.show_name() << "\n" << st2.show_address() << "\n";
  cout << st2.show_status() << "\n";
}
```

Accessing Virtual Functions Through Pointers

It's sometimes difficult to see the advantages or even the necessity of virtual functions. The mechanism is obscured by other forms of overloading in C++. An important difference must be noted, however.

Consider the simple example in Listing 8-8. It contains a class, simple_base, with a single character string variable member, info. Aside from the constructor, the only other member function is show(), which returns the value stored in info. Using simple_base as a base, the derived class simple has its own character string member. It has also a member function show() that returns this latter value. The show value in the base class has not been declared as a virtual function; however, the show() member in the derived class overloads this function name. In other words, when an object of the derived class calls this function, it executes the local member and not the function in the base class.

Listing 8-8. A simple derived class illustrating the relationship between member functions in the base and the derived class: simple.cpp.

```
#include <iostream.h>
#include <string.h>

class simple_base  {
  char info[80];
```

continues

251

8

Listing 8-8. continued

```
public:
  simple_base(char* v)  { strcpy(info, v); }
  char* show() { return info; }
};

class simple : private simple_base {
  char sinfo[80];

public:
  simple(char* v, char* b);
  char* show() { return sinfo; }
};

simple::simple(char* v, char* b) : simple_base(b)
{
 strcpy(sinfo, v);
}

main()
{
 simple x("Derived", "Base");
 simple *ptr = &x;
 simple_base *bptr =(simple_base*) &x;

 cout << "Derived Class pointer points to..." ;
 cout << ptr->show() << "\n\n";
 cout << "Base Class pointer points to..." << bptr->show() << "\n\n";
}
```

In the program defined by main() in Listing 8-8, you access the show() member through a pointer to an object of type simple. This program, however, contains an additional reference. A pointer variable of type simple_base* is declared and is assigned the address of the derived object. Note the necessary type cast. This assignment is not an error in C++. A pointer to a base class can take the address of a class object that is derived from itself. When you execute this program, the result is startling. Although the pointer variable bptr contains the address of the object x, it executes the show() function that is a member of the base class.

In Listing 8-9, you find the same pair of classes: simple_base and simple. Here, however, you declare show() to be a virtual function. Although the program defined

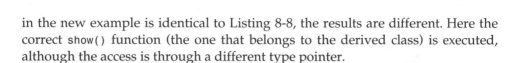

in the new example is identical to Listing 8-8, the results are different. Here the correct show() function (the one that belongs to the derived class) is executed, although the access is through a different type pointer.

Listing 8-9. A variation on the previous class: simple1.cpp.

```
#include <iostream.h>
#include <string.h>

class simple_base  {
  char info[80];

public:
  simple_base(char* v)  { strcpy(info, v); }
  virtual char* show() { return info; }
};


class simple : private simple_base {
  char sinfo[80];

public:
  simple(char* v, char* b);
  char* show() { return sinfo; }
};

simple::simple(char* v, char* b) : simple_base(b)
{
 strcpy(sinfo, v);
}

main()
{
 simple x("Derived", "Base");
 simple *ptr = &x;
 simple_base *bptr =(simple_base*) &x;

 cout << "Derived Class pointer points to..." ;
 cout << ptr->show() << "\n\n";
 cout << "Base Class pointer points to..." << bptr->show() << "\n\n";
}
```

The method of using a base class pointer to access a derived class is used often to implement a linked data structure class such as a linked list. Such a class would maintain all the mechanisms for creating the linked list. When it serves as a base, however, its pointers will need to point to different kinds of derived class objects.

There is a difference when a function in a base class is declared virtual. Sometimes the consequences of this are subtle and surprising. There is a trade-off, too, with using a virtual function. All the variations of this kind of member function are kept in a table. The binding is not done at compile time as with regular class functions, but it is done at run-time. This method provides greater flexibility in program design, but also costs some in speed and code size.

Pure Virtual Functions and Abstract Base Classes

Another important variation in the virtual function syntax is the creation of *pure virtual functions,* which are member functions that do not have a default definition in the base class. Pure virtual functions must be defined in any class derived from such a base.

To declare a virtual function as pure, instead of the code that normally would be associated with a member function, you need to make the following kind of declaration:

```
virtual show() = 0;
```

This is a legal declaration. It sets up the compiler to insist that any derived class that needs to use this function has to supply its "real" definition.

An additional consequence of using a base class with a pure virtual function is that it cannot be used to declare any objects of its type. Because there is an undefined member function, such a declaration could not be satisfied. A class that has at least one pure virtual function is called an *abstract class.* Listing 8-10 illustrates the relationship between an abstract class and its derived class.

Listing 8-10. An abstract class: abstract.cpp.

```
#include <iostream.h>
#include <stdio.h>

class abstract  {
protected:
  double value1;
  double value2;
```

```
public:
  abstract()   { value1 = value2 = 0; }
  abstract(double x, double y)  { value1 = x; value2 = y; }
  virtual void add(double, double) = 0;
  char* show();
};

char* abstract::show()
{
  char* buffer = new char[80];

  sprintf(buffer, "Value1 = %f\nValue2 = %f", value1, value2);
  return buffer;
}

class new_number : public abstract {

public:
  new_number(double, double);
  void add(double, double);
};

new_number::new_number(double x, double y) : abstract(x, y)
{
  ;
}

void new_number::add(double p, double q)
{
  value1 += p;
  value2 += q;
}

main()
{
 new_number x(1.2, 3.4);

 x.add(2,1);
 cout << "show the values:\n" << x.show() << "\n";
}
```

In abstract.cpp you see a simple numeric class with a pure virtual member function add(). You can't do anything with this class except use it to derive a more specialized version, which you did in the new_number class. Note that in this latter class, a definition has been given to the member function add(). The program defined by main() runs the new class through its limited paces.

Listing 8-11 is another program defined using the previous set of classes. The only difference in this new program is that the derived class object is accessed through a pointer variable of the base type, abstract*. Although it's not possible to declare an object of type abstract, you still can create an address reference using the pointer.

Listing 8-11. Abstract classes, pointers, and virtual functions: absrt1.cpp.

```
main()
{
 new_number x(1.2, 3.4);
 abstract* ptr = (abstract*)&x;

 x.add(2,1);
 cout << "show the values:\n" << ptr->show() << "\n";
}
```

Although not strictly necessary, abstract classes offer the software designer another tool to help control the complexity of a real-world design. The advantage is in the elegance of combining the common features of a series of special classes in a base class that is not used to create an object. This elegance leaves the designer free to defer specific implementation details until later and to concentrate on the issue of the basic design. For example, a shape class declared as abstract would focus not on how to draw a particular shape, but rather on the things that all shapes have in common: position and color. Individual shapes derived from this base then would be concerned with their own implementation on the screen or the plotter.

If, in contrast, a shape class had to be one that could give rise to objects, it couldn't be as general as the purely abstract class. Such an implementable definition would need to take one of the actual shapes as most basic and derive the rest from that. In many cases this kind of relationship would work, but in many real contexts, this derivation would be strained, at best.

In addition to the complex situations that abstract classes help to clarify, even some simple relationships are better modeled using this technique. Abstract classes are better at representing concepts and intangible relationships than are ordinary base classes and derived classes.

Serial Inheritance of Classes

The terms *base classes* and *derived classes* are relative terms. Any class can serve as a base, even a class that is itself derived from another class. It's safe and normal to have strings of classes derived from each other. This serial derivation, however, must be distinguished carefully from true multiple inheritance, which is discussed in Chapter 9. Multiple inheritance involves classes with two or more independent base classes. In serial derivation, each class has one base class.

Making a Derived Class into a Base Class

Even with the more powerful technique of multiple inheritance available, a simple string of derived classes often can serve as an effective tool for efficient program design. Each derived class can look no further than its declared base class. The ultimate origin of that base and its functions is not important to the process of derivation.

The only access that a derived class can have to its base class is through the members in the base's public section and, possibly through those in a declared protected section. As long as these members perform their stated tasks, there is no direct interaction with any previous base classes. The clearest way to explain these concepts is with an example: the record class.

Case Study: The *record* Class

In Listing 8-12, you define a series of derived classes that are used to build up a record class. The first class, name, is the initial base class. It keeps track of the first, middle and last name and supplies some public member functions to access these values.

The first derived class is address, which takes name as a base and adds the address values: number and street, city, state, and ZIP code. address also has member functions that serve as an interface to the outside world. Finally, the definition of the record class indicates that it is a derivative of address. record adds the telephone number information to the name and address information already accessible through address.

Listing 8-12. An example of serial inheritance: record.cpp.

```cpp
#include <iostream.h>
#include <string.h>

class name  {
  char first[80];
  char mid[80];
  char last[80];

public:
  name()  { first[0] = mid[0] = last[0] = '\0'; }
  void set_name(char*, char*, char*);
  char* show();
};

void name::set_name(char* f, char* m, char* l)
{
  strcpy(first, f);
  strcpy(mid, m);
  strcpy(last, l);
}

char* name::show()
{
 char* temp = new char[80];

 strcpy(temp, first);
 strcat(temp, " ");   // add a space
 strcat(temp, mid);
 strcat(temp, " ");
 strcat(temp, last);
 return temp;
}

class address : name  {
  char street[80];
  char city[80];
  char state[80];
  char zip[10];
```

```
public:
  address() { street[0] = city[0] = state[0] = zip[0] = '\0'; }
  void new_address(char*, char*, char*, char*);
  void new_name(char*, char*, char*);
  char* show_info();
};

void address::new_address(char* s, char* c, char* st, char* z)
{
 strcpy(street, s);
 strcpy(city, c);
 strcpy(state, st);
 strcpy(zip, z);
}

void address::new_name(char* f, char* m, char* l)
{
  set_name(f, m, l);
}

char* address::show_info()
{
 char* temp = show();

 strcat(temp, "\n");      // add a new line
 strcat(temp, street);
 strcat(temp, "\n");     // new line for city/state/zip
 strcat(temp, city);
 strcat(temp, ", ");      // separate city/state with a comma
 strcat(temp, state);
 strcat(temp, "  ");     //add two spaces for zip
 strcat(temp, zip);

 return temp;
}

class record : address {
     char area[4];
     char prefix[4];
     char number[5];
```

continues

Listing 8-12. continued

```cpp
public:
     record(char*, char*, char*, char*, char*, char*,
               char*, char*, char*, char*);


     char* show_record();
};

record::record(char* f, char* m, char* l, char* s, char* c,
         char* st, char* z, char* a, char* p, char* n)
{
     new_name(f, m, l);
     new_address(s, c, st, z);

     strcpy(area, a);
     strcpy(prefix, p);
     strcpy(number, n);
}

char* record::show_record()
{
 char* temp = show_info();

 strcat(temp, "\n(");  // add a new line for phone.
 strcat(temp, area);
 strcat(temp, ") ");
 strcat(temp, prefix);
 strcat(temp, "-");
 strcat(temp, number);

 return temp;
}

main()
{
  record x("Joseph", "Henry", "Green", "1234 Pearly Street",
             "Santa Cruz", "CA", "94080", "408", "556", "1234");

  cout << "** " << x.show_record() << "\n";
}
```

There is a direct link between address and name. There also is a direct link between record and address. There is no direct link between record and name. If an object of type record needs the information in name, it must go through the intermediate class address.

The example program defined in Listing 8-12 is a good example of the utility of serial inheritance. It is not, however, a perfect design. One problem with the program is that there is not an organic connection between each level. It's purely arbitrary that the name is the base to address and address is the base to record. It works fine and allows a high degree of complexity control, but it lacks the kind of relationships that would make it an obvious whole. This may seem an unimportant point in the context of a successful example. Remember that to reach the coding phase, however, it's still necessary to go through a design phase in which these relationships are neither obvious nor unimportant.

Object-Oriented Design: Inheritance

In this chapter you have reached the final requirement in the definition of object-oriented technique: inheritance. The value of this characteristic is obvious. Inheritance enables you to make connections between objects that share some (but not all) of the same characteristics. You can gather these common characteristics together into an object, write the appropriate code, and use this base object to give rise to the similar but more specialized objects that you need. It's no longer necessary to reinvent code and value members each time you create a different kind of object.

Inheritance is another tool for controlling the complexity and details of software designs. It represents a more radical version of the modularity first encountered with the creation of classes themselves. The paths and relationships between objects are mapped even more closely by this part of the object-oriented syntax.

An additional advantage of being able to derive one class from another is a simplicity of design. Often the real-world relationships that are modeled in programming languages have this kind of hierarchical structure. For example, a machine is composed of parts put together in a specific order. This syntax makes it easy to translate from the problem set to the program solution. Of course, I'm not yet finished with inheritance. Multiple base classes add another dimension to this discussion.

8

Summary

This chapter explored the capacity of C++ to create systems of related classes. The mechanism for this is the derivation of one class from another. The derived class contains all the information of its base—it "is" that class, and more. The utility of class derivation is unlimited because you can use any preexisting class as a base, even if your access to it is limited to a precompiled version. The derived class lets the designer divide a programming problem into increasingly specific modules for an easier and more comprehensible solution.

In addition to the relationship that grows out of the base-derived concept, this chapter has described other aspects of derived classes. Chief among these are protected members and virtual member functions. Both of these capabilities help generate clearer systems of classes and promote modularity. The members in a protected section of a base class are private to the rest of the program but available to the members of any derived class. Virtual functions are member functions that, when defined in the base class, can be redefined in subsequent derived classes. Pure virtual functions have no definition in the base class but must be defined in any derived classes. A base class that has one or more pure virtual functions cannot be used to create any objects. Such a class is called an *abstract* class.

Finally, this chapter has enhanced the notion of systems of classes by illustrating the creation of a series of related classes. This system is built on the premise that derived classes and base classes are relative.

9

Multiple Inheritance

9

Multiple Inheritance

In the original implementations of C++, a derived class could inherit from only one base class. Even with this restriction, the object-oriented paradigm is a flexible and powerful programming tool. Newer versions of C++ have added the capability of creating a derived class from multiple base classes. In this chapter, you'll see how this multiple inheritance complements the object-oriented nature of C++.

Expanding the Inheritance Paradigm

Juggling a derived class with a single base class gave us a powerful tool for general software design. Because any class can serve as a base, the possibility of standard class libraries customized through inheritance becomes a flexible software design technique. A designer can take a standard class (perhaps one that implements a linked list) and add the necessary members to customize the class for a particular purpose. In this case, I have taken a general solution—the linked list class—and have specialized it through the single derivation.

Adding the possibility of two or more base classes increases the flexibility and the power of the inheritance paradigm. In the past, you might have combined three classes in serial order. Now, however, you can relate all three in a single statement of inheritance. Instead of a derived class becoming a base class and then this class, in turn, being used for another class, you can combine directly the base classes into one derived class. This is illustrated in Figure 9-1.

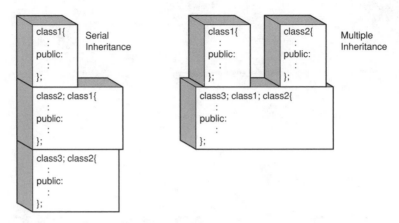

Figure 9-1. Serial derivation compared to multiple inheritance.

Of course, multiple inheritance offers us much more than this convenience. It opens the way to new kinds of designs and an enhanced ability to control details. Single derivation is a movement from a general object to a specialized one. In multiple inheritance, by contrast, each base class contributes its own properties to the derived class to produce a new kind of object. This new object is not necessarily a specialization of any of the base classes, but rather an amalgam of all of them.

Multiple inheritance is most appropriate to define objects that are composite in nature, such as a personnel record, a graphic object (remember that it has shape, color, and position), or anything that is a combination of other objects. In contrast, single inheritance is more useful in defining objects that are specializations of general concepts, such as a linked list to a queue, or a general linked list to a linked list of numbers or characters. Both techniques are necessary to successful software design.

Designing with Multiple Bases

Multiple inheritance is just an obvious extension of the derived class syntax and not a radically different notion. There are still plenty of design problems that are best solved by a single base. But some problems can be more naturally expressed using a combination of several previously designed class concepts.

The syntax of multiple inheritance is similar to the situation when only one base class is used. The line that declares the class name contains a reference to the base classes. The statement

```
class example : private base1, private base2  {
```

indicates that the class being defined has two base classes, both of them private. Listing 9-1 is a simple example of a derived class with two bases.

Listing 9-1. A simple example of multiple inheritance: smulti.cpp.

```cpp
#include <iostream.h>
#include <string.h>
#include <stdio.h>
class  base1  {
  int x;

public:
  base1()  { x = 0; }
  base1(int p) { x = p; }
  int show() { return x; }
};

class base2  {
  double z;

public:
  base2()  { z = 0; }
  base2(double p) { z = p; }
  double show() { return z; }
};

class mderived : private base1, private base2  {
  char* title;

public:
  mderived()  { title = 0; }
  mderived(char*, int, double);
  char* display();
};

mderived::mderived(char* st, int p, double q) : base1(p), base2(q)
{
 title = new char[strlen(st) + 1];
 strcpy(title, st);
}

char* mderived::display()
{
```

continues

Listing 9-1. continued

```
char* temp = new char[ strlen(title) + 1 +
                       sizeof(int) + sizeof(double) + 4];

sprintf(temp, "%s—%d—%f", title, base1::show(), base2::show());
return temp;
}

main()
{
 mderived x("this is a case of multiple inheritance", 25, 1.23);

 cout << "Result: " << x.display();
}
```

In smulti.cpp, base1 contains only an integer value as a variable member. base2 has a double. The derived class mderived declares the two base classes. One interesting thing to note about mderived is the way that it handles the calls to the two base class constructors. Just as with a single base, the name is used with parentheses to pass the expected parameters. Each constructor call is separated by a comma. Aside from this minor difference, referencing the member functions of the two base classes is the same as it would be if there was only one base class.

Abstracting Data in a Complex Environment

Until now, I have emphasized the similarities between single inheritance and multiple inheritance. I certainly don't want to minimize these similarities: The syntax is obvious and not radically new. Keep in mind, however, that there are differences. These differences are important even if they are not reflected in the syntax and programming statements.

Multiple inheritance as a design tool allows the programmer to deal naturally with a situation that is common in the process of modeling real-world entities inside the computer. Obviously, relationships and objects often have more than one characteristic that must be considered when creating a representative data structure. For example, an automobile has shape, type, and color. Each of these characteristics is, itself, a complex notion with details that need to be dealt with. The examples in this chapter (for ease of illustration) tend to be simple—well-behaved numeric quantities or character values. But when you start designing for real, you'll need some way to deal with the complexity that you face.

Classes and derived classes offer a way to control complexity by creating hierarchies of details. Multiple inheritance takes this capability further by recognizing the common situation: Any particular entity can be created by reference to more than one of these hierarchical relationships. Even basic entities can have more than one set of characteristics. The representation of a geometric figure, for example, has aspects relating to shape as well as color. Each of these aspects has details of its own with which to deal and may in turn need its own hierarchy to control complexity (see Figure 9-2).

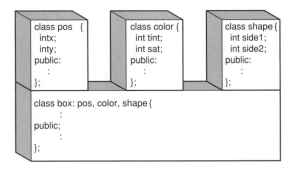

Figure 9-2. Using multiple objects to control complexity.

Coordinating Two Base Classes

The techniques for using and calling two base classes from a derived object are similar to the techniques you used with a single base class. The only problem to be on guard against is the greater opportunity for ambiguous expressions when accessing the base from the derived class. If both base classes have member functions with the same name, the scope dereferencing operator (::) has to be used to indicate which member function you wish to call. Of course, you have to pay some attention also to the coordination of constructors and destructors.

Constructors and Destructors

In creating derived classes with only one base class, you noted that the base class constructor always is called before the derived class constructor. Furthermore, you have a mechanism for passing the necessary parameter values to the base constructor from the derived class constructor.

```
derived_class(char* x, int y, double z) : base(x, y)
```

passes the character pointer x and the integer value y to the base class.

This method is expanded in a logical way to encompass more than one base class.

```
derived_class(char* x, int y, double z) : base1(x), base2(y)
```

calls the base1 constructor and passes the character string value x and the base2 constructor, supplying an integer value y. As with single inheritance, the base class constructors are called before the derived class constructor executes. Moreover, the base class constructors are called in the order in which they are listed in the derived class constructor declaration. In this example, the base1 constructor is called before the base2 constructor.

Similarly, the relationship between the derived class destructor and the base class destructor is maintained. The derived destructor is called before any base class destructors are called. The base class destructors are called in the reverse order that the base objects were created.

Listing 9-2 (record.cpp) contains an example of a class, record, that has two base classes: phone and address.

Listing 9-2. An address record with two base classes: record.cpp.

```
#include <iostream.h>
#include <string.h>
class phone  {
    char* area;
    char* prefix;
    char* number;

public:
    phone(char*, char*, char*);
    ~phone() { delete area; delete prefix; delete number; }
    char* show();
};
```

```
phone::phone(char* a, char* p, char* n)
{
 area = new char[strlen(a) + 1];
 prefix = new char[strlen(p) + 1];
 number = new char[strlen(n) + 1];

 strcpy(area, a);
 strcpy(prefix, p);
 strcpy(number, n);
}

char* phone::show()
{
 char* temp = new char[ strlen(area) + strlen(prefix) +
                        strlen(number) + 4 ];
 strcpy(temp, "(");
 strcat(temp, area);
 strcat(temp, ") ");
 strcat(temp, prefix);
 strcat(temp, "-");
 strcat(temp, number);

 return temp;
}

class address  {
  char* street;
  char* city;
  char* state;
  char* zip;

public:
  address(char*, char*, char*, char*);
~address() { delete street; delete city; delete state; delete zip;}
  char* show();
};

address::address(char* s, char* c, char* st, char* z)
{
 street = new char[strlen(s) + 1];
 city = new char[strlen(c) + 1];
 state = new char[strlen(st) + 1];
 zip = new char[strlen(z) + 1];
```

continues

Listing 9-2. continued

```
strcpy(street, s);
strcpy(city, c);
strcpy(state, st);
strcpy(zip, z);
}

char* address::show()
{
 char* temp = new char[strlen(street) + strlen(city) +
                  strlen(state) + strlen(zip) + 6];

 strcpy(temp, street);
 strcat(temp, "\n");
 strcat(temp, city);
 strcat(temp, ", ");
 strcat(temp, state);
 strcat(temp, "  ");
 strcat(temp, zip);

 return temp;
}

class record : private phone, private address  {
    char first[80];
    char mid [80];
    char last[80];

public:
    record(char*, char*, char*, char*, char*,
            char*, char*, char*, char*, char*);
    ~record() { delete first; delete mid; delete last; }
    void show_record();
};

record::record(char* f, char* m, char* l,
        char* s, char* c, char* st, char* z,
        char* a, char* p, char* n) : address(s,c,st,z),
                                        phone(a,p,n)
{
  strcpy(first, f);
```

```
  strcpy(mid, m);
  strcpy(last,l);
}

void record::show_record()
{
 cout << first << " " << mid << " " << last << "\n";
 cout << address::show() << "\n";
 cout << phone::show() << "\n";
}

main()
{
  record x("Sally", "Sara", "Smith", "12345 El Monte Road",
         "Los Altos Hills", "CA", "94022", "415", "555",
         "1234");

  x.show_record();
}
```

The two base classes are straightforward implementations of the common data processing tasks of initializing and manipulating a telephone number and an address. The record class adds the member to store the name and inherits the other information from its two base classes. The record constructor accepts the values for all three classes and passes them into each base through the constructor. Note the use of explicit addressing with the scope dereferencing operator (::) in the show_record() member of the derived class. This is necessary because both base classes have a member named show().

Virtual Function Definitions

Just as with a single base class, a multiply-derived class can redefine a virtual function. The syntax of this redefinition is the same: A function is declared virtual in the base. If it's given a default definition, it can be redefined in the derived class or the default definition can be used.

The one aspect of virtual functions that is different in multiple inheritance is the increased possibility of a member function name ambiguity. In other words, more than one base class might have a virtual function of the same name. In this case, the virtual function must be redefined in the derived class to resolve the ambiguity. Listing 9-3 contains the example of a derived class with two bases. Each base has member functions of the same name declared as virtual.

Listing 9-3. A derived class with two bases, including virtual functions: shaper.cpp.

```cpp
#include <iostream.h>
#include <stdio.h>
class shape   {
  int Top;
  int Left;

public:
  shape(int x, int y)  { Top = y; Left = x; }
  virtual void move(int, int);
  virtual char* show_pos();
};

void shape::move(int x_incr, int y_incr)
{
  Top += y_incr;
  Left += x_incr;
}

char* shape::show_pos()
{
  char* temp = new char[40];

  sprintf(temp, "Top = %d, Left = %d",Top, Left);
  return temp;
}

class rectangle  {
  int Bottom;
  int Right;

public:
  rectangle(int x, int y) { Bottom = y; Right = x; }
  virtual void move(int, int);
  virtual char* show_pos();
};

void rectangle::move(int x_incr, int y_incr)
{
  Bottom += y_incr;
  Right += x_incr;
}
```

```
char* rectangle::show_pos()
{
  char* temp = new char[40];

  sprintf(temp, "Bottom = %d, Right = %d", Bottom, Right);
  return temp;
}

class square : public shape, public rectangle  {

public:
    square(int);
    void move(int, int);
    char* show_pos();
};

square::square(int side) : shape(0,0),
                       rectangle(side, side)
{
  ;
}

void square::move(int Horiz, int Vert)
{
  shape::move(Horiz, Vert);
  rectangle::move(Horiz, Vert);
}

char* square::show_pos()
{
  char* temp = new char[80];

  sprintf(temp, "%s\n%s", shape::show_pos(),
                       rectangle::show_pos());

  return temp;
}

main()
{
  square x(10);
```

continues

Listing 9-3. continued

```
cout << x.show_pos() << "\n";

x.move(50, 20);

cout << x.show_pos() << "\n";
}
```

The square class is a specialization of the rectangle class that serves as a base. The square class is derived also from the shape class. This is a reasonable circumstance, although to be useful all three classes should be fleshed out with details. The shape class and the rectangle class both have a member function, move(), that is declared as virtual. In each case, the member function has an identical declaration, which is true also of the virtual function show_pos().

Both sets of virtual member functions are redefined in the derived class square. In the case of move(), a direct call to each of the base class functions is included to adjust each component of the derived class. The same is true of the show_pos() member. If you tried to dispense with the redefinition of either one of these member functions, the resulting ambiguity would prevent the program from working. The main() function attached to the example indicates how these functions interact.

If you declare one or more virtual functions in a class to be pure virtual functions, that class becomes an abstract class (see Chapter 8). Such a class can be used only as a base. You cannot declare any direct objects of an abstract class. An abstract class can be used also as one of the bases of a multiply-derived class. In Listing 9-4, I've rewritten the earlier example. The shape class now is an abstract class and move() is a pure virtual function. Notice that the variable members of shape have been moved to a protected section so that they can be accessed directly inside the derived class. This is necessary to make sure that the behavior of the new example is identical to that of the previous one.

**Listing 9-4. A multiply-derived class
with one abstract base class: shaper1.cpp.**

```
class shape   {
protected:
  int Top;
  int Left;
```

```
public:
  shape(int x, int y)  { Top = y; Left = x; }
  virtual void move(int, int) = 0;
  virtual char* show_pos();
};

char* shape::show_pos()
{
  char* temp = new char[40];

  sprintf(temp, "Top = %d, Left = %d",Top, Left);
  return temp;
}

class rectangle  {
  int Bottom;
  int Right;

public:
  rectangle(int x, int y) { Bottom = y; Right = x; }
  virtual void move(int, int);
  virtual char* show_pos();
};

void rectangle::move(int x_incr, int y_incr)
{
  Bottom += y_incr;
  Right += x_incr;
}

char* rectangle::show_pos()
{
  char* temp = new char[40];

  sprintf(temp, "Bottom = %d, Right = %d", Bottom, Right);
  return temp;
}


class square : public shape, public rectangle  {

public:
```

continues

Listing 9-4. continued

```
      square(int);
      void move(int, int);
      char* show_pos();
};

square::square(int side) : shape(0,0),
                   rectangle(side, side)
{
  ;
}

void square::move(int Horiz, int Vert)
{
  Top +=  Vert;
  Left += Horiz;

  rectangle::move(Horiz, Vert);
}

char* square::show_pos()
{
  char* temp = new char[80];

  sprintf(temp, "%s\n%s", shape::show_pos(),
                     rectangle::show_pos());
  return temp;
}
```

The Virtual Base Class

As long as there is only one base class, the problem of reusing a particular base class is nonexistent. But as soon as it's possible to have multiple inheritance, the question of using the same base class more than once becomes an issue.

When a derived class declares its base classes, you cannot declare the same base twice. Direct multiple use of the same base class is forbidden by the syntax of derivation. There is, however, a more subtle way you can indirectly generate this situation. Recall that any class can serve as a base class. This is true even for a class that itself is derived. The expression

```
class base2 : public base1   {
        :
    }
```

declares a simple derivation. But a subsequent declaration

```
class derive1 : public base1, public base2   {
        :
    }
```

creates a derived class that has inadvertently and indirectly called one of the base classes twice. In this case, `derive1` has `base2` as one of its base classes and `base1` as another. `base1` is attached twice, however: once directly, and once indirectly through `base2`.

The solution to this problem is the virtual base class. By using this modifier in the base class declaration, the compiler is alerted to the possibility of multiple uses of a base class. The resulting code contains only one instance of each base class rather than multiple versions. Listing 9-5 is an example that uses the concept of virtual base classes.

Listing 9-5. A derived class with a virtual base class: vclass.cpp.

```
#include <string.h>
#include <iostream.h>
class base1   {
  char title[80];

public:
  base1(char* m) { strcpy(title, m); }
  char* show1() { return title; }
};

class base2 : virtual public base1 {
  char title[80];

public:
  base2(char*);
  base2(char*, char*);
  char* show2() { return title; }
};
```

continues

Listing 9-5. continued

```
base2::base2(char* m) : base1("Default Value")
{
 strcpy(title, m);
}


base2::base2(char* m, char* n) : base1(n)
{
   strcpy(title, m);
}


class derive1 : virtual public base1, public base2  {
   char title[80];

public:
   derive1(char*, char*, char*);
   char* show3()  { return title; }
};


derive1::derive1(char* p, char* q, char* r) : base1(q), base2(r)
{
 strcpy(title, p);
}


main()
{
 derive1 x("This is the Derived class", "This is base 1",
                 "This is base 2");

 cout << "base1 = " << x.show1() << "\n";
 cout << "base2 = " << x.show2() << "\n";
 cout << "derive1 = " << x.show3() << "\n";
}
```

The class derive1 takes both base1 and base2 as base classes. The question of the multiple use of base1 is solved by the declaration of base1 as a virtual base class. When the constructor of derive1 calls its base constructors, it passes only a single character string to base2. The base2 constructor that is called, in turn, is set up to pass a default character string value into base1 if only a single character string is passed as a parameter. This would seem to conflict with the direct call of the `base1` constructor performed by `derive1`. But because this is declared as a virtual base, only the direct declaration has an effect and there is no conflict.

The virtual class declaration is a valuable tool when you are creating complicated sets of classes. The accidental reuse of a base class can lead to errors that are obscure and difficult to track down. This mechanism offers a safe and easy-to-understand way of dealing with this problem.

Manipulating the Base Class

You've already seen some examples of base class manipulation. Additional base classes increase the chance of ambiguity in a member function declaration and the complexity of the class. There are more details to deal with because the relationship involves more classes. The problems that you faced with the initial derived classes still apply here.

Public and Private Base Classes

When defining a derived class, the base classes can be declared either private or public. In a public base class, the member functions of the base class are members also of the derived class—they can be called directly through an object of the derived class. The same is true of a base class when the derivation requires more than one base class.

Similarly, if a base class is declared private—whether explicitly (the preferred way) or by default—access to the base class members is available only to the member functions of the derived class. It is impossible to access the base class member functions directly through a derived class object.

It's important to understand the relationship between the base classes and the derived class, but it's equally important to focus on the relationship between the two base classes. You could be fooled into thinking that what has been created is one amalgam with mutual access rights; this is wrong. The only meeting point between the base classes is the derived class. Individually, even as a part of a derived class they have no way to access each other directly. The relationship is clarified in Figure 9-3, which shows the logical relationship in a case of multiple derivation.

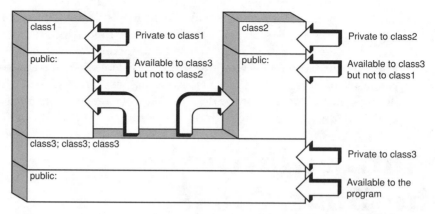

Figure 9-3. The relationship between base classes and derived classes with multiple inheritance.

Protected Sections

Because multiple inheritance is an extension of the syntax of single inheritance, the creation of protected sections in any base class still is possible. As is the case with single inheritance, these protected sections offer a special link for data abstraction. The derived class can access directly any members found in this part of the base. To the rest of the program, however, a protected section is the same as a private section.

The same caveats apply to the protected section here as do in the case of a single base class. By including a protected section in a class, you open a chink in the armor of encapsulation, which allows some class that is defined later to get into the base class. This means that later, if you want to change or update the base class, the process needs to consider subsequent class definitions more carefully than if this derived class had no special access to the base.

The Chain of Inheritance

As you've seen in earlier chapters, class objects and particularly inheritance offer the program designer ways to control the complexity inherent in complex systems. By creating independent objects that can take care of themselves, the process of design is reduced to the construction of classes and their connection into programs. Class inheritance enhances this design capacity by allowing the creation of general-purpose classes and then specializing those classes to fit specific circumstances. Multiple inheritance extends and completes this capability.

One important advantage of multiple inheritance is that it allows the creation of complicated derived classes without the necessity of a long chain of many inherited classes. Instead of the serial inheritance you saw in Chapter 8 (Listing 8-11), you can combine base classes into a derived class in a kind of "flat" structure that restricts necessary access to one level. This is preferable to going back through two or three levels of access to find a member function in an early base class. The value of multiple inheritance becomes particularly clear when you move from the simple case of two base classes and implement derived classes with three and more bases.

Moving Beyond Two Base Classes

Using multiple base classes poses no problems beyond those found when the number of base classes is restricted to two. The use of multiple base classes gives you a natural way to solve some common programming problems.

The record class in Listing 9-6 represents a common data processing problem: keeping track of an individual's personal statistics. The logical way to approach this problem is to divide the problem into the three obvious parts: the name, the address, and the telephone number. This solution is one that is used in many different programming languages. In C++, each of these parts is implemented as an object. Thus, you have a name class that handles the details of manipulating a person's name. Similarly, there is a class for the person's address (address), and one for the telephone number (phone).

Listing 9-6. Using multiple inheritance: record.cpp.

```
#include <string.h>
#include <iostream.h>
class name  {
  char first[80];
  char mid[80];
  char last[80];
public:
  name(char*, char*, char*);
  char* show();
};
```

continues

Listing 9-6. continued

```
name::name(char* f, char* m, char* l)
{
     strcpy(first, f);
     strcpy(mid, m);
     strcpy(last, l);
}

char* name::show()
{
 char* temp = new char[strlen(first)+strlen(mid)+strlen(last)+3];

 strcpy(temp, first);
 strcat(temp, " ");  // add a space
 strcat(temp, mid);
 strcat(temp, " ");
 strcat(temp, last);

 return temp;
}

class address  {
  char street[80];
  char city[80];
  char state[3];
  char zip[11];

public:
  address(char*, char*, char*, char*);
  char* show();
};

address::address(char* s, char* c, char* st, char* z)
{
 strcpy(street, s);
 strcpy(city, c);
 strcpy(state, st);
 strcpy(zip, z);
}
```

```
char* address::show()
{
 char* temp = new char[ strlen(street) + strlen(city) +
                        strlen(state) + strlen(zip) + 6];

 strcpy(temp, street);
 strcat(temp, "\n");
 strcat(temp, city);
 strcat(temp, ", ");
 strcat(temp, state);
 strcat(temp, "  ");
 strcat(temp, zip);

 return temp;
}

class phone  {
  char area[4];
  char prefix[4];
  char number[5];

public:
  phone(char*, char*, char*);
  char* show();
};

phone::phone(char* a, char* p, char* n)
{
 strcpy(area, a);
 strcpy(prefix, p);
 strcpy(number, n);
}

 char* phone::show()
{
 char* temp = new char[strlen(area)+strlen(prefix)+strlen(number)+1];

 strcpy(temp, "(");
 strcat(temp, area);
 strcat(temp, ") ");
 strcat(temp, prefix);
 strcat(temp, "-");
 strcat(temp, number);
```

continues

Listing 9-6. continued

```
 return temp;
}

class record : private name, private address, private phone {
  char job_title[80];

public:
  record(char*, char*, char*,  char*, char*, char*, char*,
      char*, char*, char*, char*);
  char* show();
};

record::record(char* f, char* m, char* l, char* s, char* c,
           char* st, char* z, char* a, char* p,
           char* n, char* jt) :  name(f, m, l),
                                 address(s, c, st, ),
                                 phone(a, p, n)
{
 strcpy(job_title, jt);
}

char* record::show()
{
 char* temp1 = name::show();
 char* temp2 = address::show();
 char* temp3 = phone::show();
 int len = strlen(temp1)+strlen(temp2)+strlen(temp3);

 len += strlen(job_title) + 11];
 char* temp = new char[ len ];

  strcpy(temp, temp1 );
  strcat(temp, "\n");
  strcat(temp, temp2);
  strcat(temp, "\n");
  strcat(temp, temp3);
  strcat(temp, "\n");
  strcat(temp, job_title);
  strcat(temp, "\n");
```

```
   delete temp1;
   delete temp2;
   delete temp3;

   return temp;
}

main()
{
   record x("John", "Jacob", "Smith",
          "1234 Pearl Street", "Santa Cruz", "CA",
          "94080", "408", "556", "1232", "Programmer");

   cout << "*************\n" << x.show() <<"\n";
}
```

The record class is used to combine these three independent classes into one. The three classes are listed in the definition of the record class. The record constructor gathers the values needed for each of the three base class constructors as well as its own needs. Each base class is given its required parameters and is called by name.

Designing with Multiple Classes

Compare Listing 9-6 to Listing 8-11, which is similar. Both of these classes solve the problem. Both give the program access to this information, and both are simple enough that neither is clearly more desirable than the other. Using independent classes for each component of the design is a clear winner, however, when you consider factors of design and control. The primary defect with the earlier example is that it combines the components of the derived class in an unintuitive way. The address class is made a part of the name class through inheritance. Then the address class is used as the base for the record class. At each point you add more of the details. The design adds complexity, too: Each base adds a new private section and a new set of member functions.

Listing 9-6, in contrast, has a more obvious design. You need to create an object with a name, address, and telephone component. You can reach into the library and pull out a class to take care of each of these components. You attach each one to the derived record class. They are all on the same level and there is no connection between the base classes. In particular, this last characteristic is different from the earlier example. In fact, the earlier serial derivation is not really an accurate representation of the algorithm that you're trying to implement. Using multiple base classes is, in fact, a better solution.

Multiple inheritance is more consistent with increasingly understood notions of reusability and software components. The ideal software development environment would contain a series of libraries of classes that could be specialized and used to create whatever software systems are necessary. This is not a new idea. Even the standard library in C is an earlier attempt to realize the kind of efficiency that this approach represents. The use of classes and object-oriented techniques is an evolutionary step up from these early attempts that ultimately builds on these earlier systems.

Avoiding Limitations and Pitfalls

The question of how to approach a particular software design problem does not have an absolute answer. There are usually many equally efficient ways of rendering an algorithm into C++ code. When you expand the meaning of efficiency to include other factors such as reliability and development time, the number of good solutions grows. There is an evolving C++ style, and you can explore some guidelines—which are more "rules of thumb" than cherished principles. It's equally important, however, not to become bogged down in someone else's style, but to develop an understanding of the language that is deep enough that a solution comes from this knowledge rather than from the thoughtless application of a received principle.

I've already discussed the question of using multiple bases to add components to a class. This is preferable not only because it makes for a cleaner and easier-to-control derived class, but it enhances also the consistency of software throughout any project. For example, whenever you need to access a name, you use the name class. Instead of three or four different sets of functions that deal with names, you have only one. Moreover, the access and the interaction are exactly the same at each point in the program at which you access name, because the class handles all of those details.

Of course, one important limitation comes from the freedom to put things together arbitrarily. Sometimes a design can be too eclectic; it has too many components combined together into the same object. Base classes should represent components of the object being created in the derived class. This latter, in turn, should not be a catch-all for miscellaneous parts. In Listing 9-6, the record object is meant to keep track of an individual. Each of its base classes represent something that needs to be recorded for an individual—the name, the address, and the telephone number.

Suppose that I take the record class and alter it by adding an invoice class, like this:

```
class invoice  {
    char* object_id;
    char* description:
    long unit_price;
    int number_ordered;
public:
    invoice(char*, char*, long, int);
    void print_invoice();
    void update();
  };

class record : private name, private address,
               private phone, private invoice  {

    :
  };
```

Nothing in the syntax forbids this combination. Yet it doesn't add to the efficiency of the program or to the clarity of the design. There is, after all, no organic relationship between the two classes.

In concentrating on the element of inheritance, it's easy to forget that class objects can communicate also with one another. You don't need to build monolithic classes to carry all the details of a program. You can write code that connects several independent classes without violating the spirit of object-oriented programming.

Choosing Between Friend Functions and Multiple Inheritance

In some ways, multiple inheritance addresses some of the same problems that you solved previously using friend functions. Friend functions often are constructed to serve as a bridge between classes, connecting them together in a way that allows communication between objects.

In Chapter 6 you saw the dangers inherent in friend functions. When you declare friend functions, you open up the class to any outside function that wants to violate the interface defined in the public section and directly manipulate the class members. Multiple inheritance reduces the need to use friend functions. A derived class often is thought of as the *product* of its bases, but you can derive a class to serve as a connecting bridge between its base functions. This is the need that the friend function previously filled.

The advantage to using a derived class as the bridge is in the fact that no special privileges are handed out to make the connection. You don't open the class definition to any other part of the program. You can maintain a carefully controlled environment in the base classes while still gaining this coordination. Listing 9-7 illustrates this method.

Listing 9-7. A derived class serving as a bridge between its two base classes: tmbridge.cpp.

```
#define COLON ":"

class tme {
  long secs;

public:
 tme(char*);
 long show_time() { return secs; }
};

tme::tme(char* tm)
{
 char *hr, *mn;

 hr = strtok(tm, COLON);
 mn = strtok(0, COLON);
 secs = (atol(hr) * 3600) + (atol(mn) * 60);
}

class dte  {
 int month,
     day,
     year;

public:
 dte(int m, int d, int y)  { month = m; day = d; year = y;}
 int show_month() { return month;}
 int show_day()  { return day; }
```

```
 int show_year() { return year; }
};


class tmbridge : private tme, private dte  {

public:
     tmbridge(char*, int, int, int);

     char* gdate();
     char* gtime();
};

tmbridge::tmbridge(char* t, int m, int d, int y) : tme(t), dte(m, d, y)
{
     ;
}

char* tmbridge::gdate()
{
 char* buffer = new char[15];
 sprintf(buffer, "%2d-%2d-%4d", show_month(), show_day(), show_year());
 return buffer;
}

char* tmbridge::gtime()
{
 char* buffer = new char[10];
 int h = show_time()/3600,
     m = (show_time() % 3600)/60;
 sprintf(buffer,"%02d:%02d", h, m);
 return buffer;
}
```

Compare Listing 9-7 to Listing 6-4. I've rewritten the example using a derived class as a bridge between the tme and dte classes. I added a simple output function to each base class. Otherwise, the examples perform identically. The functions gdate() and gtime(), which were friend functions in the earlier example, are member functions of the derived class tmbridge. The access is provided, but the integrity of the classes remains intact.

Summary

In this chapter you've explored multiple inheritance, which is just an extension of the syntax of single inheritance. The expanded capability that comes with more than one base class, however, allows us to design simple and easy-to-read derived classes.

Multiple base classes increase your ability to develop libraries of classes that you can combine to produce specialized objects to solve specific problems. They offer enhanced control over the details of a complex design, making it easier to solve complex problems.

Finally, multiple inheritance can do many of the things that you previously depended on the friend function to do. It does these things, however, in a way that does not violate the encapsulation of the class. As a result, multiple inheritance is better at creating bridges between classes than are the less controllable friend functions.

10

The C++ *iostream* Library

10

The C++ *iostream* Library

The C standard library has many well-developed input and output routines. It even contains a few massive I/O functions, such as printf(), that do all things to all kinds of data. This library is still available to the C++ programmer. C++ itself, however, adds a new and more convenient facility for getting values into and out of a program: the iostream library. This set of interlocking data types and specialized classes provides the convenience of built-in I/O statements while maintaining the flexibility of user-defined functions. Instead of having the functionality of a Swiss army knife, the iostream library has a series of smaller functions, each tied to specific data types. Furthermore, the functions in the C++ library are more efficient than those most commonly used in C. This efficiency is manifested also by the greater readability of the C++ output statements.

This chapter introduces the C++ iostream library and its most common objects—the standard I/O streams cin, cout, and cerr. It shows also how to extend the stream model to disk files and handle the issues that arise with that transformation. Finally, the chapter offers many concrete examples that show the iostream library in action.

Basic Input and Output in C++

To better understand why the `iostream` library in C++ is more convenient than its C counterpart, let's review how C handles input and output. First, recall that C has no built-in input or output statements. Functions such as `printf()` are part of the standard library, but not part of the language itself. Similarly, C++ has no built-in I/O facilities. The absence of built-in I/O gives the programmer greater flexibility to produce the most efficient user interface for the pattern of the application at hand.

The problem with the C solution to input and output lies with its implementation of these I/O functions. There is little consistency among them in terms of return values and parameter sequences. `scanf()`, for example returns the number of conversions performed, whereas `printf()` returns no useful value. Programmers tend to rely on the formatted I/O functions—`printf()`, `scanf()`, and so on—especially when the objects being manipulated are numbers or other noncharacter values. These formatted I/O functions are convenient, and for the most part they share a consistent interface. But they are also big and unwieldy because they must manipulate many kinds of values.

The C++ Approach to I/O

C++ uses the mechanism of the class to provide modular solutions to data manipulation needs. Continuing this approach, the standard C++ library provides three I/O classes as an alternative to C's cumbersome general-purpose I/O functions. These classes contain definitions for the same pair of operators (>> for input and << for output), which are optimized for specific kinds of data. These operators are overloaded so that you can add definitions to accommodate new situations without relinquishing their simple, convenient syntax. Thus, you can easily and radically modularize the input/output system with many small I/O functions that have a consistent interface. You don't need to trade convenience for code size.

To accommodate the data formatting needs included in the traditional C I/O library, C++ adds the standard `iostream` library, which contains a set of small, specific functions that are more efficient than C's massive general-purpose functions. The `iostream` library contains specific functions to perform conversions between the three supported number systems (decimal, hexadecimal, and octal), as well as specialized functions that place strings and individual characters within specified fields. In addition, special operators and functions are defined that can format these I/O streams. It's important to note that unlike C, C++ separates the notion of simply getting and putting values from the more complicated problem of formatting input and output.

C++ supports also the input of numbers, characters, and character strings more conveniently and more efficiently than C. Although you cannot format input explicitly as you can with the scanf() function, the new library contains much of the functionality of scanf(). To maintain old programs and to accommodate traditional programmers, the original C library is, of course, available to a C++ program. It's better, however, to use the iostream library when creating new code.

The << and >> I/O Operators

From the programmer's point of view, the key to the iostream library is the output operator, which replaces the more familiar function call. Instead of writing

```
printf("%d\n",x);
```

to display a message on a screen, in C++ you use the more concise form

```
int x=123;
```

```
cout << x << "\n";
```

This translates to standard output (cout) as "Output the value of x and then output a new-line character." Note that you don't need to specify a format for the value in x—the system determines the format. This form is more convenient and more obvious than the printf() function, but these are not its only advantages. In addition to its economy of expression, the C++ method introduces more significant improvements. For example, in the latter code fragment, the value stored in variable x, 123, is easily sent to the display screen. Using the traditional C library, you would first need to convert the numeric value into character string form, because a string is the only data that can be displayed on an output device such as a terminal screen. Usually you would invoke the convenient (but bloated) printf() function. As a general-purpose conversion function, printf() contains all the code needed to handle the many possible combinations of value-to-output transformations. This extra code is linked into each program whether or not it is needed. With the iostream library, C++ includes only the code needed for a specific conversion. Generally, this makes the code for I/O operations smaller and faster than the equivalent C code.

The iostream library supplies a similar input operator. The following code fragment illustrates its operation:

```
int x;

cin >> x;
```

The code places the value from the standard input, which can be typed at the keyboard or entered by some other method, in the variable x. Because x is declared as an integer variable, it expects an integer value. The input operator automatically performs the conversion. As its corollary did in the output system, this operator replaces the conventional formatted input statement, scanf(). This is not a substitution, however, because the input operator does only the data conversions. The scanf() function is a complete, formatted input facility that lets you describe the specification of the input line. C++ has no iostream input function comparable to this library resource. Remember, however, that you always can use scanf() or any of the other basic C I/O functions whenever you need them. The advantages of using the stream input operator are the same as those gained from the output functions: The resulting code is smaller, more specific, and more efficient.

An easy way to remember which operator is for input and which is for output is to remember that the C++ I/O operators are analogous to the redirection operators in MS-DOS and UNIX. Thus, just as in UNIX, the < symbol indicates that a command receives its values not from the keyboard but from a file. The << symbol indicates that the file (usually cout) receives its value from a variable or an expression. For example, the UNIX command

```
ls < file
```

executes the ls command with the arguments contained in file. Similarly, the C++ command

```
cout << x;
```

sends the value stored in x to the standard output cout. The same relationship exists between > and >>. The MS-DOS command

```
dir > file
```

sends the results of the command to a file, whereas the C++ statement

```
cin >> x;
```

puts the value from the standard input into the variable x (see Figure 10-1).

As a notational convenience, these operators offer economy of expression, and their implementation is more efficient than C's general-purpose approach. The full impact of this new iostream library, however, goes far beyond these advantages. Let's unlock the full power of these routines.

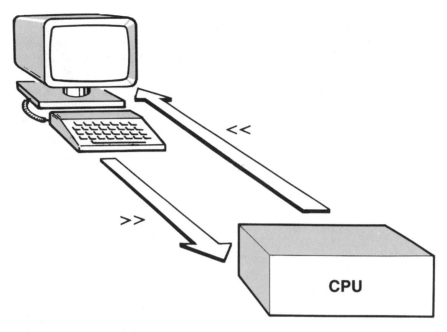

Figure 10-1. Data flow with the << and >> operators.

The *iostream* Class

Chapter 3 showed how a C++ class integrates data and related functions into a single structure or object. Therefore, you should not be surprised that the power and simplicity of the iostream library comes from its implementation as a series of related classes. These classes include input and output routines defined for each standard data type in C++. In addition to these, by using member functions and derived classes (see Chapter 8), you easily can add your own I/O routines for user-defined data types. Naturally, these facilities extend to disk I/O as well as to other devices.

The Stream I/O Model

C++ is as consistent with its progenitor language as possible. It therefore treats all I/O as a character string operation. This is the origin of the term *stream*—a stream of characters. Both languages also treat disk files as streams, even when they include binary (nontext) values. Remember this useful metaphor as you examine some of the more subtle and potentially confusing parts of the library.

As with operating systems such as UNIX, C++ uses the file as a basic model for all input and output, even that which goes to the display terminal rather than to the disk. In fact, C++ automatically opens the standard input and output files called `cin` and `cout` whenever you load a program for execution. You can manipulate these files exactly as you would any user-defined data files.

Access to the `iostream` library is through the header file, iostream.h. The header file must be included at the top of each file that contains any objects that depend on the `iostream` classes. This header file contains the necessary declarations for creating the standard objects (`cin`, `cout`, and `cerr`), as well as provides support for many different types of input and output situations.

The header file iostream.h is complicated and confusing. The everyday library functions, however, are based on the following classes:

`streambuf`	A buffer type that creates and manages a stream for I/O
`ios`	An interface between `streambuf` and the I/O classes that contains the common interface methods
`istream` and `ostream`	Classes that define the I/O operators and functions for each type of stream

These interrelated classes can be used to handle a large variety of both ordinary and special-case I/O.

The `streambuf` class is the simplest and most basic of the classes. It contains the most general functions for buffering data, such as allocating a buffer and keeping track of the current position in the buffer. Note that the `streambuf` type merely handles a buffer. It doesn't know where the values come from or where they are going. The everyday designer rarely uses directly any of the member functions of this class.

The `ios` class creates an interface between the `streambuf` class and the more specialized I/O classes that follow. One of the key members of this class is of type `streambuf`. It contains members that control the format and operation of the various kinds of I/O. This class is responsible for reporting on the performance of the stream (when it is successful, when it fails, how it fails), as well as defining the various modes of operation of the stream.

The input operators are defined in the `istream` class, which is derived from the `ios` class. It contains definitions for the various overloaded forms of the >> operator, as well as some more traditional statements such as `get()` and `read()`. A specialized version of this class, `istream_with_assign`, is used to create the `cin` object. Figure 10-2 illustrates the relationship between these classes. The arrows denote derivation.

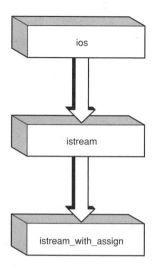

Figure 10-2. The istream hierarchy.

Similarly, ostream defines the output associated with the << operator. As with the istream class, additional member functions such as write() also perform output operations. The objects cout and cerr are created through an additional derived class, ostream_with_assign. Figure 10-3 shows the origin of these classes.

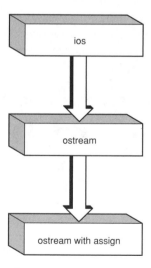

Figure 10-3. The ostream hierarchy.

Other classes defined in iostream.h handle various kinds of specialized cases. In a later section, I talk about files and the fstream class. Most of the interest in this chapter, however, revolves around the two classes: istream and ostream.

When each program begins execution, C++ automatically opens three streams—cin (standard input), cout (standard output), and cerr (standard error). These streams become the interface between the program and the user. Almost every program must use these streams to some extent.

The cin stream handles all the input from the terminal keyboard. In contrast, cout manipulates the terminal display screen. Another standard stream, cerr, provides the programmer with a secondary means for reporting error conditions when mixing error messages and normal display output might cause problems. These three standard streams correspond to C's stdin, stdout, and stderr files.

You can manipulate the standard streams as you would their C counterparts.

- You can redirect them to other devices, even a disk file.

- You can close and reopen them.

- You can combine them with each other or with other files.

In fact, because both cerr and cout are connected to the terminal display subsystem, most programs actually display error messages through a different stream than ordinary output. The two streams are logically separate and could be assigned to different devices, or even to a disk file. (You can conveniently assign cerr to a disk file in programs designed to be run as batch jobs.) In programs that must open several input or output files during the course of processing, you merely declare the additional files and treat them as though they were cin and cout streams.

The Input Operator >> and the Standard Input Stream

Let's use the standard input stream, cin, to examine the operation of the input operator >> in detail. Most of the following discussion applies also to other istream objects.

Note that >> is an overloaded operator. C++ supplies a separate function definition for the input of each standard data type—integer, real, and character-oriented. You can use the >> operator to direct the input of any value from the keyboard. Because this operator is overloaded, the correct function definition for that data type always executes. (Of course, you still have to be sure that the user has entered a valid value, but that is an axiom of real-world programming.) You no longer need to do explicit type conversion or type checking, which is an improve-

ment over the standard C library, in which input that is not character-oriented must be converted to the required data type.

Flexibility of the >> Operator

The convenience of the input operator is obvious. For the user to enter an integer value, the program requires only the following simple code:

```
int x;

cin >> x;
```

Remember that the >> symbol was chosen as a mnemonic device for the direction of flow, which is from the input stream (cin) to the variable. This operator can do much more, however. For maximum flexibility, you can cascade operators. For example, the code fragment

```
int x,y;

cin >> x >> y;
```

lets the user enter two integer values into a program. One goes into the x variable and the other goes into y. This type of cascading has no built-in or practical limit. The code

```
cin >> x >> y >> z;
```

introduces three values to the program. The same procedure holds true for the float or double real number types.

```
double x,y;

cin >> x >> y;
```

Note that you always use the same operator and the identical syntax, regardless of the type of data involved. When you use multiple input values, the order of operation is simple and not surprising: The first variable mentioned is the first filled. The others are filled in the order of their appearance.

Because the >> operator is overloaded with explicit operational code for each supported data type, there are no restrictions on the kinds of input lines that you can construct inside a cin expression. C++ supports any combination of data types in the same line of code. For example, the lines

```
char ch;
double x;

cin >> ch >> x;
```

generate the expected values in the correct variables.

10

The General-Purpose *istream* Input Function

As useful as the input operator is, it does not handle all kinds of input. To create a flexible and useful library, the designer of C++ chose an implementation that reflects the most common usage of such a routine. This is a simple, no-nonsense input routine. The individual programmer must create the flourishes and the code for special cases. The basic nature of the input operator becomes most evident when you use it to handle character string input. Its operation with this data type might surprise an unwary programmer.

Like scanf() in the C library, >> reads in a string only to the first occurrence of white space. Consider the following code fragment:

```
char ch[80];

cin >> ch;
```

If the user enters the character string this is only a test from the keyboard, only the first word (this) is placed in the string variable ch. The input operator sees the blank space after a word as a signal to end input. The null character that conventionally marks the end of a string in C is then affixed to the end of ch. Thus, the >> operator is inadequate for any line-oriented input that might contain embedded spaces or other white-space characters.

The istream class contains a character string function, get(), which serves as a basic input routine that can retrieve a complete string, blank spaces and all. The get() function performs no conversions. It merely accepts a character string and places it in the specified variable. Actually, get() consists of a family of overloaded functions that perform basic uninterpreted input. The following box lists the general form of these functions. In addition to its character string function, get() supports basic input to a single character variable. Note that all versions of get() let you specify a character that terminates input. When you use the default terminator, '\n', the function accepts input (including spaces) until the specified length of the variable or buffer is exceeded or until a new-line is entered.

For example, the program

```
#include <iostream.h>

main()
{
  char ch;
```

```
  cout << "Enter a Character-->";
  cin.get(ch);
  cout << "ch = " << ch << '\n';
}
```

uses the single character form of get() while

```
#include <iostream.h>

main()
{
  char str[80];

  cout << "Enter a String-->;
  cin.get(str, 79);
  cout << "str = " << str << '\n';
}
```

reads a character string from the standard input.

The *get()* Function in the Class *istream*

```
istream& get( char *string, int length, char terminator)
```

in which
   string is a character string variable;
   length is the maximum length of the input string; and
   terminator indicates a particular character that causes termination of input. The default value is \n.

This function accepts characters until the maximum length is reached or the terminating character is entered.

```
istream& get(char& c)
```

in which *c* is a reference to a character variable.

This function produces simple character input.

NOTE: char and char* can be either signed or unsigned.

The Output Operator <<
and the Standard Output
Stream

As a complement to the istream object that imports values into a program, the iostream library defines also an ostream type that exports values from the program. The heart of this class is the overloaded output operator <<, which lets you display built-in data types. This operator can perform the basic output function for most programs.

If you cascade the output operator, it displays values in the order in which they are specified in the line. Thus, the output expression

```
int x=123;
```

```
cout << "x = " << x;
```

displays

```
x = 123
```

on the screen or on any other output destination that you specify (by redirecting cout). As with the input operator, there is no built-in limit to the number of elements that you can cascade. Common sense and good programming practice, however, might dictate a limit of three or four. Of course, you can combine different data types freely on one line. For example, the code

```
int x=123;
double f=1.23;
```

```
cout << "x = " << x << "f = " << f;
```

creates a display with the appropriate labels. Note that this code is much simpler than a comparable printf() statement, which would require format specifiers for each data type used.

The *ostream* Output Functions

The ostream class contains two primitive output functions. The first of these, put(), performs the most basic output operation: It outputs a single character. The put()

routine accepts an expression that yields a single character and sends the character to the specified display device. This function is the equivalent of the `putchar()` macro associated with the C standard library. It uses the following syntax:

```
char ch='a';
```

```
cout.put(ch);
```

Recall that `cout` is an object of the `ostream` class. The `put()` function is a member of this class, so you must access it either through the dot notation (`.`) or through the arrow notation for pointer variables (`->`). `cout` is the most common object used in this way.

The second primitive `ostream` output function, `flush()`, clears the output buffer of any characters waiting to be sent to the output destination. Usually, you use this routine with an `ostream` attached to a disk file to ensure that all buffered characters have been written explicitly to a file before you close the file or rewrite to it. Because C++ automatically calls the `flush()` function before it destroys an `ostream` object, however, you rarely need to explicitly call this function. (This is another example of the useful actions of a class destructor.)

Formatted Output Functions

Included in the `iostream` library are a series of format functions—usually called *manipulators*—that can be positioned in the stream to give the programmer greater control over value conversion and display mechanics. These manipulators are divided into two broad categories: those with parameters and those without.

One important characteristic of a stream that must deal with numeric values is the *base* or *radix* of those numbers. Inside the computer, of course, everything is stored as a binary number. You need to worry about converting a value only when you want to see it on the screen. The `iostream` library has three manipulators to control this situation. The default conversion is to base 10, the familiar decimal notation. This is covered by the `dec` manipulator. If `dec` appears in a stream, as in

```
cout << dec << x  << y;
```

any number output after this appearance is displayed in base 10. Of course, because base 10 is the default, the explicit use of `dec` is necessary only if a previous manipulator has set the conversion base to some other value. This conversion works also for `cin`.

Setting the Conversion Base

`dec`   Forces the conversion base to be 10—decimal

`hex`   Forces the conversion base to be 16—hexadecimal

`oct`   Forces the conversion base to be eight—octal

Another common base number used in programming is 16. This conversion can be set by using the `hex` manipulator. Both

```
cout << hex << x << y;
```

and

```
cin >> hex >> x;
```

force a conversion to base 16 format. The former displays the two values using hexadecimal notation, whereas the latter converts keyboard input (if it is a string of digits) into a hexadecimal value before storing it in `x`. Similarly, `oct` converts either input or output into octal (base eight) notation. In this case, the option of input in a format other than base 10 is convenient if your program manipulates octal or hexadecimal values.

Note that these base converters work the same with both input and output streams—they are defined in the class `ios`. The converters work within the syntax of the stream, going from left to right as they apply their conversion. After a conversion specification has been made, it takes another number base manipulator to change it.

Setting the base for the conversion of numeric values is not the only stream characteristic you need to control. Another important factor is the width of the display field, or how many character positions a particular number or character string will occupy on the screen. The `setw()` manipulator gives you control over this field width. This manipulator, however, takes a parameter.

```
setw(int size);
```

The value of `size` is used to specify the number of characters to be given to the display of the next object. For example,

```
cout << setw(10) << x;
```

displays the value of `x` in a field 10 spaces wide. If more spaces are needed, it grabs just enough to display the number. In this situation, `setw()` works in a way analogous to `printf()`.

Common Manipulators

`setw(int sz)`	Sets the width of the stream to the value of *sz*.
`setprecision(int dg)`	Sets the number of digits after the decimal point to the value in *dg*.
`setfill(int ch)`	Uses the value of *c* instead of the default fill characters.
`ws`	Removes white space from the stream.
`endl`	Inserts a new-line and flushes the output stream.

(These manipulators require iomanip.h for proper declaration.)

The `setw()` manipulator has a unique characteristic. Whereas the other manipulators are toggles (they stay on until you turn them off), `setw()` specifies the width only for the next item in the stream. After that item is displayed, the field width reverts to the default value of 0. For example, the expression

```
cout << setw(10) << x << y;
```

prints the value of x in a field that is 10 characters wide. The y value, however, uses just enough space to display itself. As with the earlier numeric base converters, `setw()` works with `cin` as well as `cout`.

If you are dealing with real numbers (`float` or `double`), you need to control not only the field width, but also the number of digits that appear to the right of the decimal point—the *precision*. This task is handled by `setprecision(int)`. The parameter indicates the number of fractional digits. For example,

```
cout << setprecision(3) << setw(10) << x;
```

shows the value of x with three numbers after the decimal point. Note that setting the number of digits does not guarantee the significance of those digits. Mathematical precision is a function of the data type implementation. `setprecision()` indicates only the numbers to be displayed.

`setfill(int)` sets the fill character. This is the character that will be used in a field to fill the spaces that are not used to display a value. The default value is a space, but you can use any character from the ASCII set.

```
cout << setfill('#') << setw(10) << 123;
```

prints a line that looks like

```
#######123
```

In some data processing circumstances, such as printing checks, this kind of fill is necessary.

Other manipulators remove white space from a stream or attach a new-line character. The manipulators enable you to control the format of both output and input.

General-Purpose Format Control: The *ios* Class

As noted previously, the `ios` class serves as a kind of control interface between the `ostream` and the `istream` classes and the `streambuf` class. Its members perform a variety of housekeeping tasks that facilitate the smooth execution of `iostream` class objects. One of the most important of these support tasks is to exert fine control over the format of these two streams. This control is available to the user.

Commonly Used *ios* Format Flags	
`ios::skipws`	Skip white space during input.
`ios::left`	Left-justify.
`ios::right`	Right-justify.
`ios::dec`	Make the conversion base decimal.
`ios::oct`	Make the conversion base octal.
`ios::hex`	Make the conversion base hex.
`ios::showbase`	Indicate base on output.
`ios::uppercase`	Display hexadecimal digits in uppercase.
`ios::showpos`	Show a plus sign (+) with positive numbers.
`ios::scientific`	Use floating-point notation for real numbers.
`ios::fixed`	Use fixed-point notation for real numbers.
(These format flags require iostream.h for proper declaration.)	

The manipulator function `setiosflags(long)` takes the `ios` format flags as commands and toggles on the particular flag that is passed as a parameter. For example, the expression

```
cout << setiosflags(ios::left) << setw(10) << x << endl;
```

causes the output of the x value to be left-justified in a field of 10 spaces. If two or more flags need to be set simultaneously, the bitwise or operator (¦) is used to combine the flags. The line

```
cout << setiosflags(ios::left¦ios::fixed) << setw(15) << x;
```

displays its value using both left-justification and fixed-point numbers.

To turn off one of the characteristics associated with these ios flags, you need recourse to another manipulator function, resetiosflags(long). Just as with setiosflags(), you need to use the ios flags to indicate which characteristics you want to turn off. In

```
cout << setiosflags(ios::left) << x << resetiosflags(ios::left) << y;
```

the value of x is printed as a left-justified value. Before y can be displayed, however, the left-justification characteristic is toggled off by restiosflags().

These two functions, setiosflags() and resetiosflags(), give the programmer more direct control over display formats. A glance at the list of commonly used flags indicates the usual kinds of functions: setting justification, showing the conversion base, and specifying floating-point notation. There is some overlap with the simpler manipulators discussed previously, but for the most part these ios flags offer additional possibilities. The simpler manipulators are easier to use and are preferable if they can do the job. setiosflags() and resetiosflags() should be reserved for times when you need finer control.

Disk File Input and Output

One important consequence of using classes to implement the stream library is that the same model that performs I/O for the keyboard and terminal works just as well when you apply it to a disk file. The same operators and operations perform in precisely the same way. This greatly simplifies a programming task that has always been difficult and confusing.

To facilitate disk file I/O, the stream library defines a series of classes that are related in ways similar to the classes used with the standard I/O objects cin, cout, and cerr. Some of the same classes are involved, although there are also new class definitions to consider. Class definitions and other declarations that are necessary for file access are found in the header file fstream.h, which must be included with any code that will access the disk.

As with the earlier iostream library, the fstream library contains some specialized classes optimized for file manipulation. The most basic of these specialized classes is filebuf, which is a derivative of the standard streambuf type. Like its progenitor type, filebuf manages a buffer. In this case, however, the buffer is attached to a disk file. filebuf, in turn, is used as a member of a new file-oriented stream class, fstreambase. This latter stream is derived from ios.

fstreambase is used as the base class for a variety of classes related to file input and output. The one of particular interest here is fstream. This class has both fstreambase and iostream as its base classes. From the former it inherits the necessary functionality to manipulate a disk file. The other base class, iostream, gives it access to the operators that it needs to put values into the file and take them from it. The perhaps confusing relation among these classes is more clear in the simplified diagram in Figure 10-4.

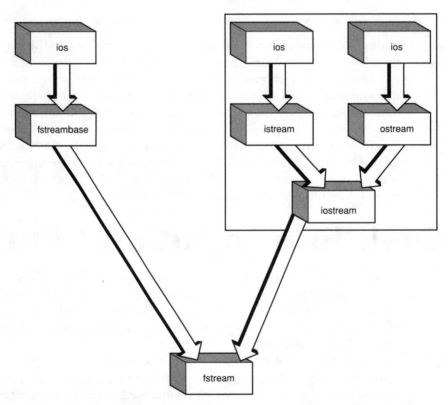

Figure 10-4. The fstream class.

The fstream class derives its buffering capabilities from the fstreambuf class and, indirectly, from filebuf. The formatting and other functionality associated with a stream is inherited from the iostream class, which is part of the standard iostream library. iostream is derived from both the istream and ostream classes that I discussed earlier. The same functionality found in the standard object (cin, cout,

and so on) also is part of the file class objects created by the fstream class. Before I discuss these important similarities, however, I need to cover the basic file operations associated with this class.

Opening a File

The first interaction that a program has with a disk file is to attach it to the program. With an fstream object, this can be done in one of two ways:

- Through the fstream constructor
- Explicitly with a call to the member function open()

It's important to note that the fstream object in a program is independent of its attachment to a file. It exists even after any particular attachment is broken (the more normal case), or you can create a file object without opening a particular file.

The rules for opening a file follow familiar practice. You need to supply a file name in the local format. MS-DOS requires an eight-character name, whereas UNIX allows up to 14 characters. You need to supply an access mode as well. The access mode tells the system what kind of access to allow: read, write, read and write, or variations on these basic modes. The basic form for opening a file with a constructor is

```
fstream  object_name ( file_name, access_mode);
```

In contrast, an explicit call to the member function open() would look like this:

```
fstream object_name;

object_name.open(file_name, access_mode);
```

In both cases the result is the same: The object is attached to the name file and can interact with it.

The access mode flags are members of the ios class. The three major access modes are

ios::in	For read-only access
ios::out	For write access
ios::app	For append access

Other modes are summarized in the following box. These modes are modifiers to the base modes. If you want to open a file for read access, the statement you need is

```
fstream fobject("file1.dat", ios::in);
```

To combine flags, you use the same technique that you used previously with the formatting flags: You use the bitwise or (¦) operator.

```
fstream fobject("file1.dat", ios::in¦ios::binary)
```

attaches the object fobject to the file file1.dat for read access. It then sets the file type as binary, rather than text.

The File Access Flags in *ios*

`ios::in`	Opens the file for read access.
`ios::out`	Opens the file for write access.
`ios::ate`	Causes a seek to end when the file is opened.
`ios::app`	Opens the file for append access.
`ios::trunc`	If the file exists, it is truncated.
`ios::nocreate`	Open fails if the file doesn't exist.
`ios::noreplace`	Open fails if the file does exist.
`ios::binary`	Opens the file as a binary file.

After a file has been opened and attached to an object of type fstream, access is achieved through the use of the same operators that you used with cin and cout. To send things out to the file, the << operator is used. To receive values from the file, the complementary >> is put to service. All of the conversion and formatting associated with these operators is still in effect for the file.

Finally, to detach a file from a file object, you need to use the member function close(). close() takes no parameter. It severs the attachment between the program and the disk file in a graceful manner that prevents information loss. It's important to note that executing the close() member function does not destroy the fstream object. A call to open() could attach it to a new file. The object exists according to the rules of its scope and storage class. If the associated variable is automatic, it is destroyed as soon as the function is terminated. You can remove a dynamically allocated file object by using the delete operator. Other than in these two cases, the stream persists through the program. Listing 10-1 shows a simple program using the fstream class.

Listing 10-1. A simple file access program: filstrm.cpp.

```
#include <iostream.h>
#include <fstream.h>

main()
{
 fstream x;
 x.open("fubar.dat",ios::out);

 x << "This is only a test ";
 x << "Nothing can go wrong ";
 x << "...nothing can go wrong.";

 x.close();

 x.open("fubar.dat", ios::in);
 char buffer[80];

 for( ; !x.eof() ; )  {
    x >> buffer;
    cout << buffer << "\n";
  }
}
```

In the filstrm.cpp program, I create a read-write file object using the fstream class. I open the file object x in the constructor for write access using the flag ios::out. Several applications of the << operator put information onto the disk file. Finally, I detach x by a call to the member function close().

In the second part of the main(), I read the information back from the file. I use an explicit open call to reattach it to the previous file—this time for input mode, ios::in. The for loop reads through the file, displaying each character string on through cout as soon as it is read from the file. A new member function used here, eof(), is one of a series of functions that enable the programmer to test the state of the stream. In the case of x.eof(), it returns 0 until the end of file is reached. It makes an ideal test for this kind of loop. I talk more about these test members in the next section.

Testing the State of a File Stream

One important attribute of a file object is its current state. C++ defines five possible conditions.

goodbit	Indicates that the last access was successful.
eofbit	Signals that the end of the file has been reached.
failbit	Is set for an unsuccessful access without data loss.
badbit	Indicates an invalid operation was attempted.
hardfail	Indicates a catastrophic failure of the file.

These values are flags in the ios class. You can access the current state of the fstream most easily, however, through a series of specific member functions. For example, if the stream is at the end of the file, eof() returns a value of true. Similarly, fail(), bad(), and good() test for their particular conditions. As an example, the following code might read the contents of the file stream in_file:

```
for(;;)  {
    if(in_file.eof())
        break;

    in_file >> ch;

    cout << ch;
}
```

This loop continues until the end-of-file condition exists, at which time the break statement exits the loop. You saw a similar construction in Listing 10-1.

In addition to the Boolean functions available within the stream, one function actually lets the programmer access the internal structure of the stream itself. The clear() function directly sets the state of the stream. The default value is goodbit, but you can pass any other legal value as a parameter to the function. Use clear() sparingly and carefully because it changes the value of a variable that is ordinarily set to reflect the condition of the stream. Circumstances in which you would use the function include handling a recoverable failure, as in

```
if(in_file.fail())  {
    cout << "recoverable failure\n";

    in_file.clear();
}
```

or forcing a condition that the program requires, such as a premature end-of-file.

```
while(!in_file.eof())  {
    if(test())  {
        cout << "exiting file early\n";
        in_file.clear(_ios::eofbit);
    }
    .
    .
    .
```

In both examples, the `clear()` function offers an orderly and efficient way to change the state of the stream.

A Practical File Program

The comp.cpp program (Listing 10-2) illustrates the use of file streams. This program accepts two file names and compares the files character-by-character. It reports any differences it finds, listing the position and the contents of each file at each point of difference. The program terminates when it reaches the end of the shortest of the two files.

**Listing 10-2. A program that compares
two files and reports their differences: comp.cpp.**

```
#include <iostream.h>
#include <fstream.h>
#include <stdlib.h>

main(int argc,char* argv[])
{
 if(argc < 3 )  {
    cout << "Error! You must specify two files to compare\n";
    exit(1);
 }

 fstream file1(argv[1], ios::in);

 if(file1.bad())  {
    cout << "Sorry! I couldn't open " << argv[1] << endl;
    exit(1);
  }
```

continues

Listing 10-2. continued

```
fstream file2(argv[2], ios::in);

if(file2.bad())  {
    cout << "Sorry! I couldn't open " << argv[2] << endl;
    exit(1);
 }

cout << "comparing files: " << argv[1] << " " << argv[2] << endl;

char ch1,ch2;

int n=0;

for(;;n++)  {
    if(file1.eof() || file2.eof())
      break;

    file1 >> ch1;

    file2 >> ch2;

    if(ch1 != ch2)
      cout << "\nposition: " << n << "\t" << ch1 << "\t" << ch2;

 }
}
```

Note that the program takes input from the command-line arguments (this procedure is the same in C++ as it is in C). First, the program checks the count variable argc to see if the user supplied sufficient input. If the count does not indicate that two file names were entered, the program exits with an error message. Otherwise, the program attempts to open the first file by creating and opening an fstream variable. A test is done to see if this worked. If the attempt fails, the program prints an error message and exits. This procedure is repeated with the second file.

Next, the program prints an information banner on the screen and begins to read the files character-by-character. Note that the temporary variables, ch1 and ch2, are declared before entering the loop, which is in keeping with good C++ programming practice. The for loop increments the line counter n and terminates when it reaches the end of either file. The heart of the loop is the conditional that tests each character for equality. If it fails, the program displays the position and the differing characters. No explicit call to the `close()` member function is performed because the end of program sequence gracefully closes all files.

This particular program is written as a UNIX-style *filter*. The user enters file names through the standard input device, and the result comes back through standard output. You can use the operating system to redirect both of these. For example, the program could take input from one disk file and return it to another without any change to the program code.

Direct File Access Member Functions

Until this point, you have dealt with files on a straightforward basis: Open a file, read or write through to the end, and close the file. You can write many useful programs even under this restriction. But often you need to be able to move back and forth within a file. This is particularly important in updating or changing the values already in the file.

In C, the standard library contains functions that enable this kind of direct access: `tell()` and `lseek()`. `tell()` reports on the current position of the file pointer as an offset value from the beginning of the file (remember that a C file is a collection of bytes). This is a `long` value. `lseek()` positions the file pointer at a specified offset preparatory to a read or write operation.

The C++ `iostream` library contains similar capabilities, but in the form of member functions of either the `ostream` or `istream` class. By making them class members, their access and use is facilitated. As you will see, they represent an efficient and effective way to handle this specialized I/O.

One additional complication with direct access in C++ is the fact that a file potentially can have two pointers: one for read operations and one for write operations. As a result, both `ostream` and `istream` have their own set of member functions.

The *ostream* and Direct Access

The `ostream` class is responsible for putting values into a disk file. It contains the overloaded operator definitions and the other member functions that put value into a file. In addition to these write functions, it contains two member functions that control position. The first of these position control members is `tellp()`, which reports on the current position of the write pointer in the file. This function indicates the offset in the file at which the next value will be placed.

In contrast to tellp(), seekp() takes as a parameter a position or offset value and moves the write pointer to that location. This member has a direct effect on where the next write operation will be performed and is vital when you are trying to design a file update program. It's important to note that seekp() comes in two forms: the more common absolute form, and a form that enables the designer to specify an offset value relative to a particular location (see the following table). This latter form is similar to the lseek() function found in the C standard library.

File-Oriented *ostream* Member Functions

```
streampos tellp()
```

This member returns the current position of the output stream pointer in terms of the absolute position. streampos is defined earlier as a long value.

```
ostream& seekp(streampos pos)
```

This member changes the current position of the output stream pointer to the absolute value indicated by the parameter pos.

```
ostream& seekp(streamoff offset, ios::seek_dir anchor)
```

An alternative form of output stream pointer positioning, this member function moves the stream cursor to a position specified by an offset value (in bytes) from an anchor position (specified by an enum definition found in the ios class).

NOTE: streampos is a specialized data type that is equivalent to long in most current implementations.

The *istream* and Direct Access

istream, too, has a tellg() member to report offsets within a file. In this case, the offset refers to the read pointer in the file. Similarly, seekg() works the same as seekp(), directly positioning the read pointer in the file. Like seekp(), seekg() has both an absolute form and a relative form, which are shown in the following box.

File-Oriented *istream* Member Functions

```
streampos tellg()
```

This member returns the current position of the input stream pointer in terms of the absolute position. `streampos` is defined earlier as a `long` value.

```
istream& seekg(streampos pos)
```

This member changes the current position of the input stream pointer to the absolute value indicated by the parameter `pos`.

```
istream& seekg(streamoff offset, ios::seek_dir anchor)
```

An alternative form of input stream pointer positioning, this member function moves the stream cursor to a position specified by an offset value (in bytes) from an anchor position (specified by an `enum` definition found in the `ios` class).

NOTE: `streampos` is a specialized data type that is equivalent to `long` in most current implementations.

Some Case Studies of Direct File Access

Both `ostream` and `istream` support the kind of direct access that a programmer needs to do any serious work with disk files. Seeing the member functions described, however, is not the same as seeing them in action. You need practical examples to reinforce and to demonstrate how to program with these resources. In the next section, I show some examples of file access designs.

Using *fstream* with Traditional Programming Design

The `fstream` class can be used in simple and traditional contexts to provide access to disk files. In Listing 10-3, a simple file read-write program is constructed using the `iostream` library.

Listing 10-3. A simple file I/O program: filprog1.cpp.

```cpp
#define SPA " "

#include <stdio.h>
#include <iostream.h>
#include <fstream.h>
#include <string.h>
#include <stdlib.h>

class record  {
    char first[80];
    char mid[80];
    char last[80];
public:
  record()
    { for ( int q = 0; q < 80; q++) first[q] = mid[q] = last[q] = 0; }
  void update(char*, char*, char*);
  void show()
     { cout << first << SPA << mid << SPA << last << " "; }
  char* show_last() { return last; }
};

void record::update(char* f, char* m, char* l)
{
  if(f)
    strcpy(first, f);
  if(m)
    strcpy(mid, m);
  if(l)
    strcpy(last, l);
}


void fill_file(char*);
void read_file(char*);
char menu();

main()
{
 char fname[80];
```

```
  for( ; ; )
   switch(menu())  {
     case 'f': cout << "\nWrite Data To File\n";
               cout << "File Name: ";
               cin >> fname;
               fill_file(fname);
               break;
     case 'r': cout << "\nRead Entire File\n";
               cout << "File Name: ";
               cin >> fname;
               read_file(fname);
               break;
       case 'h':
       case 'H': exit(0);
   }
}

char menu()
{
 char xh;
 cout << "\n";

 cout << "=======Menu======\n";
 cout << "f(ill file)\n";
 cout << "r(ead entire file)\n";
 cout << "h(alt program)\n";
 cout << "==================\n";
 cout << "Command: ";
 cin >> xh;
 return xh;
}

void fill_file(char* fname)
{
  fstream fd(fname, ios::out);
  record rec;

  char fr[80];
  char md[80];
  char ls[80];
```

continues

Listing 10-3. continued

```cpp
  for(;;)  {
   cout << "\n\nEnter Name Below\n";
   cout << "First...";
   cin >> fr;
   if(!strcmp(fr, "stop"))
     break;
   cout << "Middle..";
   cin >> md;
   if(!strcmp(md, "stop"))
     break;
   cout << "Last....";
   cin >> ls;
   if(!strcmp(ls, "stop"))
     break;

   rec.update(fr, md, ls);
   cout << "Saving...";
   rec.show();
   fd.write((unsigned char*)&rec, sizeof(rec));
  }
 fd.close();
}

void read_file(char* fname)
{
  fstream fd(fname, ios::in);
  record x;

  for( ; ; )  {
    fd.read((unsigned char*) &x, sizeof(record));
    if(fd.eof())
      break;
    x.show();
    cout << endl;
  }
  fd.close();
}
```

To keep the detail at a manageable level, the record class is defined to store and manipulate only a name—first, middle, and last—as a series of character strings.

The class record stores these names in its private section. Note that there is only a default constructor for the class, which sets each component of the name to a null (0) value. No explicit initialization is done when a record object is created.

The record class has three member functions in addition to a constructor: an update() function that puts values into the name members, a generalized show() function that displays the contents of record, and a specialized show_last() function that returns only the last name. The latter two members are simple inline expanded functions. show() uses the iostream library to display, in a traditional order, the contents of the three variable members. show_last() returns the address of the last name member field.

The update() member function is used to put values into a record or to change those currently stored. This function takes three character strings as parameters and uses the strcpy() library function to copy their values into the name members. A simple mechanism enables the user to change only some of the values: Only parameters that are nonzero are copied into the member. By putting a 0 in place of an argument, you can guarantee that the old value remains. For example, in

```
record x;
        x.update("Thomas", "Richard", "Harry");
                    :                           :
        x.update(0, 0, "Jones");
```

the first call of update() places three values into the record object. The subsequent call to this member function changes only the last member in the record object x. first and mid retain their original values.

The heart of this program is two I/O functions: fill_file() and read_file(). Because this is a simple and traditional design, these functions are defined outside of any class definition. Nonetheless, they serve to illustrate the advantages of using the fstream class. A little later in this chapter, I discuss how you can incorporate disk-based I/O in a more orthodox C++ style.

fill_file() uses a record object to gather name values and store this information in a disk file. This function takes a single parameter: a character string that contains the name of the disk file that is to be used. The body of this function consists of a series of question and answer statements that take information from the keyboard and place it into some local variables: fr, md, and ls. These variables become the parameters for a call to the record member function update(). After this object has been loaded with a specific set of names, you can manipulate just the record variable to accomplish the task.

File access in file_fill() is gained through the declaration of an fstream object. In this case, the variable is fd and the file is opened in the declaration. To simplify the example, no explicit error checking is included here. In a production program, it would be necessary to include some guarantee of success before allowing the program to continue. The mode value, `ios::out`, specifies a write-only access and starts writing at the beginning of the file, destroying any previous values. A simple call to the `fstream write()` member function puts the contents of the `record` object in the file. Note that the `record` pointer is cast to `unsigned char*`, which is necessary because there is no `void*` defined as a possible parameter for an `fstream write()` call. Putting the entire class in the file simplifies the output and takes advantage of the object-oriented nature of class objects. The call to the `close()` member is not essential, because the `fd` variable is destroyed as soon as the function is exited. Closing files is a good habit to maintain, nonetheless.

`read_file()` performs the complementary action to `fill_file()`: It reaches into the file and pulls out the contents of a `record` object. As in the earlier function, an object of type `fstream` is created, and the constructor opens the file. The file name is found in the parameter `fname` and the access mode comes from the `ios` member `in`. I create also a temporary `record` object, `x`, to hold the values that come from the file. As in the earlier function, an explicit call to the `close()` member of `fstream` is made just before the function terminates.

The operation of `read_file()` is controlled by a `for` loop without any conditions, which loops forever. Within the range of this statement is a call to the `read()` member of `fstream` through the file id `fd`. Note that again I cast the address of the `record` variable `x` to `unsigned char*` to make it consistent with one of the overloaded definitions of `read()`. As with `write()`, no definition has a `void*` parameter. The statement immediately after the `read()` function involves a call to the member function `eof()`. This returns `true` if the program has reached the end of the file. Here this member is used within an `if` statement to decide whether or not to end the loop. If you are not finished getting values from the file, you ask the `frecord` object `x` to display its value.

Rounding out the program is a `menu()` function that displays the choices (in this case there are only three: `fill`, `read`, and `halt`), and a `main()` that contains the controlling statements. `menu()` is another simple function. Besides displaying a list of the program's functions, it prompts for the user's choice. After the user enters this choice, a `return` statement sends it back to `main()`, which contains the loop that controls the program—a `for` statement that creates a forever loop. Inside this loop is a `switch` statement that sets up and calls the necessary functions to perform each task. The only declaration is a string variable, `fname`, to hold the file name that serves as the parameter to `fill_file()` or `read_file()`.

The filprog1.cpp program is too simple to be of much more use than illustrating the basic concepts of file I/O. A more practical program must do more than just read and write data to a file. One useful addition to a file program is a function that searches through the file for a particular record. A search like this usually is based on some particular value or *search key*. For example, you could modify filprog1.cpp to search for a particular last name. A search like this always yields one of two possibilities:

- A match to the key value will be found.

- The entire file will be searched but no match will be found.

In the former, successful case, the entire record is displayed. The failed case usually elicits an appropriate error message.

After you establish the utility of searching a file for a particular record, you must turn your attention toward different methods for conducting this search. Perhaps the least desirable is the brute force method of reading each record in turn from the file and comparing its value to the key. Although this method has the virtue of simplicity, it is potentially time-consuming with a large file. There are alternative designs that can improve the performance of this basic method. For example, buffering several records at one time in memory allows a more rapid search (memory is much faster than the disk) and an increased efficiency in reading from a file. Buffering is used commonly, but for this program I utilize another technique to improve performance: an index file. I should point out before I continue the discussion that both techniques often are used together. In this demonstration program, however, I use only indexing.

An index file serves as a companion to a data file. The index file contains a selection of the values in the original file coupled with information about the position of those values. In the case of the record file, for example, the index file contains the last name from each record and the *offset* or position of the record entry that contains that last name. The relationship between an index file and its main file (or data file) is illustrated by Figure 10-5.

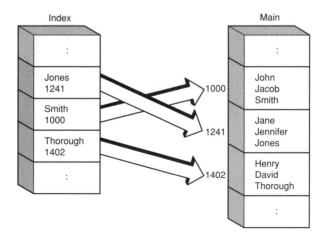

Figure 10-5. The relationship of an index file and a main file.

10

The value of an index file is that it enhances the performance of file acquisition. Instead of having to read through the entire data file, comparing the key value to each record until a match is found, you read through the much smaller index file and use the position information in conjunction with the main file to access directly the desired record. The smaller size of the index file makes the search process less time-consuming.

Additional design choices can further enhance the performance of an index file. Among these choices are keeping the file sorted on the key value, using some specialized searching algorithms, and even creating a hierarchy of *indices*, which are index files pointing to other index files. A discussion of these techniques is beyond the scope of this book.

To implement an index file in the example, you need to use the fstream member functions tellp() and seekg(). Utilizing an index file is a two-stage process. First you must create an index file with values from the file of record objects. After the index is available, you can use it to access the main file directly. Listing 10-4 contains a function, build_index(), that accomplishes the former task.

Listing 10-4. The function build_index().

```
struct index  {
   char key[80];
   long position;
};

void build_index(char* fname, char* iname)
{
 index idx;
 record x;
 fstream fr(fname, ios::in);
 fstream ir(iname, ios::out);

 for(;;)  {
   idx.position = fr.tellg();
   fr.read((unsigned char*) &x, sizeof(record));
   if(fr.eof())
     break;
   strcpy(idx.key, x.show_last());
   ir.write((unsigned char*) &idx, sizeof(idx));
 }
 fr.close();
 ir.close();
}
```

I start by defining the structure of the index file. I use a simple class created with the struct keyword and without any member functions. This class consists of a character string that holds the key value (in this case this is a last name) and a long integer that contains the position of the matching record object in the main file. The algorithm is simple. I declare both a variable of the new type index (idx), and one of type record (x). After this is accomplished, I create an fstream variable for both the main file and the index file. In the case of the former, the access mode is read-only, so the designator is ios::in. The index needs write access, so ios::out is used. The name of each file is passed into build_index as a parameter.

The main part of the build_index() function is the loop defined by the for statement. This loop continues until it reaches the end of the main file by reading through each record entry in turn. Again I use the eof() member of fstream to signal this end. The first statement in the loop uses the tellg() member to put the current position of the file pointer into the position member of index. Then the read() member function makes the last name value available to be copied into the index object's key member. Finally, the index object is written out to the index file.

When an index exists for the file, I can construct a function that finds and displays specific objects on the file. This function is contained in Listing 10-5.

Listing 10-5. A function to find and display records: query().

```
void query(char* fname, char* iname, char* kvalue)
{
 fstream fr(fname, ios::in);
 fstream ir(iname, ios::in);
 record x;
 index idx;

 for(;;)  {
   ir.read((unsigned char*) &idx, sizeof(index));
   if(ir.eof())
     break;
   if(!strcmp(idx.key, kvalue))  {
     fr.seekg(idx.position);
     fr.read((unsigned char*) &x, sizeof(record));
     x.show();
     cout << endl;
     fr.close();
     ir.close();
     return;
   }
 }
```

continues

Listing 10-5. continued

```
cout << "Record Not Found\n";
fr.close();
ir.close();
}
```

The query() function requires three parameters: fname, iname, and kvalue. fname and iname contain the main and index file names respectively. kvalue is the character string value that is used as the search argument. As with the build_index() function, I start by creating two fstream objects: fr and ir. The former is associated with the main file, whereas the latter is associated with the index file. The constructor opens these files for read-only access. In addition, a record object (x) and an index object (idx) are declared.

The for statement defines a loop that continues until the function reaches the end of the index file. An if statement that tests the member function ir.eof() breaks out of the loop as soon as an attempt is made to read beyond the end of the file. The function will close both files before it returns to its calling environment.

Inside the loop, a call to ir.read() loads the idx object with the next index value from the index file. The strcmp() function from the standard library is used to compare kvalue to the index value idx.key. If these two values match, the idx.pos value is used in a call to the fstream member, fr.seekg(). This positions the pointer in the main file at the desired record value. A call to fr.read() fills x with that value. After the record object has been retrieved, x.show() displays the contents on the screen and the program can exit the loop and, ultimately, the function.

Another useful addition to the program is an *update function,* which enables the user to change some or all of the values in a particular record object and store the result back onto the file. There are a number of different possible designs for such a function. Listing 10-6 shows a simple solution.

Listing 10-6. A function to alter record values: update().

```
void update(char* fname, char* iname, char* keyvalue)
{
  fstream fr(fname, ios::in¦ios::out);
  fstream ir(iname, ios::in);
  record rec;
  index idx;

  for(;;)  {
    ir.read((unsigned char*) &idx, sizeof(index));
```

```
        if( ir.eof() )
          break;
        if(!strcmp(idx.key, keyvalue))  {
          fr.seekg(idx.position);
          fr.read((unsigned char*) &rec, sizeof(record));
          rec.show();
          cout << endl;
          cout << "1...First Name\n" << "2...Middle Name\n";
          cout << "3...Last Name\n" << "Change Which Item: ";
          int ans;
          char temp[80];

          cin >> ans;
          switch(ans)  {
            case 1 : cout << "New First Name: ";
                      cin >> temp;
                      rec.update(temp, 0, 0);
                      break;
            case 2 : cout << "New Middle Name: ";
                      cin >> temp;
                      rec.update(0, temp, 0);
                      break;
            case 3 : cout << "New Last Name: ";
                      cin >> temp;
                      rec.update(0, 0, temp);
                      break;
          }
          fr.seekp(idx.position);
          cout << "Altering Record...\n";
          rec.show();
          cout << "\n";
          fr.write((unsigned char*) &rec, sizeof(record));
          fr.close();
          if(ans == 3)
            build_index(fname, iname);
          return;
        }
    }

  fr.close();
  ir.close();
}
```

The update() function bears some resemblance to query(), which was defined earlier. In both cases, you need to search through the index and try to match a key value. The important differences between functions occur when a match is found. As in the case of query(), you need to create two file objects, as well as a record object and an index object. One important difference at this point is in the access mode specified for the main file: ios::in¦ios::out. This flag value opens the file for both read and write access.

The update() function reads through the index file until it either finds a match or reaches the end of the file. If no match is found, the files are closed and the function terminates. If a match is found, however, the value of the position member of the index object is used to position the pointer in the main file. It's necessary to read the old contents of the record so that the program can prompt the user for any changes that are needed. A call to the read() member of fstream object fr accomplishes the former, whereas the show() member of x takes care of the latter.

Changes entered by the user are first sent to x through the update() member. After this object has been changed and displayed to the user, the file pointer associated with fr is repositioned and the new record object replaces the existing one in the file.

Finally, the changes to the main() and menu() functions are shown in Listing 10-7. These changes reflect the addition of the new functions.

Listing 10-7. The main() and menu() functions that define a new file access program: filprog2.cpp.

```
void fill_file(char*);
void read_file(char*);
void build_index(char*,char*);
void query(char*, char*, char*);
void update(char*, char*, char*);
char menu();

main()
{
 char ch;
 char fname[80];
 char iname[80];
 char keyvalue[80];

 for( ; ; )
  switch((ch = menu()))  {
    case 'f': cout << "Write Data To File\n";
```

```
                cout << "File Name: ";
                cin >> fname;
                fill_file(fname);
                break;
    case 'r': cout << "Read Entire File\n";
                cout << "File Name: ";
                cin >> fname;
                read_file(fname);
                break;
    case 'b': cout << "Build Index File\n";
                cout << "File Name: ";
                cin >> fname;
                cout << "Index File Name: ";
                cin >> iname;
                build_index(fname, iname);
                break;
    case 'q': cout << "Query On Last Name\n";
                cout << "Enter File Name: ";
                cin >> fname;
                cout << "Enter Index File Name: ";
                cin >> iname;
                cout << "Last Name: ";
                cin >> keyvalue;
                query(fname, iname, keyvalue);
                break;
    case 'u': cout << "Update Record\n";
                cout << "File Name: ";
                cin >> fname;
                cout << "Index File Name: ";
                cin >> iname;
                cout << "Last Name: ";
                cin >> keyvalue;
                update(fname, iname, keyvalue);
                break;
    case 'h':
    case 'H': exit(0);
  }
}

char menu()
{
 char xh;
```

continues

Listing 10-7. continued

```
cout << "=======Menu======\n";
cout << "f(ill file)\n";
cout << "r(ead entire file)\n";
cout << "b(uild an index)\n";
cout << "q(uery by last name)\n";
cout << "u(pdate)\n";
cout << "h(alt program)\n";
cout << "==================\n";
cout << "Command: ";
cin >> xh;
return xh;
}
```

File Programming with Classes

The program that you studied previously was designed to show you how to use the fstream library with traditional programming problems. Certainly, creating a file access and management program is typical of that large class of software designs that make up a programmer's repertoire of techniques. These old-fashioned techniques are important to explore, particularly for the programmer who needs to integrate C++ into an existing system of C source code. You can accomplish the same task, however, in a way that takes greater advantage of the benefits offered by C++.

Instead of writing a file management program, you can create a file management class. You already have the basic algorithms and designs, but you need to repackage them in the form of a class. This method offers you the maximum flexibility for creating customized file programs.

You need to start with a data type that handles the information that you want to keep and enables you to access it on the file. Listing 10-8 contains the declaration of a record class along with the definitions of its member functions. The record class is similar to its namesake in the earlier examples, but some additional functionality has been added, including one new member function.

Listing 10-8. The definition of a class to hold name information: record.

```
#define SPA " "

#include <stdio.h>
#include <iostream.h>
```

```
#include <fstream.h>
#include <string.h>
#include <stdlib.h>

class record  {
    char first[80];
    char mid[80];
    char last[80];
public:
  record()
    { for ( int q = 0; q < 80; q++) first[q] = mid[q] = last[q] = 0; }
  int fill();
  void change(char*, char*, char*);
  char* show();
  char* show_last() { return last; }
};

void record::change(char* f, char* m, char* l)
{
  if(f)
    strcpy(first, f);
  if(m)
    strcpy(mid, m);
  if(l)
    strcpy(last, l);
}

int record::fill()
{
  cout << "\n\nEnter Name Information Below\n";
  cout << "First Name:  ";
  cin >> first;
  if(!strcmp(first, "stop"))
    return 0;
  cout << "Middle Name: ";
  cin >> mid;
  if(!strcmp(mid, "stop"))
    return 0;
  cout << "Last Name:  ";
  cin >> last;
  if(!strcmp(mid, "stop"))
    return 0;
```

continues

335

Listing 10-8. continued

```
  return 1;
}

char* record::show()
{
  char* temp = new char[250];

  strcpy(temp, first);
  strcat(temp, SPA);
  strcat(temp, mid);
  strcat(temp, SPA);
  strcat(temp, last);

  return temp;
}
```

As in the earlier record class, only a default constructor initializes the variable members to a null value. The change() and show_last() members also are unchanged from the earlier example.

The fill() function now has become a member of the class instead of being a stand-alone function in the program. This design change makes sense because it concentrates in the record class all the functions and tasks that pertain to this part of the design—an orthodox C++ style. The fill() member prompts the user for input and then stores that input in the appropriate variable member.

Although show() appears as a member in both versions of record, it takes on a new form in this design. Instead of being responsible for directly displaying the contents of the object, show() repackages the contents in the form of a character string and passes the string to the world outside the class. This involves the allocation of a new character string every time a call is made to the show() member function, requiring that the program outside of the class must take responsibility for deallocating this resource when the string is no longer used.

After you have defined the record class, turn your attention to the creation of a class that handles disk I/O transparently. This class is defined in Listing 10-9.

Listing 10-9. A file access class: db.

```
struct index  {
  char key[80];
  long position;
};
```

```
class db  {
  record x;
  char fname[80];
  char iname[80];

  int build_index();
  long search_index(char*);

public:
  db(char* m, char* i) { strcpy(fname, m); strcpy(iname, i); }
  int fill_file();
  int read_file();
  void query(char*);
  void update(char*);
};

int db::fill_file()
{
  fstream fd(fname, ios::out);
  if(fd.fail()|fd.bad())
    return 0;

  for(; x.fill() ;)
    fd.write((unsigned char*) &x, sizeof(record));

  fd.close();
  build_index();
  return 1;
}

int db::read_file()
{
  fstream fd(fname, ios::in);

  if(fd.fail()|fd.bad())
    return 0;

  for( ; ; )  {
    fd.read((unsigned char*) &x, sizeof(record));
    if(fd.eof())
      break;
    if(fd.fail()|fd.bad())
```

continues

Listing 10-9. continued

```
        return 0;
      cout << x.show() << endl;
    }
  fd.close();
  return 1;
}
```

The listing contains, first of all, the definition of a simple class (without any member) that I use later to create and access an index file. As before, there is a character string key field as well as a position member. The declaration of the main class, db, follows. Notice that a record object is an important member of the private part of this class. You have also fname and iname, both character strings, which hold the name of the main file and the name of the index file. These values are part of the class object definition.

The first two member functions also are in the private portion of the class: build_index() and search_index(). These are meant as auxiliary functions and are not part of the user interface. These functions are good candidates for eventual change and development—perhaps to a more efficient index structure. There is ample reason to keep them in the private section.

The defined class constructor sets both the file name and the index file name, which means that a particular db object always is associated with a specific pair of files. No member function is supplied that allows the alteration of the fname and iname members. A class destructor might be defined here to make sure that files are closed. Because this is a demonstration program, each function using a file takes care to call the fstream member close(). No destructor is supplied.

Basic file output is supplied by the member function fill_file(). This function is similar in operation to the function in the earlier example, but note that now it returns an integer value. This value is used to signal success or failure back to the calling environment. There are some other differences. Chief among these differences is the addition of error checking. A call to the fstream members fail() and bad() reassures you that the file has been opened successfully. If it has not, a value of 0 is returned through the member name. The for loop that controls the member function is itself controlled by calls to the fill() member of x, the record object, which returns a 0 value if the user enters stop instead of a valid value. Aside from these differences, fill_file() uses the same algorithm as the earlier example.

Similarly, read_file() repeats the design of the earlier read function. There are even fewer differences between this function and its predecessor than there are between the two versions of fill_file(). Error checking has been added (as with `fill_file()`), and the output of each instance of x has been altered to reflect the fact that the record member show() now returns a character string and does not display the value.

Neither `fill_file()` nor `read_file()` need the services of the index file that is also a part of the db class. Each deals directly with the file as a whole. The other two member functions in the public interface part of db, query() and update(), need to use the index file, however. Even `fill_file()` calls the `build_index()` member before returning to the function that called it. Listing 10-10 shows the construction of the `build_index()` member.

Listing 10-10. Creating an index file: `db::build_index()`.

```
int db::build_index()
{
  fstream fd(fname, ios::in);
  if(fd.fail()|fd.bad())
    return 0;
  fstream id(iname, ios::out);
  if(id.fail()|id.bad())  {
    fd.close();
    return 0;
   }
  index xrec;
  for ( int q = 0; q < 80; q++) xrec.key[q] = 0;
  for(;;)  {
    xrec.position = fd.tellg();
    fd.read((unsigned char*) &x, sizeof(record));
    if(fd.eof())
       break;
    strcpy(xrec.key, x.show_last());
    id.write((unsigned char*) &xrec, sizeof(index));
   }
  id.close();
  fd.close();
  return 1;
}
```

build_index() opens both the main file and an index file. The former is for read-only access, whereas the latter requires write access. The index class definition that I discussed previously is used to create an object that stores both the location of a record object on the file and the value of its last name member. Again some error checking has been added to an algorithm that is similar to the earlier example. As with `fill_file()` and `read_file()`, the return value of the function is used to indicate success or failure.

In the earlier example, each function that needed to use the index file contained its own search loop. Because I've moved the whole file access mechanism into a class, I can extract that search loop and make it a member function that can be shared by the other members. Listing 10-11 shows the code for this search.

Listing 10-11. Accessing the index file: `db::search_index()`.

```
long db::search_index(char* key_value)
{
  fstream id(iname, ios::in);
  if(id.fail()¦id.bad())
    return -1;

  index idx;

  for(;;)  {
   id.read((unsigned char*) &idx, sizeof(index));
   if(id.eof())
      break;
   if(!strcmp(key_value, idx.key)) {
      id.close();
      return idx.position;
    }
  }
  id.close();
  return -1;
}
```

The `search` member must return a `long` value to be compatible with the `seek` members that are defined in `fstream`. In this version, the search `key` value is passed into the function as a parameter. If the opening of the index file is successful, the function reads through the file and checks for a `key` value to match the last `name` member of some object. One of two outcomes is assured: A successful match is made or the end of the file is reached. In the latter case, a negative value—0 is a legitimate file position—is returned, just as is the case with a failed attempt to open the index file. If a match is found, the value from the `position` member of the `index` object is returned. Both `query()` and `update()` depend on `search_index()` to furnish a record position in the main file.

query() takes a last name as a parameter and uses it to find and display the other two names associated with its key value. Notice that a call to the search_index() is done first, and this value is tested to make sure that the value is found in the index. If no record matches the search argument, query() goes no further. It displays an error message and stops. Otherwise, it positions the file pointer, reads the full record, displays it, and then continues.

The update() member shares an important algorithm with query(): It, too, makes a call to search_index() before it opens any file. If the name that was passed in through key_value has a match in the index, the main file is opened, the file pointer is moved to the correct place, and the record object is retrieved from the file. After retrieval, the value is displayed. Note that the main file is opened for both read and write access, using ios::in¦ios::out.

After the record object is displayed to the user, however, a prompt for a possible change is made. Unlike the earlier update() function, this function enables the user to change everything in stages. The changes are written to the file only when the user chooses to take this step. The same pointer variable is used to position the file. This time, however, a call to the write() member is performed. These two member functions are illustrated in Listing 10-12.

Listing 10-12. Reading and updating individual records: db::query() and db::update().

```
void db::query(char* key_value)
{
  long pos = search_index(key_value);

  if(pos < 0)  {
    cout << "Record Not Found\n";
    return;
  }

  fstream fd(fname, ios::in);
  if(fd.fail()¦fd.bad())  {
    cout << "File Open Failure\n";
    return;
  }
  fd.seekg(pos);
  fd.read((unsigned char*) &x, sizeof(record));
  cout << x.show() << "\n";
  fd.close();
}
```

continues

Listing 10-12. continued

```
void db::update(char* key_value)
{
  long pos = search_index(key_value);

  if(pos < 0)  {
    cout << "Record Not Found\n";
    return;
   }

  fstream fd(fname, ios::in¦ios::out);
  if(fd.fail()¦fd.bad())  {
    cout << "File Open Failure\n";
    return;
   }

  fd.seekg(pos);
  fd.read((unsigned char*) &x, sizeof(record));
  cout << x.show() << endl;

  char f[80];
  char m[80];
  char l[80];
  int cmd = 0;
  int flag = 0;

  for(; cmd != 4 ;)  {
     cout << "Change Which Item\n";
     cout << "1........First Name\n";
     cout << "2........Middle Name\n";
     cout << "3........Last Name\n";
     cout << "4........Save Changes\n";
     cout << "Choice: ";
     cin >>cmd;
     switch(cmd)  {
       case 1 : cout << "\nNew First Name: ";
                cin >> f;
                x.change(f, 0, 0);
                break;
       case 2 : cout << "New Middle Name: ";
                cin >> m;
```

```
                    x.change(0, m, 0);
                    break;
          case 3 : cout << "New Last Name: ";
                    flag = 1;
                    cin >> l;
                    x.change(0, 0, l);
                    break;
        }
   }

  fd.seekp(pos);
  fd.write((unsigned char*) &x, sizeof(record));
  fd.close();
  if(flag)
    build_index();
}
```

To complete this example, Listing 10-13 contains a menu() function that
prompts a user for the various tasks that the db class can perform. Included in this
listing is a main() function that defines a program to test and experiment with this
class definition.

**Listing 10-13. A menu() and main() function
to illustrate the use of record and db: filprog2.cpp.**

```
char menu();

main()
{
 db rec("rbar.dat", "rbar.idx");
 char kname[80];

 for(;;)
   switch(menu())  {
     case 'f': cout << "Filling File With Data\n\n";
                if(rec.fill_file())
                  cout << "Successfully saved data\n";
                else
                  cout << "Data was not saved to disk\n";
                break;
```

continues

Listing 10-13. continued

```
        case 'r': cout << "Reading File\n\n";
                  if(!rec.read_file())
                    cout << "Problem reading the file\n";
                  break;
        case 'q': cout << "Query File\n\n";
                  cout << "Last Name: ";
                  cin >> kname;
                  rec.query(kname);
                  break;
        case 'u': cout << "Update Record\n\n";
                  cout << "Last Name: ";
                  cin >> kname;
                  rec.update(kname);
                  break;
        case 'h': exit(0);
    }

}

char menu()
{
  char ans;
  cout << "============MENU==========\n";
  cout << " f)ill file with data\n";
  cout << " r)ead entire file\n";
  cout << " q)uery on last name\n";
  cout << " u)pdate a record\n";
  cout << " h)alt the program\n";
  cout << "==========================\n";
  cout << "===> ";
  cin >> ans;
  return ans;
}
```

You can make many additional modifications to the preceding program. The menu() function and switch sections, for example, could be packaged in a class. The important point to note is that by wrapping the file access functions in a class, you gain maximal flexibility in program design, particularly when you're dealing with more than one file. This advantage is not new. Throughout this book, you've seen how encapsulation leads to better designs and more readable programs. It's important to see, however, that the object-oriented structure of C++ carries through even to the I/O library. The temptation is too great to see the I/O library as the same as the C library: a collection of compiled and unchangeable functions. This would be a mistake. Although the I/O library is supplied with the compiler, it is no less flexible than if you designed and coded it yourself. In the next section, you see this point driven home as I use the fstream class to derive more specialized I/O structures.

Using *fstream* as a Base Class

One of the defining characteristics of C++ is its capacity for inheritance, which is a necessary factor in C++'s object-oriented nature. Until this point, my examples of class derivation have described situations in which the designer has control over the source code for both the base class and the derived class. You know that this kind of control is not necessary to produce a derived class. All you need to create an inheritance relationship is the class declaration. Access to the function definition, except as a compiled library or object file, is not necessary.

Examples of defining derived classes without the control of the base class have been scarce. In this section, I show two example programs that supply an opportunity to derive a class from a preexisting one. I use the fstream class as a base and a modified form of the file access program from the previous section as the derived class. It may seem strange to modify a supplied library in this way. The object-oriented nature of C++, however, makes this modification as natural as any other programming task.

Listing 10-14 has a class, db, derived from an earlier example (Listing 10-8 through Listing 10-13). This simplified design has only two options: Fill the file with name information or display the name information already in the file. The record class and its functions are the same as they were in the earlier example. The menu() function and the switch statement in main() have been modified to reflect the fact that there are only two choices available to the user. The big difference, however, is that db is a derived class, and its base is fstream.

Listing 10-14. A program that uses fstream as a base class.

```
#define SPA " "

#include <stdio.h>
#include <iostream.h>
#include <fstream.h>
#include <string.h>
#include <stdlib.h>
```

continues

Listing 10-14. continued

```cpp
class record  {
    char first[80];
    char mid[80];
    char last[80];
public:
  record() { first[0] = mid[0] = last[0] = 0; }
  int fill();
  void change(char*, char*, char*);
  char* show();
  char* show_last() { return last; }
};
void record::change(char* f, char* m, char* l)
{
  if(f)
    strcpy(first, f);
  if(m)
    strcpy(mid, m);
  if(l)
    strcpy(last, l);
}

int record::fill()
{
  cout << "\n\nEnter Name Information Below\n";
  cout << "First Name:  ";
  cin >> first;
  if(!strcmp(first, "stop"))
    return 0;
  cout << "Middle Name: ";
  cin >> mid;
  if(!strcmp(mid, "stop"))
    return 0;
  cout << "Last Name:  ";
  cin >> last;
  if(!strcmp(mid, "stop"))
    return 0;
  return 1;
}
```

```
char* record::show()
{
  char* temp = new char[250];

  strcpy(temp, first);
  strcat(temp, SPA);
  strcat(temp, mid);
  strcat(temp, SPA);
  strcat(temp, last);

  return temp;
}


class db : private fstream {
  record x;
  char fname[80];


public:
  db(char* m) { strcpy(fname, m); }
  int fill_file();
  int read_file();
};

int db::fill_file()
{
  open(fname, ios::out);
  if(fail()¦bad())
    return 0;

  for(; x.fill() ;)
    write((unsigned char*) &x, sizeof(record));

  close();
  return 1;
}
```

continues

Listing 10-14. continued

```
int db::read_file()
{
  open(fname, ios::in);

  if(fail()|bad())
    return 0;

  for(; ; )  {
    read((unsigned char*) &x, sizeof(record));
    if(eof())
       break;
    cout << x.show() << endl;
   }
  close();
  return 1;
}

char menu();

main()
{
 db rec("pbar.dat");

 for(;;)
   switch(menu())  {
     case 'f': cout << "Filling File With Data\n\n";
               if(rec.fill_file())
                 cout << "Successfully saved data\n";
               else
                 cout << "Data was not saved to disk\n";
               break;
     case 'r': cout << "Reading File\n\n";
               if(!rec.read_file())
                 cout << "Problem reading the file\n";
               break;
     case 'h': exit(0);
   }

}
```

```
char menu()
{
  char ans;
  cout << "=============MENU===========\n";
  cout << " f)ill file with data\n";
  cout << " r)ead entire file\n";
  cout << " h)alt the program\n";
  cout << "===========================\n";
  cout << "===> ";
  cin >> ans;
  return ans;
}
```

The db class is declared with fstream as a private base class, which makes sense because the derived class supplies access to the files through fill_file() and read_file(). You do not need to make the fstream member functions members of db. Low-level access like read() and write() is handled transparently by the program using this class.

As a result of being derived, a db object is also a file object. This is in contrast to the earlier example, in which each time an access was made, an entirely new object was created. The constructor supplies the name of the file that is to be accessed and copies it into a private variable member. Note that the constructor does not send the file name to the fstream part of the class. Instead, this part of the class is created using the default constructor, which creates db as an unassigned file object. It is necessary to use the open() member before any actual access can take place.

The differences created by deriving the class from fstream are visible in the fill_file() member. open() is used to attach the db object to a specific disk file. A call to close() breaks this connection. Similarly, write() sends the values out to the file. In each case, the function is not a member of an independent object, but is a member function of the calling object. The same thing is true of the read_file() member function. open(), close(), and read() are accessed directly and not through an intermediary object.

The program described in Listing 10-15 builds on the last example. This example puts back the index file mechanism, but within the context of a db class that is derived from fstream. Besides defining an index record, the member functions build_index(), search_index(), query(), and update() have become part of the class.

Listing 10-15. A file program with query() and update(): filprog3.cpp.

```
#define SPA " "

#include <stdio.h>
#include <iostream.h>
#include <fstream.h>
#include <string.h>
#include <stdlib.h>

struct index  {
  char key[80];
  long position;
};


class record  {
    char first[80];
    char mid[80];
    char last[80];
public:
  record() { first[0] = mid[0] = last[0] = 0; }
  record(char* f, char* m, char* l)  { change(f, m, l); }
  int fill();
  void change(char*, char*, char*);
  char* show();
  char* show_last() { return last; }
};

void record::change(char* f, char* m, char* l)
{
  if(f)
    strcpy(first, f);
  if(m)
    strcpy(mid, m);
  if(l)
    strcpy(last, l);
}

int record::fill()
{
```

```
    cout << "\n\nEnter Name Information Below\n";
    cout << "First Name:   ";
    cin >> first;
    if(!strcmp(first, "stop"))
      return 0;
    cout << "Middle Name: ";
    cin >> mid;
    if(!strcmp(mid, "stop"))
      return 0;
    cout << "Last Name:   ";
    cin >> last;
    if(!strcmp(mid, "stop"))
      return 0;
    return 1;
}

char* record::show()
{
  char* temp = new char[250];

  strcpy(temp, first);
  strcat(temp, SPA);
  strcat(temp, mid);
  strcat(temp, SPA);
  strcat(temp, last);

  return temp;
}

class db : private fstream {
  record x;
  char fname[80];
  char iname[80];

  int build_index();
  long search_index(char*);

public:
  db(char* m, char* i) { strcpy(fname, m); strcpy(iname, i); }
  int fill_file();
  int read_file();
  void query(char*);
```

continues

Listing 10-15. continued

```
  void update(char*);
};

int db::build_index()
{
  open(fname, ios::in);
  if(fail()¦bad())
    return 0;
  fstream id(iname, ios::out);
  if(id.fail()¦id.bad())  {
    close();
    return 0;
   }
  index xrec;
  for(intq = 0; q < 80; q++) xrec.key[q] = 0;
  for(;;)  {
    xrec.position = tellg();
    read((unsigned char*) &x, sizeof(record));
    if(eof())
       break;
    strcpy(xrec.key, x.show_last());
    id.write((unsigned char*) &xrec, sizeof(index));
   }
  id.close();
  close();
  return 1;
}

long db::search_index(char* key_value)
{
  open(iname, ios::in);
  if(fail()¦bad())
    return -1;

  index idx;

  for(;;)  {
   read((unsigned char*) &idx, sizeof(index));
   if(eof())
      break;
```

```
   if(!strcmp(key_value, idx.key)) {
      close();
      return idx.position;
   }
 }
 close();
 return -1;
}

int db::fill_file()
{
 open(fname, ios::out);
 if(fail()|bad())
   return 0;

 for(; x.fill() ;)
   write((unsigned char*) &x, sizeof(record));

 close();
 build_index();
 return 1;
}

int db::read_file()
{
 open(fname, ios::in);

 if(fail()|bad())
   return 0;

 for(;;) {
   read((unsigned char*) &x, sizeof(record));
   if(eof())
      break;
   cout << x.show() << endl;
  }
 close();
 return 1;
}

void db::query(char* key_value)
{
```

continues

Listing 10-15. continued

```
  long pos = search_index(key_value);

  if(pos < 0) {
    cout << "Record Not Found\n";
    return;
   }

  open(fname, ios::in);
  if(fail()|bad())  {
    cout << "File Open Failure\n";
    return;
   }
  seekg(pos);
  read((unsigned char*) &x, sizeof(record));
  cout << x.show() << "\n";
  close();
}

void db::update(char* key_value)
{
  long pos = search_index(key_value);

  if(pos < 0) {
    cout << "Record Not Found\n";
    return;
   }

  open(fname, ios::in|ios::out);
  if(fail()|bad())  {
    cout << "File Open Failure\n";
    return;
   }

  seekg(pos);
  read((unsigned char*) &x, sizeof(record));
  cout << x.show() << endl;

  char f[80];
  char m[80];
  char l[80];
```

```
    int cmd = 0;
    int flag = 0;

    for(; cmd != 4 ;)  {
        cout << "Change Which Item\n";
        cout << "1........First Name\n";
        cout << "2........Middle Name\n";
        cout << "3........Last Name\n";
        cout << "4........Save Changes\n";
        cout << "Choice: ";
        cin >>cmd;
        switch(cmd)  {
          case 1 : cout << "New First Name: ";
                   cin >> f;
                   x.change(f, 0, 0);
                   break;
          case 2 : cout << "New Middle Name: ";
                   cin >> m;
                   x.change(0, m, 0);
                   break;
          case 3 : cout << "New Last Name: ";
                   flag = 1;
                   cin >> l;
                   x.change(0, 0, l);
                   break;
        }
    }

    seekp(pos);
    write((unsigned char*) &x, sizeof(record));
    close();
    if(flag)
      build_index();
}

char menu();

main()
{
 db rec("rbar.dat", "rbar.idx");
 char kname[80];
```

continues

Listing 10-15. continued

```
for(;;)
  switch(menu())  {
    case 'f': cout << "Filling File With Data\n\n";
              if(rec.fill_file())
                cout << "Successfully saved data\n";
              else
                cout << "Data was not saved to disk\n";
              break;
    case 'r': cout << "Reading File\n\n";
              if(!rec.read_file())
                cout << "Problem reading the file\n";
              break;
    case 'q': cout << "Query File\n\n";
              cout << "Last Name: ";
              cin >> kname;
              rec.query(kname);
              break;
    case 'u': cout << "Update Record\n\n";
              cout << "Last Name: ";
              cin >> kname;
              rec.update(kname);
              break;
    case 'h': exit(0);
  }

}

char menu()
{
  char ans;
  cout << "============MENU==========\n";
  cout << " f)ill file with data\n";
  cout << " r)ead entire file\n";
  cout << " q)uery on last name\n";
  cout << " u)pdate a record\n";
  cout << " h)alt the program\n";
  cout << "==========================\n";
  cout << "===> ";
  cin >> ans;
  return ans;
}
```

The `fill_file()` and `read_file()` functions are the same as in Listing 10-14. `query()` and `update()` are similar to their namesake member functions in filprog2.cpp (Listing 10-9 through Listing 10-13). The difference is that they make direct use of the `fstream` member functions and do not create a separate file object. `build_index()` and `search_index()`, however, offer some interesting insights into the new design structure.

The `build_index()` member offers a special problem for the designer. It requires that two files, the main file and the index, be open at the same time. The problem is that the `db` object is associated with only one file at a time. You can open the main file by direct application of the `fstream` members. You can open the index file this way, also. Remember that the file object is unattached until you execute an `open()`. You cannot open both files simultaneously. The solution is to import a second file object. In this case, the declaration

```
fstream id(iname, ios::out);
```

serves to attach the index file to the `fstream` object `id`. The `db` object itself is associated with the main file. The index file has its own identifying object independent of the class.

In `search_index()` there is no problem of double file reference because only one file, the index, is open. The `db` object is attached to the index file using the `open()` member. When the function is finished, the `close()` member makes `db` available for attachment to the main file. Note that the `query()` member does not open the main file until the call to `search_index()` has been completed.

The programs described in this section and the previous section are not meant as complete solutions to the problems they address. They all lack sophistication, and certainly require more error checking and exception handling. They are offered, rather, to illustrate the `fstream` class and how it can be used in conjunction with the rest of C++ to design programs that access files. The best thing to do with these examples is to experiment with them. Changing them, compiling them, and noting the differences will help you to understand the underlying structure of the `iostream` library.

The Standard I/O Functions and the *iostream* Library

This chapter should not give you the impression that the `iostream` library is meant to replace the carefully developed (and debugged) set of input and output functions in the C library. These functions are available in C++. When mixing these functions with the iostream library, you should take care not to produce code that is obscure or difficult to read. One solution might be to build a class around a function like scanf() to hide its details from the rest of the program. This method would make for a cleaner design.

The stream data type was developed to solve a particular problem: basic program I/O. Because the emphasis is on convenience and modularity, complex data input requirements or sophisticated output designs might not be possible using this library alone. For the large group of programs that require only simple input and output from keyboard to screen, however, stream objects offer a safe and convenient tool for rapid software development.

Using the *iostream* Library with User-Defined Data Types

The programmer can tap the full power of the iostream library not only for built-in data types, such as integers and real numbers, but also for classes that are defined within programs. The same convenience and concise notation can be shared by user-defined types. You can use cout and cin and the operators << and >> with these types as you would use them for more ordinary output.

The advantage of using a consistent I/O scheme is clear: It makes the basic algorithm obvious, particularly to someone reading the program code for the first time. Using I/O functions is often a complicated procedure. Frequently, these operations are unique to a specific implementation or are tied to some operating system or hardware peculiarity. Even in the absence of these kinds of problems, programs filled with specialized I/O function calls tend to be convoluted and confusing. The iostream library—true to the philosophy of C++—enables a programmer to hide these details within a standard interface.

As the program designer, you face only one issue: The examination of the new data type to decide what constitutes an appropriate I/O format for it. After you make this decision, you need only to write the code that implements this format. Because both the output operator (<<) and the input operator (>>) are overloaded functions, your code becomes simply another version of these functions. Thus, you don't need to alter anything in the iostream library itself. Your new function merely adds an alternate interface to the stream.

Redefining *ostream*

To create an output function for a new class, you must redefine the function

```
ostream& operator<<(ostream&, class)
```

to create the desired output for the new class. In this syntax, *class* represents a class declaration. You can accomplish this redefinition in one of two ways.

The simplest situation occurs when a class already has an output function. The dateout.cpp program (Listing 10-16) illustrates this case with a julian date class. In this example, the new << operator function merely calls the existing output function.

Listing 10-16. A date class that uses the << output operator: dateout.cpp.

```cpp
#include <iostream.h>
#include <string.h>
#include <stdio.h>

const int months[]={0,31,59,90,120,151,181,212,243,273,304,334,365};

const char* mnames[]={"","January","February","March",
                      "April", "May","June","July",
                      "August","September","October",
                      "November","December"};

class julian  {
   int days;
public:
   julian(int =0,int =0);
   char *current_date();
};

*julian::julian(int mon,int day)
{
 days=
      (mon < 1 || mon > 12) ? 0 : (mon == 1) ? day : months[mon-1]+day;
}

char* julian::current_date()
{
```

continues

Listing 10-16. continued

```
int mn;
int dy;
int i;

if(days <= 31)  {
    mn=1;
    dy=days;
 }
else
    for( i = 2 ; i <= 12 ; i++)
        if(days <= months[i])  {
            mn = i;
            dy = days - months[i-1];
            break;
        }

  char *buffer = new char[20];

  sprintf(buffer,"%s %d",mnames[mn],dy);

  return buffer;
}

ostream& operator<<(ostream& op,julian x)
{

 return op << x.current_date();

}

main()
{

 julian today(6, 17);

 cout << today;
}
```

This example uses a simplified julian class. Its constructor initializes a variable declared to be of type julian. The date is stored as the number of days since the first of January (for the sake of simplicity, the program does not recognize leap years). The output member function current_date() returns the current value of an object of the class. This value is put into a character string in the form *month day*.

Although the member function current_date() can produce output by itself, you can call it also with an ostream operator function. The function

```
ostream& operator(ostream& op,julian x)
```

redefines the output operator so that output is available directly through cout. Instead of using this format

```
julian x(1,2);
```

```
cout << x.current_date();
```

you now can use this version

```
cout << x;
```

which maintains the consistency of the interface created by the stream library. The reference type is used here because the operator function must pass the stream down the line to other operators. This mechanism allows more than one value to be output in a single operation.

The operator<<() function calls the current_date() member to retrieve a converted form of the value stored in the days member of the class. The value is retrieved as a character string, which in turn is sent back to the stream through the return statement. The main() function is a simple driver that illustrates the use of these new operators.

Listing 10-16 suffers from a lack of adequate error checking. It does illustrate, however, the techniques required for adding user-defined types to the stream interface.

The Direct Input of User-Defined Types

Just as you can redefine the stream output operators to handle newly created class types, you also can customize input. The techniques are similar. For example, the function

```
istream& operator>>(istream&,class&)
```

has a reference variable to a user-defined class and the appropriate code to convert normal keyboard input into the values necessary for that class. The reference variable lets a function return a parameter value by setting up a call by reference situation. As with the ostream, this operator function can either stand alone or be a friend of the new class. The datein.cpp program (Listing 10-17) illustrates the latter case.

Listing 10-17. A date class that uses the >> input operator: datein.cpp.

```cpp
#include <iostream.h>
#include <string.h>
#include <stdio.h>
#include <stdlib.h>

const int months[]={0,31,56,90,120,151,181,212,243,273,304,334,365};

const char* mnames[]={"","January","February","March",
                      "April", "May","June","July",
                      "August","September","October",
                      "November","December"};

class julian  {
  int days;

public:
  julian(int =0,int =0);

  void new_date(char*);

  char *current_date();
};



julian::julian(int mon,int day)
{
 days=
    (mon < 1 || mon > 12) ? 0 : (mon == 1) ? day : months[mon-1]+day;
}

void julian::new_date(char* rdate)
{
 char* mon;
 char* dy;
```

```
    mon=strtok(rdate," ");
    dy=strtok(0," ");

    for(int i=1 ; i <= 12 ; i++)
        if(!strcmp(mnames[i],mon))
          break;

    if(i > 12)
        days=0;
     else if(i == 1)
         days=atoi(dy);
     else
        days=months[i-1]+atoi(dy);
}

char* julian::current_date()
{
 int mn;
 int dy;
 int i;

 if(days<=31)  {
     mn=1;
     dy=days;
  }
 else
     for( i = 2 ; i <= 12 ; i++)
       if(days<=months[i])  {
             mn=i;
             dy=days-months[i-1];
             break;
         }

  char *buffer = new char[20];

  sprintf(buffer,"%s %d",mnames[mn],dy);

  return buffer;
}

ostream& operator<<(ostream& op,julian x)
{
```

continues

Listing 10-17. continued

```
return op << x.current_date();

}

istream& operator>>(istream& ip,julian& x)
{

 char *temp = new char[20];

 ip.get(temp,20);

 x.new_date(temp);

 delete temp;

 return ip;
}

main()
{
 julian today(1,31);

 cout << today << "\n";

 cout << "enter new date: ";

 cin >> today;

 cout << today << "\n";
}
```

Listing 10-17 requires a member function that is capable of changing the value in the data portion of the class, because the operator>>() function is defined outside of the class. This member function is called new_date(). It accepts a character string of the form *month day* and converts it to the Julian date required as the days value. The operator>>() function receives keyboard input from the stream ip through the get() function. (Recall that this member of istream permits the entry of a character string that includes embedded blank spaces and that the >> operator accepts input only to the first white-space character.) The date format includes a space between the name of the month and the day of the month. Keyboard input is stored in the variable temp, which the program deletes after the change is made. Note that the stream ip must be returned to maintain the consistency of the operator. If you cascade the input operator >> as follows:

```
cin >> x >> y;
```

the return statement guarantees that the chain is not broken.

To parse the parameter string, new_date() first strips off the month number by using the standard library function strtok(). (The month value is the first part of rdate and is separated from the rest of the string by a space.) The program then uses strcmp() to compare each cell in the constant array mnames to the string mon. When it finds a match, the number of the index represents the number of the month. This value is then used with the integer array, months, to extract the Julian date at the beginning of the previous month. The program then adds this value to the day of the month. The calculation yields the Julian date.

Working with *fstream* Objects

So far in this chapter, I've discussed the iostream and the fstream as independent topics. A casual reading of this matter might even lead the naive reader to assume that these are totally independent systems for accessing the two important parts of the I/O subsystem. In C, for example, one set of functions controls the screen and keyboard I/O (in general terms, stdin and stdout), whereas a completely different set is responsible for disk file manipulation. For formatted I/O, printf() and scanf() are used in the former case, whereas fprintf() and fscanf() are necessary when dealing with a file. But you have seen already that this is not the case. In fact, the fstream class is derived in part from the same two classes that are used with the standard I/O: istream and ostream. Anything from these classes that applies to cin and cout applies also to any fstream object.

One of the important design goals of the C++ iostream library is to break down even further any distinction between I/O systems. The idea is to create a common set of objects to handle any kind of interaction with the outside world. This has already been shown to you in the fact that, on one hand, the iostream library can be reconfigured to directly output user-defined types. The same << and >> operators that work for int and double work also for classes. You have seen that fstream objects also use these operators. There is a fundamental symmetry between all classes of I/O.

When you are successful in reconfiguring the basic I/O operators to work directly with a class definition, you can use this new capability also with `fstream` class objects. In other words, if you can write this:

```
new_class x;
cin >> x;
cout << x;
```

you can write this:

```
new_class x;
fstream fd;
cin >> x;
fd << x;
```

Additional capability is given to the operators in the `istream` and `ostream` classes, which are base classes for both standard I/O objects and the file type. Listing 10-18 illustrates the use of these overloaded operators.

Listing 10-18. Using << and >> with disk files: filprog4.cpp.

```
#define SPA " "

#include <stdlib.h>
#include <iostream.h>
#include <fstream.h>
#include <string.h>
#include <sysent.h>

class record  {
    char first[80];
    char mid[80];
    char last[80];
public:
  record() { first[0] = mid[0] = last[0] = 0; }
  record(char* f, char* m, char* l)  { change(f, m, l); }
  int fill();
  void change(char*, char*, char*);
  char* show();
  char* show_last() { return last; }
};

void record::change(char* f, char* m, char* l)
{
```

```
  if(f)
    strcpy(first, f);
  if(m)
    strcpy(mid, m);
  if(l)
    strcpy(last, l);
}

int record::fill()
{
  cout << "\n\nEnter Name Information Below\n";
  cout << "First Name:  ";
  cin >> first;
  if(!strcmp(first, "stop"))
    return 0;
  cout << "Middle Name: ";
  cin >> mid;
  if(!strcmp(mid, "stop"))
    return 0;
  cout << "Last Name:  ";
  cin >> last;
  if(!strcmp(mid, "stop"))
    return 0;
  return 1;
}

char* record::show()
{
  char* temp = new char[250];

  strcpy(temp, first);
  strcat(temp, SPA);
  strcat(temp, mid);
  strcat(temp, SPA);
  strcat(temp, last);

  return temp;
}



ostream& operator << (ostream& op, record r)
```

continues

Listing 10-18. continued

```
{
  return op.write((unsigned char*) &r, sizeof(record));
}



istream& operator >> (istream& ip, record* r)
{
  ip.read((unsigned char*) r, sizeof(record));
  return ip;
}



class db  {
  record x;
  char fname[80];

public:
  db(char* m) { strcpy(fname, m); }
  int fill_file();
  int read_file();
};



int db::fill_file()
{
  fstream fd(fname, ios::out);
  if(fd.fail()¦fd.bad())
    return 0;

  for(; x.fill() ;)
    fd << x;

  fd.close();
  return 1;
}

int db::read_file()
{
  fstream fd(fname, ios::in);
```

```
    if(fd.fail()¦fd.bad())
      return 0;

  for(; ; )  {
    fd >> &x;
    if(fd.eof())
        break;
    if(fd.fail()¦fd.bad())
      return 0;
    cout << x.show() << endl;
   }
  fd.close();
  return 1;
}


char menu();

main()
{
 db rec("qbar.dat");

 for(;;)
   switch(menu())  {
     case 'f': cout << "Filling File With Data\n\n";
               if(rec.fill_file())
                 cout << "Successfully saved data\n";
               else
                 cout << "Data was not saved to disk\n";
               break;
     case 'r': cout << "Reading File\n\n";
               if(!rec.read_file())
                 cout << "Problem reading the file\n";
               break;
     case 'h': exit(0);
   }

}

char menu()
{
  char ans;
  cout << "============MENU==========\n";
```

continues

Listing 10-18. continued

```
cout << " f)ill file with data\n";
cout << " r)ead entire file\n";
cout << " h)alt the program\n";
cout << "============================\n";
cout << "===> ";
cin >> ans;
return ans;
}
```

The filprog4.cpp program is another variation on an earlier class. It fills or reads through a disk file. The difference here is in the fact that I have overloaded the << and >> operators so that they can produce direct file output of the record class. The fill_file() and read_file() members are the same as in the earlier example, with the exception that they use these I/O operators to send the information to the file.

In the earlier examples in this section, I have redefined the ostream operator << to perform direct output of a class object. I do the same thing here.

```
ostream& operator << (ostream& op, record r)
{
  return op.write((unsigned char*) &r, sizeof(record));
}
```

The preceding code causes this operator to call a write() member whenever it is used with a record object. Similarly,

```
istream& operator >> (istream& ip, record* r)
{
  ip.read((unsigned char*) r, sizeof(record));
  return ip;
}
```

executes a read() member within this context. After these two overloaded definitions have been executed, you can use these operator symbols with a file object for direct output to the disk, which I did in fill_file() and read_file(). In a context like this, in which an entire object is being put into a file, the simplicity offered by the use of operators is compelling.

Summary

This chapter explored the operation of the iostream library, a standard C++ library of classes and associated functions that can be used to generate simple input and output. The iostream library was devised as an adjunct to those functions common to C and C++, such as printf(), scanf(), and, more importantly, file manipulation routines.

In the realm of simple I/O, the iostream library offers substantial advantages.

- The functions are less general and more specific. Thus, they produce smaller, more efficient program code.

- The syntax is more straightforward, particularly with its use of overloaded operators.

- A more controlled and consistent interface model unifies both device file and disk file operations.

Nearly every function found in the traditional C library has a counterpart in the iostream library, including

- Character, integer, and real number input

- Character and character string I/O

- A basic set of formatting and manipulation capabilities

In addition to these basic I/O functions, C++ has a full set of disk file manipulation members, which are found in the fstream class. They include

- tellp() and seekp() to position the write pointer

- tellg() and seekg() to position the read pointer

- read() and write()

You've seen also how these members can be used in combination with user-defined classes to provide access to the file system.

The benefits of the iostream library can be extended also to user-defined classes by redefining the ostream& operator<<() and istream& operator>>() functions. This redefinition includes file access through the fstream class.

11

Object-Oriented Programming and Reusability

Object-Oriented Programming and Reusability

You've seen what you can do in C++, and what is difficult or perhaps impossible to do. You've explored the syntax and even covered some of the dangerous (yet undeniably useful) features of the language, such as operator overloading and friend functions. This final, summary chapter explores the issues of C++ and the process of software design.

The Idea of Generic Building Blocks

Two related threads run through C++. One is the obvious support C++ gives to the techniques of object-oriented design. These techniques represent a new way of approaching the creation of software systems. Underlying them, however, is the old notion of modularity and the reusability of software. The issue of reusability goes back almost to the first days of programming. Object-oriented technique is the latest and most successful implementation of this venerable theory.

The important consideration when you are designing for reusability is to create something that can be used easily in more than one program. Following this standard often means extra initial effort and a more complicated algorithm. If your program needs a function that squares or cubes numbers, you could create the function to perform the task that the program needs. With extra effort, you could create a function that could raise any number to any power. You could save such a general-purpose tool and use it on a variety of occasions.

The advantages of reusability are obvious. If you can draw on a library of resources that already have been designed and debugged, the design of subsequent programs goes not only faster, but also more smoothly. If a component has been written and debugged properly, new software does not need to take this code into consideration during the debugging phase.

One important difficulty with creating fully reusable code is in implementing a general-purpose design that works identically in all contexts—even those not anticipated at the time of design. This difficulty is particularly severe if the design vehicle is a function that must be placed within the context of a program. In contrast, the C++ class object is an ideal vehicle for implementing this kind of reusability because it is self-contained.

Objects and Reusability

The C++ class creates an autonomous object—one that is complete in itself. If properly designed, it has a well-behaved interface defined in a public section, and all its details of internal implementation are hidden in a private (or protected) section. Because communication is done exclusively through the public sections, the class is more robust in the face of changes in programming context, especially those that were not anticipated at the time the class was designed.

Recall how a C++ program is constructed. Classes are defined, class objects are created, and connections between classes are established. Most of the work of the program is done inside the class. In contrast, a traditional stand-alone function must be imbedded in code that arranges to send variables and other values into it and handles values that are returned. A finished and debugged class does a substantial amount of the work within a program. A function, even a debugged one, contributes only a small part to the overall design. The class doesn't require the extra connecting code that a function requires; instead, it contains its own methods internally.

You can harness the power inherent in the reusability of the object-oriented technique to design new classes as well as new programs. The capability of inheritance greatly simplifies this process and guarantees that you easily can add to the list of resources. You can pluck a generic class from the pool of existing classes, and add specialized characteristics through the process of creating a derived class. The derived class then becomes a new resource to be used.

Inheritance is a process that enhances the reusability of class components. It adds an even more powerful tool for building "off-the-shelf" software. Sometimes inheritance allows you not to bother with interacting classes, and instead restrict yourself to a single specialized class.

Reusability as a Design Tool

Consider a practical example of reusing class definitions. Listing 11-1 contains a class that implements a linked list. The algorithm is similar to the linked list classes that I created earlier in the book. Included in this listing is a main() function that defines a small driver program.

Listing 11-1. A linked list class object: llist.cpp.

```cpp
#include <iostream.h>
#include <string.h>
#include <stdlib.h>

class node  {
  void* info;
  node* next;
public:
  node(void* v)  {info = v; next = 0; }
  void put_next(node* n) { next = n; }
  node* get_next()  { return next; }
  void* get_info()  { return info; }
};

class list  {
  node* head;
  int node_num;
```

continues

Listing 11-1. continued

```
public:
  list()  { node_num = 0; head = 0; }

  void  remove(int);
  void  insert(void*, int);
  void  append(void* v)  { insert(v, node_num + 1); }
  void* find(int);
  void  display();
};

void list::remove(int pos)
{
 node *prev, *cursor = head;
 if(pos == 1)  {
     head = cursor->get_next();
     delete cursor;
  }
 else  {
   for(int i = 1 ; i < pos ; i++)  {
     prev = cursor;
       cursor = cursor->get_next();
      }

     prev->put_next(cursor->get_next());
     delete cursor;
     node_num--;
 }
}

void list::insert(void* val, int pos)
{
 node *prev, *cursor = head,
      *temp = new node(val);

 if(!head)
   head = temp;
 else if( pos == 0) {
     temp->put_next(head);
     head = temp;
  }
```

```
else  {
    for(int i = 1 ; (i < pos) && cursor->get_next() ; i++)  {
      prev = cursor;
      cursor = cursor->get_next();
     }

    if(!cursor->get_next())
      cursor->put_next(temp);
    else  {
      temp->put_next(cursor);
      prev->put_next(temp);
     }
  }
 node_num++;
}

void* list::find(int pos)
{
 if(!head)
   return 0;

 node* cursor = head;

 for(int i = 0 ; i < pos ; i++)
    cursor = cursor->get_next();

 if(cursor)
    return cursor->get_info();
 return 0;
}

void list::display()
{
 void* temp;

 for(int i = 0 ; ; i++)  {
   if(!(temp = find(i)))
     break;
     cout << "*" << (char*)temp << "\n";
  }
}
```

continues

Listing 11-1. continued

```
main()
{
 list x;

 x.insert("Tom", 0);
 x.insert("Dick",1);
 x.insert("Harry",2);

 x.display();
}
```

The list class as just defined becomes your software resource. You can use it whenever you need to include linked list functionality in a new class or a new program. For example, you can build a stack using list. This data type (illustrated in Figure 11-1) is an important component of many software designs. A stack allows input and output at only one end. Stacks often are described as Last-In, First-Out (LIFO) data structures.

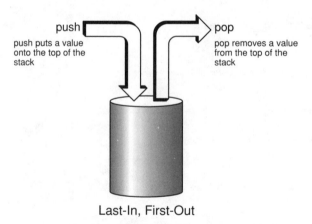

push — push puts a value onto the top of the stack

pop — pop removes a value from the top of the stack

Last-In, First-Out

Figure 11-1. The stack data type.

In Listing 11-2, the list is used as a base class to derive a stack data type (in this listing, and subsequent listings, I've left just the declarations associated with the list class as an easy reference). As with the earlier example, a main() function has been included to demonstrate how the new class can be used.

Listing 11-2. A derived class based on the list class in llist.cpp.

```
                        a stack:   vstack.cpp

#include <iostream.h>
#include <string.h>
#include <stdlib.h>

class node  {
  void* info;
  node* next;
public:
  node(void* v)   {info = v; next = 0; }
  void put_next(node* n) { next = n; }
  node* get_next()  { return next; }
  void* get_info()  { return info; }
};

class list  {
  node* head;
  int node_num;

public:
  list()  { node_num = 0; head = 0; }

  void  remove(int);
  void  insert(void*, int);
  void  append(void* v)  { insert(v, node_num + 1); }
  void* find(int);
  void  display();
};

class stack : private list  {
  int top;

public:
  stack()  { cout << "Building a stack object...\n"; top = -1; }
  void display();
  void push(double);
  double pop();
};
```

continues

Listing 11-2. continued

```
void stack::display()
{
 void* temp;

 for(int i = 0 ; ; i++)  {
   if(!(temp = find(i)))
      break;
  }
}

void stack::push(double x)
{
 double* ptr = new double;
 *ptr = x;

 top++;
 append((void*)ptr);
}

double stack::pop()
{
 void* temp = find(top);
 remove(top+1);
 top--;
 return *((double*)temp);
}

main()
{
 stack x;

 cout << "============================\n";
 x.push(3.2);
 x.push(6.4);
 x.push(12.8);
 x.display();
 cout << "============================\n";
 cout << "q = " << x.pop() << "\n";
 cout << "============================\n";
```

```
  x.display();
  cout << "============================\n";
  cout << "q = " << x.pop() << "\n";
  cout << "============================\n";
}
```

You can use a linked list to create a queue in the same way you defined a stack. A queue is a data type that allows values to enter at one end and to be taken out at the opposite end. It can be described as a First-In, First-Out data structure (FIFO). The queue is illustrated in Figure 11-2.

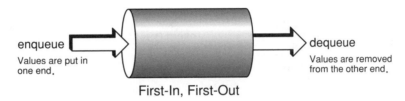

enqueue

Values are put in
one end.

dequeue

Values are removed
from the other end.

First-In, First-Out

Figure 11-2. A queue.

In Listing 11-3, I use the same `list` class to derive a class that implements a queue data type. No changes have been made to `list` to accomplish this new definition. Again, I include a `main()` function to illustrate the use of objects of this type.

Listing 11-3. A new class derived from the earlier `list` class that implements a queue: queue.cpp.

```
#include <iostream.h>
#include <string.h>
#include <stdlib.h>

class node  {
  void* info;
  node* next;
public:
  node(void* v)  {info = v; next = 0; }
  void put_next(node* n) { next = n; }
  node* get_next()  { return next; }
```

continues

Listing 11-3. continued

```
   void* get_info()  { return info; }
};

class list  {
  node* head;
  int node_num;

public:
  list()  { node_num = 0; head = 0; }

  void  remove(int);
  void  insert(void*, int);
  void  append(void* v)  { insert(v, node_num + 1); }
  void* find(int);
  void  display();
 };

class queue : private list  {

public:
  queue() { enqueue(0); }
  void enqueue(void*);
  void* dequeue();
};

void queue::enqueue(void* x)
{
 append(x);
}

void* queue::dequeue()
{
  void* temp = find(1);
  remove(1);
  return temp;
}

main()
{
 queue x;
```

```
x.enqueue("Tom");
x.enqueue("Dick");
x.enqueue("Harry");

cout << (char*) x.dequeue() << "\n";
cout << (char*) x.dequeue() << "\n";
cout << (char*) x.dequeue() << "\n";
}
```

Although the design is relatively simple, these three listings serve as a reminder of how easily you can use existing classes to design new software.

The Future of Object-Oriented Programming

It is safe to argue that C++ and the future of object-oriented technique are secure. We are in the early stages of a paradigm change that will alter the way we approach software development. Programmers no longer will approach a design as a monolithic structure and arbitrarily divide it into modules and subtasks. Instead, they will begin with a library of models or objects that perform specific functions. Design will be a process of either combining these objects to produce programs or adding specialized characteristics to existing objects to create new resources.

A

Using C++ with UNIX

Programming in UNIX

Summary

Using C++ with UNIX

In this book you have explored the syntax and theory of C++. One of the advantages of using a high-level programming language like C++ is its portability. Programs that are written under one operating system are easy to import to a different one. Sometimes only a recompilation is necessary, or perhaps some adjustment in variable sizes is required in addition to recompilation. The examples and explanations in this book do not apply to any particular implementation of C++, nor to any particular operating system environment. They will compile and run under MS-DOS, UNIX, or any other operating system.

Even as you focus on the portability of C++, you should recognize that some programs and techniques are basic to a particular environment. You can write programs that work only under MS-DOS or only in UNIX. The possibility of environment-specific programs does not mean that C++ is not a portable platform. Rather, it underscores the fact that C++ is powerful enough to enable the designer to reach down to the level of system resources and create software that can take advantage of these features.

Programming in UNIX

UNIX and C++ have a mutual affinity that stems from their common origin. C++ compilers were first available for the UNIX environment, and much of the development work is still performed under this operating system. Moreover, the structure and object-oriented nature of C++ make it an almost ideal platform for UNIX development. In this appendix, I briefly discuss some simple examples of this affinity.

UNIX System Calls and Programming

One important difference in programming under the UNIX operating system is in the use of *system calls*. System calls are requests that a program makes to the operating system to perform one of the many important tasks over which this system software has control. A program might request that memory be allocated, a program be loaded, or even a disk file be created. These things are not done directly by the user software; rather, they are done indirectly by the operating system kernel. System calls are important in every operating system, but in UNIX they are used extensively, even by applications programs.

One reason that system calls are used so much in UNIX is that they have a simple format that is easy to integrate into a C++ program. In other operating system environments, a system call usually involves a somewhat obscure mechanism often involving the setting of register memory in the central processing unit and an explicit jump to a memory location. In contrast, a UNIX system call has the same format as a function call. For example, to open a file for read and write access, a program executes the following statement:

```
fd = open(filename, O_RDWR);
```

The open() function is a system request to allocate a system data structure to the file that has its name in the variable filename and then pass an identifier back to the program making the request. Like an ordinary function, the open() system call can be used in an expression with an assignment operator. In fact, the only way that the system calls in a program can be identified is by reference to the system manual. Using system calls in a program is no more difficult than using standard library functions like strcpy(). The use of operating system services optimizes the program in terms of speed and resources, which makes for more efficient and elegant programs.

Multitasking in UNIX

Another important attraction of UNIX is its ability to execute multiple tasks simultaneously. Even at the user level, this capability is a convenience. Many developers run the compiler and an editor together so that they can continue to make changes to a file while earlier changes are being compiled and tested. Multitasking can be controlled by a program, however, and can serve as a design tool. Multitasking actually can simplify the creation of complicated software systems.

At the heart of multitasking is the notion of a *process*. A process is created when a program is loaded into memory and begins to execute. In a singletasking system, only one program executes at a time. This is true even in a task-switching system, which allows several programs to be in memory at the same time. In a multiprocessing system, several processes can run simultaneously, share resources, and produce output.

A complete discussion of processes and multitasking is beyond the scope of this book. In UNIX, however, it's relatively easy to start and maintain a process. All the processes in a UNIX system are organized in a hierarchy. Each process has a parent process of its own and is the parent to one or more child processes. A process can be started only by an existing process, which is accomplished by a call to int fork().

When a program executes this system call, a new process is created that is identical to the original one. For example, the code fragment

```
if( (pid = fork())
    cout << "Original process \n";
  else
    cout << "Child process\n";
```

results in two executing processes: the original process that made the call to fork(), and the new process created by it. Each process can distinguish itself by the unique value that fork() returns to it. The original process is given the process identification number of the child process. The fork() system call returns 0 to the child process.

Loading and Running a Program in UNIX

One important programming design issue in any multitasking system is loading and running programs from inside executing processes. The fork() system call is one element of this process. All it can do, however, is create a clone of its calling process. What you need is a way to load specific program code into a process so that different programs can be run. This loading process is accomplished by using one of the members of the exec family of system calls.

The format for an exec system call is

```
execvp(char*  file_name, char* argv[]);
```

in which file_name is the name of the file that contains the executable code and argv[] is a character string array. argv[0] contains the name of the program (the same as in file_name). Subsequent elements in argv contain any arguments that are to be passed to the program as it begins to execute. If the specified file_name cannot be found in the current directory of the process, the PATH variable is used to find the file. execvp() is one of the exec calls.

execvp() and the other members of this family of system calls overlay the current process with the code from the specified program file. When this is accomplished, the altered process begins to execute using the new code. It's important to note that loading and running a program is destructive to the calling process; its code is overwritten by the new program.

fork() and execvp() can be used together to overcome the problem created by the destructive nature of execvp(). A process that is going to load and start a new program first uses fork() to create a child process. This new process then uses execvp() to load the new code. You can modify the earlier code fragment as follows to illustrate this arrangement:

```
if((pid = fork())
    cout << "Original Process\n";
  else
    execvp("new_program", argv);
```

Using this format, loading a new program is not destructive to the existing process, because it is the child process that is overlaid with the new code.

A C++ Example: The *shell* Class

Although a complete discussion of C++ and UNIX programming is beyond the scope of this book, a simple example illustrates how well these two work together. Listing A-1 illustrates a C++ program that uses the two system calls I discussed previously.

Listing A-1. A shell class: comint.c.

```
#include <iostream.h>
#include <string.h>
#include <sysent.h>
#include <sys/signal.h>
#include <fcntl.h>

class shell  {
  int pid;
  int fd;
  int parser(char*[],char*);
```

```
public:
  shell()              { fd = -1;}
  shell(char*);
 ~shell();
  void run();
};

shell::shell(char* fname)
{
    fd = open(fname, O_WRONLY|O_CREAT);
}

shell::~shell()
{
  if(fd > 0)
    close(fd);
  cout << "Exiting Shell\n";
}

int shell::parser(char* cmd[], char* buf)
{
  char* temp;
  temp = strtok(buf, " ");
  if(temp)  {
    cmd[0] = new char[strlen(temp) + 1];
    strcpy(cmd[0], temp);
   }
  else
   return 0;

  for(int i = 1 ; (temp = strtok(0, " ")) ; i++ )  {
    cmd[i] = new char[strlen(temp) + 1];
    strcpy(cmd[i], temp);
  }
  cmd[i] = '\0';
  return i;
}

void shell::run()
{
  char buffer[80];
  char* cmdline[10];
```

continues

Listing A-1. continued

```
  for(buffer[0] = '\0'; strcmp(buffer, "halt") ; )  {
   cout << "=>";
   cin.getline(buffer,80);
   if(fd > 0)  {
     write(fd, buffer, strlen(buffer)+1);
     write(fd, "\n", 1);
    }
   if(strcmp(buffer, "halt"))  {
     parser(cmdline, buffer);
     if( (pid = fork()) )  {
        wait((int*)0);


      }
     else
        execvp(cmdline[0], cmdline);
    }
   else
     kill(-1,SIGTERM);
 }
}

main()
{
 shell x("log.dat");
 x.run();
}
```

The shell class implemented in comint.c serves as a simple command interpreter. When initialized and loaded, it continues to ask the user to enter commands. These commands are then parsed for the actual program name and the command-line arguments, which are in turn put into a character string array. After the command name and arguments are separated, a new process is created and a call to execvp() loads the specified program. The process associated with the shell class waits until the new command terminates and then asks the user for a new one. A halt command will stop the program.

The private section of the shell class contains a variable, pid, to hold the identification number of the child process. Another variable, fd, serves as a file handle. Finally, the member function parser() processes the command lines. parser() is in the private section because it is not a member that is called outside of the class.

The public section of shell defines the interface to any program using the class. The constructor and destructor define the initialization and deinitialization of shell. The constructor is overloaded. One simply initializes fd to a negative value, whereas the other is supplied with a character string parameter. This parameter is the name of a disk file that receives a record of each command passed into the constructor as an argument. The action of the class is controlled by the member function run().

At the heart of run() is a for loop that continues as long as the user doesn't enter the string halt. On each iteration, the loop prompts for a command and accepts input from the keyboard into the variable buffer. This input is passed to parser() along with the character string array, cmdline. parser() uses the standard library function strtok() to break the contents of buffer into individual substrings. These are placed into individual elements of cmdline. cmdline[0] contains the name of the program to be executed. Note that the last element in the array is set to 0, which is a requirement of execvp() and indicates the end of the list of parameters.

When the cmdline array has been prepared, run() creates a new process by calling fork(). The parent process then calls wait(). This system call suspends the calling process until the child process completes. At the same time, the child process calls execvp(), which loads and executes the command in cmdline[0]. After this is complete, the process terminates and the original process is awakened. The loop continues until the user enters halt.

Command logging is enabled by a call to the second constructor. The value of the file handle, fd, is used to indicate to run() whether or not to store the value of buffer as it is entered. The constructor opens the log file by using the UNIX system call open(). The destructor closes the file using the system call close(). write() is used to put the contents of buffer on the file.

Summary

In this appendix you have seen how C++ can be used to program in a UNIX operating system environment. In particular, you saw how you can use UNIX system calls within class definitions to produce objects that use system resources efficiently. As a case study, you investigated a shell class that implemented a small command interpreter.

C++ and UNIX are natural partners. This appendix has only scratched the surface of an important connection.

Index

Symbols

A

I

J-K

L

M

N

O

P

I

V

va_arg( ) macro, 105
va_end( ) macro, 105
va_start( ) macro, 105
values, constant, 10-11
variables
  automatic, 9
  declaring, comparing C++ and
    ANSI C, 23-24
  extern, 10
  pointer, 11-13
  reference, 38-39, 98-103
  register, 10
  scope, comparing C++ and ANSI
    C, 24-26
  static, 9-10

virtual base classes, 278-281
virtual functions, 247-248
  accessing through pointers,
    251-254
  pure, 254-256
  redefining in multiple inheritance,
    273-278
void pointers, 13-14
void* data type, 165

W-Z

word class, 147-149
words, 78
write( ) function, 341-343

Dear Reader:

Thank you for considering the purchase of our book. Readers have come to know products from The Waite Group for the care and quality we put into them. Let me tell you a little about our group and how we make our books.

It started in 1976 when I could not find a computer book that really taught me anything. The books that were available talked down to people, lacked illustrations and examples, were poorly laid out, and were written as if you already understood all the terminology. So I set out to write a good book about microcomputers. This was to be a special book, very graphic, with a friendly and casual style, and filled with examples. The result was an instant best-seller. Today the Waite Group has over 70 computer books on the market, and many more are published each year. And no matter what your level of computer interest and expertise, we think The Waite Group has a title you'll like. Our books cover the DOS and Unix operating systems, as well and the C, C++, BASIC, and 80x86 assembler languages. Our titles cover the most popular compilers including those from Microsoft and Borland.

THE
WAITE
GROUP

We have honed the reader levels of our books into a number of best-selling approaches: our *Primer Plus*® and *Programming Primers* guide beginners from the introductory concepts through to a working knowledge of writing professional programs. Our *Bibles* have evolved into comprehensive reference books that appeal to intermediate and advanced programmers and power users. They include standard formats that make looking up any command or function quick and easy, provide clear examples, compatibility information, understandable syntax statements, jump tables and concise tutorials. Power users and programmers should check out our *Tricks of the Masters* books. These titles provide hints, tips, examples, and in-depth discussions that go far beyond the basic principles and facts found elsewhere. You'll discover obscure nuggets of information, work-arounds, and compelling discussions by experts that will hone your programming skills.

We're sure that you'll get to know the signature of "The Waite Group" on a book title as a stamp of a first quality book. A catalog of our titles can be obtained by filling out our reader response card, found in this book.

Thanks again for considering the purchase of this title. If you care to tell me anything you like (or don't like) about the book, please use our reader response card.

Sincerely,

Mitchell Waite
President

Primer Plus is a registered trademark of The Waite Group, Inc.

100 Shoreline Highway   Suite A-285   Mill Valley,   California   94941   415-331-0575   Fax 415-331-1075

Enhance Your Operating System With Books From The Waite Group!

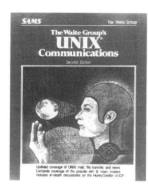

Waite Group Reader Feedback Card
Help Us Make A Better Book

To better serve our readers, we would like your opinion on the contents and quality of this book. Please fill out this card and return it to *The Waite Group*, 100 Shoreline Hwy., Suite A-285, Mill Valley, CA, 94941.

Name _____

Company _____

Address _____

City _____

State _____ ZIP _____ Phone _____

1. How would you rate the content of this book?

    ☐ Excellent   ☐ Fair
    ☐ Very Good   ☐ Below Average
    ☐ Good   ☐ Poor

2. Please mark an L for things you liked and a D for things you disliked about this book.

    ___ Pace   ___ Examples   ___ Cover
    ___ Content   ___ Index   ___ Price
    ___ Writing Style ___ Listings   ___ Quizzes
    ___ Accuracy   ___ Ease of Use   ___ Construction
    ___ Jump Tables   ___ Design   ___ Appendixes
    ___ Compat. Boxes ___ Illustrations ___ Ref. Card

3. Please explain the one thing you liked *most* about this book. _____

4. Please explain the one thing you liked *least* about this book. _____

5. How do you use this book? For work, recreation, look-up, self-training, classroom, etc? _____

6. What is your level of computer expertise? _____

7. How did you learn about this book? _____

8. Where did you purchase this particular book?

    ☐ Book Chain   ☐ Direct Mail
    ☐ Small Book Store   ☐ Book Club
    ☐ Computer Store   ☐ School Book Store
    ☐ Other: _____

9. Can you name another similar book you like better than this one, or one that is as good, and tell us why? _____

10. How many Waite Group books do you own? _____

11. What are your favorite Waite Group books? _____

12. What topics or specific titles would you like to see The Waite Group develop? _____

13. What operating system and version are you using? _____

14. What programming languages do you know? _____

15. Any other comments you have about this book or other Waite Group titles? _____

16. ☐ Check here to receive a free Waite Group catalog.

Title of this book _____ ISBN: _____

From:

The Waite Group, Inc.
100 Shoreline Highway, Suite A–285
Mill Valley, CA 94941

Staple or tape here